The Politics of Sustainability

Responsibility for future generations is easily postulated in the abstract but it is much more difficult to set it to work in the concrete. It requires some changes in individual and institutional attitudes that are in opposition to what has been called the 'systems variables' of industrial society: individual freedom, consumerism, and equality.

The Politics of Sustainability: Philosophical Perspectives seeks to examine the motivational and institutional obstacles standing in the way of a consistent politics of sustainability and to look for strategies to overcome them. It argues that though there have been significant changes in individual and especially collective attitudes to growth, intergenerational solidarity and nature preservation, it is far from certain whether these will be sufficient to encourage politicians to give sustainable policies priority over other legitimate concerns. Having a philosophical approach as its main focus, the volume is at the same time interdisciplinary in combining political, psychological, ecological and economic analyses.

This book will be a contribution to the joint effort to meet the theoretical and practical challenges posed by climate change and other impending global perils and will be of interest to students of environmental studies, applied ethics and environmental psychology.

Dieter Birnbacher is Professor of Philosophy at the University of Düsseldorf, Germany.

May Thorseth is Professor of Philosophy at the Norwegian University of Science and Technology, Trondheim, Norway.

Routledge Studies in Sustainability

The Politics of Sustainability

Philosophical Perspectives

Edited by Dieter Birnbacher and
May Thorseth

Routledge
Taylor & Francis Group

LONDON AND NEW YORK

earthscan
from Routledge

First published 2015
by Routledge
2 Park Square, Milton Park, Abingdon, Oxfordshire OX14 4RN

and by Routledge
711 Third Avenue, New York, NY 10017

First issued in paperback 2017

Routledge is an imprint of the Taylor & Francis Group, an informa business

British Library Cataloguing-in-Publication Data
A catalogue record for this book is available from the British Library

Library of Congress Cataloging-in-Publication Data
The politics of sustainability : philosophical perspectives / edited by Dieter
Birnbacher and May Thorseth.
pages cm
Includes bibliographical references and index.
ISBN 978-1-138-85429-1 (hardback) — ISBN 978-1-315-72120-0 (ebook)
1. Sustainability—Philosophy. 2. Sustainability—Political aspects. 3. Climate
change mitigation—Political aspects. I. Birnbacher, Dieter, editor of compilation,
author. II. Thorseth, May, 1957– editor of compilation, author.
GE195.P66 2015
338.9'2701—dc23
2014042314

ISBN 13: 978-1-138-06434-8 (pbk)
ISBN 13: 978-1-138-85429-1 (hbk)

Typeset in Goudy
by FiSH Books Ltd, Enfield

Contents

Contributors

Dieter Birnbacher, Professor of Philosophy, Heinrich-Heine-Universität Düsseldorf, Germany.

Bernward Gesang, Professor of the Ethics of Economics, University of Mannheim, Germany.

Ludger Heidbrink, Professor of Philosophy, University of Kiel, Germany.

Adrian-Paul Iliescu, Professor of Philosophy, University of Bucharest, Romania, and director of DIRESS – Research Center on Intergenerational Justice, Social Responsibility and Sustainability.

Karsten Klint Jensen, Associate Professor, Institute of Food and Resource Economics, Faculty of Life Sciences, University of Copenhagen, Denmark.

Roland Mees, Ph.D. student, University of Utrecht, the Netherlands.

Dominic Roser, Research Fellow, Oxford Martin Programme on Human Rights for Future Generations, University of Oxford, UK.

Joachim H. Spangenberg, Research Coordinator, Vice-Chair, Sustainable Europe Research Institute SERI Germany e.V., Cologne, Germany.

May Thorseth, Professor of Philosophy at the Norwegian University of Science and Technology, Trondheim, Norway.

Jörg Tremmel, Associate Professor, Institute for Political Science, University of Tübingen, Germany.

Ivo Wallimann-Helmer, Centre for Ethics, University of Zurich, Switzerland.

Kerri Woods, Lecturer in Political Theory, School of Politics and International Studies, University of Leeds, UK.

Introduction

Though "sustainability" can look back on a particularly successful career as a political slogan, central dimensions of the concept remain either unclear or controversial, or both. There are plenty of open questions, some of them conceptual, others ethical and still others political. Not only have the "Why" and "How" of sustainability never ceased to be the object of lively discussion, but also the "What," the very content of what is intended by the term. Part of the difficulty derives from the fact that on its way from forestry economics to world politics the meaning of the concept underwent a number of transformations, each of them enlarging its scope and successively blurring its contours.

The roots of the concept lie in traditional hunting practices and the implicit rule to cull no more animals from a given population than is allowed by keeping the stock constant. Its international career started in 1713 when Hans Carl von Carlowitz in his *Sylvicultura oeconomica* made it a rule of forestry to harvest no more wood than is allowed by the capacity of the wood to regenerate and yield the same harvest in continuity. A more sophisticated variant of the same rule was formulated by another forester, Georg Ludwig Hartwig in 1791 in terms of utility flows: forests should be harvested only to an extent compatible with later generations deriving the same utility from their use as the present one. This idea was later generalized to all kinds of exchanges between man and nature involving nature as a resource. "Sustainability" became a general maxim of intergenerationally responsible use of finite resources and the economic analogue of the famous proviso in John Locke's theory of property, according to which the original appropriation of land must be compatible with leaving "enough, and as good to others."

In our days, the interpretations given to "sustainability" have transcended the framework of the man–nature relationship and are typically formulated, not in terms of harvests or yields, but in terms of present and future needs. This tendency is highlighted by the often quoted definition of the World Commission on Environment and Development – better known as the Brundtland Commission – of sustainability in combination with development: "Sustainable development is development that meets the needs of the present without compromising the ability of future generations to meet their own needs." Evidently, this compromise formula, issued in 1987, lies at the root of a number of problems that many scientists have thought grave enough to turn away from the concept altogether. By taking its starting-point from human needs, present and future, the scope of the concept is radically enlarged, comprising not only natural but, in addition, economic, human, social, moral and political resources. At the same time, it opens the way to a wide variety of interpretations considerably reducing its usefulness as term of national and international consensus, and making it easy for national and international agents to pay lip service to the idea without taking steps to basically alter their dealings with nature. Not surprisingly, the recent history of the use of the term has shown how much it is susceptible to inflationary tendencies and to the temptation to "sell" under this label whatever one happens to find important. Another worry about the concept is whether it might not ultimately harbor a contradiction: Development implies growth, but it is an open question whether growth is compatible with the restraint in resource use required to conserve resources for later generations. How much realism is there in the project to steer global development in a direction that is compatible with the long-term maintenance of the natural parameters on which it depends, especially climate stability and availability of a sufficient quantity of water and arable land? Up to the present, at least, the concept has proven to be a fig-leaf of untrammeled expansion and exponential depletion rather than the basis of a serious and concerted effort of conservation.

The present volume differs from the plethora of existing publications on sustainability in that it shifts the focus from the explication and justification of the concept of sustainability to its national and international political implementation. Though the idea of sustainability might be seen as a conservative and, indeed, modest conception of what we owe to future generations, the difficulties to transform the idea in practical politics have been shown to be formidable. After all, the idea is that sustainability demands much less than, for example, maximizing conceptions like utilitarianism, which ask for policies that have a chance of maximizing the utilities later generations reap from whatever they inherit from earlier generations. Sustainability requires much less – no more than allowing later generations to reap the same benefits from these sources as earlier generations. But in fact, though less demanding than maximizing conceptions, sustainability is a highly ambitious idea, at least in a world characterized by expectations of continuously rising standards of living and a global population estimated to amount to 9 billion people during our children's lifetime.

In fact, sustainability shares a number of features with conceptions generally held to be "overdemanding," first of all its temporal and horizontal universality. Sustainability is a principle for the long term, and it is intended to apply to all people living on Spaceship Earth. Another feature that makes it "demanding", if not "overdemanding," is its incompatibility with the dominant pattern of resource use. It cannot be seriously doubted that present patterns of resource use in the industrialized world do not meet the Lockean standard to leave "as much, and as good" to others. They are not universalizable in the precise Kantian sense that they are not compatible with their hypothetical generalization. It seems strictly impossible that the practices of production and consumption to which people in the rich countries have grown accustomed are practiced by 9 billions of people in a finite world constrained by very narrow climatic margins.

It is not to be wondered, therefore, that there are obstacles standing in the way of a sustainable politics. Two stand out as being particularly important: motivational and institutional. As far as motivation is concerned, it is well known that responsibility to future generations is readily affirmed in the abstract but rarely lived in the concrete. There is a long way to go from ideal principles to concrete motivations, both on the level of the individual and of the collective. There are not a few difficulties that have to be overcome in following high-minded principles of intergenerational justice under the dictates of economic growth, increasing burdens for social security and habitualization to wasteful consumption patterns. Though there have been significant changes in individual and collective attitudes to nature conservation and intergenerational solidarity, it is far from certain whether these will be potent enough to pressure politicians into giving priority to sustainable policies over short-term challenges such as fighting economic crises, providing working opportunities to the workless, and maintaining the national position in the international rat-race. On the individual as well as on the collective levels, the gap between what used to be called "velleitas" – the wish that does not necessarily materialize in willing – and "voluntas" – the willing that manifests itself in action – is wide open, especially on the background of relatively stable cultural practices that resist modification by ethical appeals.

There are, then, good grounds to raise the question whether present political institutions are particularly well-suited to put ideas of long-term responsibility into action. In democracies, the motivation of politicians to consistently pursue long-term and global objectives essentially depends on the motivations of their constituencies, and as far as these exhibit myopia and limitations of sympathies these features can be expected to be reflected on the collective level as "short-termism" and concentration on national interest irrespective of global consequences. Are there ways to correct this imbalance? Are there potential institutional arrangements and political strategies that might redress the balance in favor of long-term goals like climate stability, maintenance of ecological carrying capacity and the conservation of essential resources like water, soil, and fuels? Here lies a major challenge for political philosophy, and an incentive for philosophers and political scientists to search for feasible institutional arrangements and social and political strategies by which the transition from the wasteful practices of present societies to a sustainable future might be effectuated or made easier.

The contributions of this volume make an effort to meet this challenge. They are partly diagnostic, partly therapeutic. They analyze the obstacles standing in the way of a transition to sustainable politics, both on the individual and the collective level, and they present and evaluate potential remedies. It becomes apparent that both diagnosis and therapy are highly complex affairs, which require inputs from many disciplines. No discipline is by itself comprehensive enough to provide a holistic view encompassing psychology, sociology, political science and ethics. This volume documents the efforts of philosophers, most of them working in this interdisciplinary field for a long time, to provide at least building-stones for such a comprehensive view.

Philosophy is relevant to the politics of sustainability for many reasons. There are some fairly fundamental problems of political philosophy that any theory of sustainability has to face. One is to ask how inevitable it is that the republican principle of the sovereignty of the people is bound up with the sovereignty of the present over future generations. If citizens must not tolerate the tyranny of princes, how fair is it that later generations must tolerate the "tyranny of the present" of their predecessors? On the other hand, there does not seem to be an irresolvable incompatibility between democratic principles and a representation of the interests of future generations. On the contrary, the record of non-democratic rule in regard to the future is in general much worse than that of democracies. Only in an open society is there a chance of changing attitudes and motivations in a more future-oriented direction. One means is to confront citizens with the prospects for their offspring in a not too far away future, such as a massive increase in the wave of refugees from climatically disadvantaged, overpopulated and badly governed regions like sub-Sahara Africa.

Another reason for why philosophy is relevant to the politics of sustainability is that exploring ways to overcome the motivational obstacles to future-oriented action is not a purely technical matter but has a moral dimension. Prospective effectiveness has to be balanced with ethical acceptability. For example, many of the modifications proposed by contemporary authors to the institutional structure of democracies in order to overcome "short-termism" in politics face the dilemma of being either only cosmetic and ineffective or normatively unacceptable because of their being incompatible with the very idea of democratic rule. The same holds, on the societal level, for strategies directed at changing attitudes by emotional factors. On the one hand, as ferment of change, emotions are much more powerful than cognitions. Studies and observations show that personal capacity to adapt depends crucially on motivational factors, which in turn react much more to emotional confrontations than to pure information. On the other hand, a line must be drawn between morally legitimate "nudges," recommended by so-called Libertarian Paternalism, and morally more problematic forms of social pressure.

The structure of the present volume follows as far as possible the medical rule that diagnosis precedes therapy. The first section identifies the obstacles standing in the way of a change in attitudes and motivations in a more future-oriented direction. How far are the failures of states and other collectives to adequately address the problems of climate change and long-term environmental deterioration conditioned by motivations inherent in their institutional structure? How far is the relatively short election cycle of democracies responsible for the "short-termism" and populism of the policies of democratic states? Does democracy embed a "liberal tragedy of the commons"? In this section, pessimistic views prevail. Karsten Klint Jensen suggests that the lack of action can be explained as a contributor's dilemma. The complex of obstacles to action leaves no clear ways out. He then analyzes two types of possible solutions – appeal to ethics and use of incentives. Each type is linked with a specific framing, has its own motivational characteristics and involves specific consequences. Similar conclusions are reached in Ivo Wallimann-Helmer's chapter. He identifies the main source of failure of a global climate politics as the normative framework of liberal democracy and develops the view that there is high probability that at least some democracies will not consent to an international agreement to mitigate greenhouse gas emissions. Though, in this situation, the institution of judicial review would be crucial to overcome the risk of a tragedy of the commons, the chances are low that such an institutional change comes about within the normative framework of liberal democracy. A different diagnosis of the same ills is given by May Thorseth. She develops the view that part of the problem of non-sustainable dealings with nature is that economic ways of thinking and moral self-conceptions are increasingly at variance. As an illustration, she draws on an example from the context of Chinese fisheries. Three proposals of how a new balance might be attained are discussed: by the role of the public (Dewey), reflective judgment (Kant, Arendt), and deliberative democracy (Dryzek). In contrast, Bernward Gesang sees grounds for cautious optimism. Gesang defends the view that in spite of the obvious dysfunctionalities of the democratic system for ecological policies that adequately take into account the interests of future people, there is leeway for solutions of the dilemma by institutional changes short of constitutional reform, such as, on the European level, the introduction of Future Councils or ombudspersons. According to Gesang, the pending reform process in Europe holds the prospect of creating a climate in which citizens and politicians may be much more open to institutional innovations than they are at present.

The second section examines central notions in contemporary views about the present generation's responsibility to the future that can be expected to influence the willingness to act for the benefit of future generations and to avoid burdening them with long-term and possibly irreversible losses and risks. One of these is the notion of *feasibility*, examined by Dominic Roser. Roser points at the intricacies and pitfalls inherent in the notion of feasibility as used in discussions on political strategies and shows that the suggestive maxim of choosing "the least unjust policy from the feasible set" clouds the issue in several ways. He also highlights a number of ways in which there are unexploited opportunities to "squeeze more justice" out of a given level of political will. The following chapter by Kerri Woods examines another notion pervading discussion of climate justice: the notion of harm and the appeal to harm avoidance that goes with it. Her claim is that this way of characterizing climate justice relies on a notion of harm that is at odds with conventional understandings of the concept of harm and obscures the character of the duties resulting from it. Roland Mees elaborates on Stephen Gardiner's thesis, that what Gardiner calls "moral corruption" lies at the root of the prevailing attitudes of complacency and procrastination when it comes to taking environmentally friendly action. Mees follows Gardiner in seeing the present climatic crisis as being mainly due to deficiencies in public morality. "Moral corruption" is interpreted as a consequence of sticking to an attitude of staying away from morality in its entirety. It is argued that a renewed formulation of the concept of moral integrity could lead us to live up to our obligation to care for the distant future, and simultaneously, see our lives as morally good. Even more radical is the diagnosis given by Joachim H. Spangenberg in his chapter. According to him, morality will not suffice to change the ways of the industrialized world. What is needed to support successful sustainability policies is no less than a change in fundamental world view. Nothing much is to be hoped for from problem-solving strategies developed by an environmental economics that trusts in solutions from market forces, unknown technologies, and the commodification of nature.

The third section is devoted to potential remedies. Its central question is whether the apparent incompatibility between democratic principles and a representation of the interests of a future generation is irresolvable. How far can the weaknesses of democracies in consistently pursuing long-term strategies be compensated by mechanisms of self-binding, such as international contracts and the delegation of discretional power to supranational bodies? Does Sunstein's and Thaler's Liberal Paternalism offer a way out of the dilemma? Or are more radical changes in the institutional structure of modern democracies called for, such as a future court or the addition of a "fourth branch" to the classical division of powers? Dieter Birnbacher's chapter starts from the observation that it is inevitable that there is a more striking discrepancy between the motivation to accept moral principles and the motivation to act in accordance with them in future ethics than in other branches of ethics. There are not only general psychological obstacles associated with obligations to the future, these are also reinforced by three "system variables" specific to the present industrialized world: individual freedom, consumerism, and egalitarianism. The remedy is seen in internal and external self-binding. In either case, an attempt is made to control in advance the extent to which future motivations that deviate from one's principles result in undesired behavior, either by making deviations more difficult or less attractive, or by restricting future options. This route is further explored by Ludger Heidbrink in his chapter, which enters on a systematic review of the pros and cons of Libertarian Paternalism and its program of how to make actors achieve what is in their own long-term interest, despite behavioral deficits, by influencing their decisions though "nudges." Heidbrink argues that "nudges" are a legitimate and effective means of control if they are designed openly and transparently, support the self-responsibility of actors, and allow for learning processes. They should be complemented, however, by embedding consumption processes in sustainable milieus, by promoting self-responsible decision processes and by involving citizens in the administration of scarce public resources. Another option to influence political decisions that affect future generations, the institution of "trial by jury" procedures, is explored in the subsequent chapter by Adrian-Paul Iliescu. He argues that such procedures are superior vis-à-vis other kinds of procedures such as law courts, ombudspersons, commissioners, and citizens' juries but they cannot be developed inside existing law courts. They should be implemented by specialized bodies. In the concluding chapter, Jörg Tremmel goes even further in modifying the established democratic order. He suggests that the centuries-old separation of powers between the legislative, executive and judicial branch may no longer be appropriate in a world threatened by global disaster. In order to make the political system future-oriented, a new (fourth) institution might be called for that ensures that the interests of future generations are more consistently taken into account in today's decision-making process.

This volume originated from the work of the ESF-funded scientific network *Rights to a Green Future*, which brings together philosophers, natural scientists and social scientists from all over Europe concerned about the future of man's natural environment. The editors thank the European Science Foundation and the co-ordinators of the network, especially Marcus Düwell (Utrecht), for their support and valuable advice.

Part 1

Determinants of non-sustainable behavior

1 Climate change and motivation

The obstacle from conflicting perspectives

Karsten Klint Jensen

This chapter argues that the normative framework of liberal democracy is the main source of failure of a global climate politics and that there is high probability that at least some democracies will not consent to an international agreement to mitigate greenhouse gas emissions. In this situation, the institution of judicial review is crucial to overcome the risk of a tragedy of the commons. However, in the case of climate change, an institutional change of the required sort cannot be derived from within the normative framework of liberal democracy itself.

1. Introduction

Anthropogenic climate change involves a threat of serious harm in the future, and some harm is already occurring. Many people are convinced about this, and many believe that the present generation has a duty to do something about it. However, when it comes to action, the progress made so far has not been impressive.

This chapter is concerned with problems of motivation in the face of climate change. It starts from the suggestion that the lack of action can be explained as a so-called contributor's dilemma. It then analyzes two types of possible solutions: appeal to ethics, and use of incentives. Each type is linked with a specific framing; it has its own motivational characteristics and it involves specific consequences. The analysis reveals a complex of obstacles to action with no clear ways out.

2. Contributor's dilemma

Insofar as the required action involves sacrifices for the present generation for the sake of reducing the risk of harm to future generations, it seems likely that everybody will have the preferences of a free rider. This means that, regardless of what others do, everybody prefers not to contribute. If some person contributes, while others do not, this person bears some costs alone, and not much progress is being made. If others contribute, one can enjoy the progress but avoid the costs by not contributing. Thus, even if everybody prefers to act collectively rather than no-one acts – i.e. everybody prefers to contribute their part – if everyone else also does it, the worst outcome will come about, because nobody will contribute.[1]

Some people suggest that this model of an explanation gets things wrong. The reason why people are reluctant to contribute is not that they act from self-interest. Rather, most people accept a moral duty to contribute, but they fail to act out of moral weakness. However, the model does not really assume anything substantial about peoples' beliefs and motivation. It merely claims that, when it comes to the actual choice, there is, in a technical sense, a preference for not contributing, that is, this is what the person will end up choosing.

In my view, it is to stress the notion of moral weakness too far to use it as an explanation of a massive collective failure to contribute. Other explanations could be that people end up concluding that there is no ethical reason not to free-ride, or they end up concluding that self-interested reasons have more weight than ethical reasons. But even if it were the correct explanation, it does not violate the model, because people in the end will have a preference for not contributing anyway. Of course, the model is still rather rough, because evidently, some people contribute to some degree. I shall sidestep possible refinements and keep the model simple for the sake of the argument.

A contributor's dilemma arises when people have the specific preferences of a free-rider. The solution is therefore to change the choice situation or to change peoples' preferences so that the dilemma will not arise. Roughly, the literature knows two types of solutions to contributor's dilemmas: political and moral. Political solutions typically use various forms of positive or negative incentives, while moral solutions appeal to moral motivation and thus involve a psychological change.

The particular nasty thing about a contributor's dilemma is its asymmetrical nature. Those who bear the costs (the present generation) are not the same as those who enjoy the benefits (future generations). Hence, it is not possible to motivate people to contribute by pointing at the benefits they will obtain by doing so. This difficulty will affect both types of solutions. Politically, the constituency is unlikely to be motivated by one-sided sacrifices, and morally, an appeal to engage in a social contract is also likely to fail because future generations cannot benefit us for doing so. John Broome has suggested a solution to this latter problem, to which I shall return later. But first I shall introduce what I consider the dominant ethical outlook and discuss its properties as a solution to the contributor's dilemma.

3. The dominant ethical outlook

What I propose as "the dominant ethical outlook" in face of climate change is based on my personal observations of the public debate and my experiences as a teacher in applied ethics. I am afraid I have no hard sociological evidence to offer, so I have to ask the reader to accept these observations as a premise of my argument.

My first observation is about framing. In discussions concerning what we are to do about climate change, mitigation by reduction of emissions of greenhouse gases (as opposed to adaptation and compensation for actual harm and damage) is the dominant theme and what comes first to mind to many people. Within this framing, many people accept that there is room for collective political decision-making, and some ethical outlooks will of course also support this approach.

However, and this is my second observation, at some stage it will be asked "what can I (each of us) do as an individual?" and to many people, this question is essentially ethical, implying that each of us has a duty to do what we can. Or it goes the other way round through the question "What does ethics demand in the face of climate change?" and for many people (I claim) this question amounts to the same as "What should I do?"

Clearly, the questions "What can I do?" and "What should I do?" are not equivalent, and I do not claim that people give the same answer to them – I believe many people are in fact in doubt about the exact answers, and I shall say more about this later. But I do claim that many people frame a distinctively ethical approach to climate change as a matter of individual ethics, and that they also consider individual decision making in the face of climate change to be distinctively ethical in nature.

My third observation is that, for many people, the ethical duty in face of climate change can be reconstructed along the following lines: Some of my actions lead to serious risk of harm to future generations. I have a duty not to cause harm. I should therefore act so that I do not cause serious risk of harm. This is a very simplistic reconstruction as it stands, and I shall make some refinements during the following discussion. However, my overall claim in this section is that if we want to appeal to individual ethical consciousness in order to solve the contributor's dilemma, this is pretty much what it will tell us.

There are similar reconstructions of our individual ethical responsibility in face of climate change in the literature (e.g. Baer 2006; Broome 2008, 2012). And it seems that the responsibility not to cause harm has reasonably strong appeal. But as a solution to the contributor's dilemma, this appeal also involves some problems to which I turn next.

4. What is our duty as individuals?

The first problem I shall raise is that, given the framework developed so far for an individual ethical approach to climate change, there is indeterminateness as to what our precise duties are, and this might frustrate people and lead them to take the ethical demands less seriously and perhaps even give up on them.

Looking at the literature, the answers to what is our duty as individuals span from "Each of us has a clear duty to emit no greenhouse gas" (Broome 2012: 96) to "We are left with no defensible principle to support the claim that I have a moral duty not to drive a gas guzzler just for fun" (Sinnott-Armstrong 2005: 288).

The answer that we have no duties (regardless of what others do) is primarily based on the consideration that if I drive the gas guzzler on a Sunday afternoon, no one will ever perceive any harm. Broome, on the other hand, looks at the consequences of a (Western) person's average lifetime emissions, and this is probably more appropriate since we are interested in the demands to our lifestyle and not merely isolated choices; he claims that these lifetime emissions will roughly "wipe out more than six months of a healthy life" (Broome 2012: 74). Broome takes this to be a serious harm, so for him it matters what an individual does. However, this calculation shows the consequences if they were aggregated to hit one person only; but in reality the consequences of one person's emissions will be dispersed over a very large number of individuals, and it is less clear that any of these are harmed in any perceptible way.

I am not sure which conclusion to draw from this discussion. But either way, the attempt to justify an individual ethical responsibility from the harm an individual will cause by their emissions looks somewhat bleak; and if people in general come to think that, the ethical approach might lose its appeal.

There is a related discussion about which of my emissions are unnecessary. According to Broome, all avoidable emissions are unjust. But how much emission can we avoid as individuals? We can probably cut a good deal. The problem is, however, that our lives are intertwined with society in ways that cause emissions we cannot influence directly as individuals. Do we have to step out of society? And would it be more efficient if each of us produced our own energy rather than purchasing it in the available form? These questions do not have simple answers, and lead again to some indeterminateness about our precise duties.

It seems evident that anthropogenic climate change is caused by collective action, and that it also has to be addressed by collective action. This observation leads to the next problem.

5. Efficiency and coordination

Appealing to individuals' ethical motivation works as a solution to the contributor's dilemma, if individuals come to believe that they *should* contribute (and expect others to contribute) and they act accordingly, even though strictly speaking it is not in their self-interest. In this way, ethical motivation can ensure coordinated collective action for the common good rather than people acting out of individual motives.

However, if people still frame their decision from an individual perspective, and from this perspective do their best to act in the way they believe to be right, this might lead to a sub-optimal outcome from a collective perspective. The reason is that they might choose inefficient means.

One aspect is that intuitive perceptions of what it takes to most effectively reduce emissions of a given individual are not always reliable. Thorough calculations of consequences of actions in terms of their effect on emissions are complicated and often lead to surprising results. Of course, this problem could to some extent be solved by more information for individuals, but that would require that people perceive this information as reliable and are willing to act upon it.

Another aspect is the lack of coordination that follows if the individual perspective is taken strictly as "How can I change *my* lifestyle and consumption pattern?", i.e. spending time and resources exclusively on reducing one's own emissions. Sometimes it might be more efficient (in collective terms) to spend time and resources on reducing other people's emissions. For instance, a person wanting to further insulate his already rather well insulated house will thereby not obtain the same reduction of emissions as he could if he spent his resources on insulation of less well insulated houses. In spite of stressing the individual duty not to emit any greenhouse gas, Broome (2012: 73) recognizes that only governments can achieve significant progress.

This leads us to consider an alternative method of ensuring coordinated collective action, namely relying on the market mechanism and thereby ensuring that prices are corrected through incentives to correspond to the collectively chosen goal for reductions. Use of incentives may change our preferences and thus solve the contributor's dilemma. And governments might possess better knowledge of the efficiency of means than isolated individuals.

However, this solution also has its problems. For one thing, it depends on political decisions to put the correct incentives in place. But because of the asymmetrical nature of the contributor's problem, politicians and their constituencies might not be sufficiently motivated to take the necessary decisions. It is a widespread complaint that democracy is not sufficiently concerned about long-term consequences such as those following from current level of emissions of greenhouse gases. However, there are some exceptions to this pessimistic expectation; the Kyoto Protocol, however deficient it may be, has after all been agreed on. But of course, this does not necessarily translate into compliance.

Another problem is that many people perceive economic incentives as an unethical means. Most people probably accept pragmatic political compromises concerning reduction of emissions as a necessary lesser evil than nothing being done. But once the problem has been framed as a moral problem, I believe many people consider the use of economic incentives morally dubious. Emission permits can be traded. But if emissions are morally wrong, they should not be traded. Many people perceive these two spheres as incommensurable.

Some years ago, I observed a group of students in an agricultural university listening to a panel discussing the use of tradable emission permits as a means in climate policy. On the panel was an economist arguing in favor, and a biologist arguing against. It was striking that only a minority of students, which happened to be economist students, perceived tradable emission permits as a good thing; all other students perceived it as wrong.

I suggest that what is perceived as wrong about tradable emission permits is that they accept self-interested economic calculations where moral motivation is called for. Emissions are perceived as morally wrong. Tradable emission permits accept that one can act wrongly by paying one's way. But this is not perceived as morally acceptable behavior. I believe a similar skepticism can be observed regarding economic valuation of environmental goods. Economists argue that these goods will not be properly protected unless they are priced according to their true value. When economists put a market price on environmental goods, they simulate that there are private goods, but people perceive them as public goods that should be valued through political priorities (see the seminal Diamond and Hausman 1994). Hence, to treat them as objects for private consumption is again to frame them as open for self-interested calculations where concern for the common good is called for.

6. Poverty

Framing the issue concerning what to do about climate change as primarily a matter of mitigation through reduced emissions, and asking what each of us as an individual has a duty to do in this regard, has another consequence, namely to draw away attention from poverty.

There was an ironic illustration of this when the Danish Council of Ethics some years ago arranged a meeting on climate change and food. In accordance with my claims, the meeting to a large degree concentrated on how each of us, as a consumer, can reduce our emissions from food consumption (currently responsible for approximately 20 percent of total emissions in Denmark). The fact that climate change threatens food security in poor regions was hardly mentioned. And to the extent it was, it could not be seriously addressed at the meeting because the Third World somehow is not part of the Council's remit.

In 2000, the United Nations set the goal, as one of the so-called "millennium goals", to halve, before 2015, the percentage of those living in 1990 in severe poverty, where 1250 million people out of 5200 lived on less than 1 dollar a day. There has been some success: in 2008, in spite of population growth, both the number of people living in extreme poverty and the poverty rates fell in each developing region compared with 2005 (UN 2012). In developing regions, the proportion of extremely poor fell from 47 percent in 1990 to 24 percent in 2008. However, in 2007 there was still a group of 192 million people left behind, who live for less than ½ dollar a day. And with estimates of a poverty rate just below 16 percent in 2015, there is still some way to go. Moreover, the proportion of undernourished has not decreased at the same rate as income poverty, and has even stalled in many regions.

According to the IPCC (2007) and WHO (2005), there is a clear tendency that the world's poor are experiencing and will continue to experience the most serious consequences of climate change. This is due to two main reasons. First, the population in developing countries often lacks the necessary resources to be able to adapt and protect themselves against even the smallest fluctuations in climate. Second, because of their geographical location in subtropical or tropical climate zones where climate changes are predicted to have the biggest impact, the world's poor are, and will be, more exposed to changes in the climate (e.g. IPCC 2007; UNFCCC 2011; European Commission 2011). This means that climate change will probably counteract the goal of eradicating severe poverty and increase vulnerability to further poverty (Ahmed et al. 2009; Nelson et al. 2010). Moreover, there will be an increased tendency for the extremely poor to remain in poverty.

The relative success of fighting severe poverty since 1990 appears to be unsustainable in the sense that it has been accompanied by increased emissions in greenhouse gases. A major factor underlying the relative success of poverty eradication has been the economic growth experienced in many developing countries. Perhaps not surprisingly, this growth has been accompanied by an increase in greenhouse gas emissions. Thus, emissions from developing countries more than doubled from 1990 to 2008. In 2009, when the economic crisis hit, emission levels in developing countries slowed down. The total level of greenhouse gas emissions in developing countries in 2009 nevertheless became larger than the total level of emissions from developed countries. Still, the *per capita* level of emissions remains far higher (more than a factor 3) in developed countries.

Another problem, also related to climate change, is decreasing forest areas. Forest areas in Asia increased from 2000 to 2010, but continue to decrease in Africa and South America, resulting in a worldwide net loss. Hence, climate change threatens to counteract poverty eradication, while the mitigation of climate change conflicts with economic growth in poor countries.

It seems then, that to some extent, reducing emissions worldwide and fighting poverty are conflicting goals. Hence, there is an important and complex weighing-up to be made between justice *between* generations (requiring the present generation to mitigate climate change) and justice *within* generations (requiring us [the rich] to fight poverty). However, the individual ethical perspective and its exclusive focus on reducing emissions tends to overlook this problem with the consequence that it risks increasing poverty in the future.

In a sense, there is nothing new or surprising about poverty being overlooked. As Broome (2012: 54) says, "justice has a stronger emotional appeal than goodness." Or, in other words, the appeal not to harm others has much stronger appeal than the appeal to help others out of poverty. It is perceived as a clear responsibility not to cause harm. Poverty is not perceived as our responsibility. Though it is clearly acceptable to help the poor, it is not similarly perceived as a clear duty.

Still, it is a bit odd that the richer nations in the Kyoto Protocol have accepted to hold developing countries free of the costs of mitigation, but choose to ignore the adverse effects of climate change on current and future poverty.[2]

7. Conclusion

Appeal to personal responsibility not to cause harm appears to represent the strongest motivation to solve the contributor's dilemma. However, if this motivation stands alone, it will have some serious drawbacks. One drawback is the risk that it will be undermined by its indeterminateness. But given that a determinate version can work, it will have some adverse consequences. It is likely not to be the most efficient way to reduce emissions of greenhouse gases, and hence it will lead to sub-optimal outcomes. It tends to ignore the present poor and thereby risks increasing and prolonging present poverty. From this perspective, the ethics of personal responsibility can appear somewhat obsessed with securing one's own freedom from guilt at the cost of ignoring the consequences.

The only remedy to these drawbacks appears to be solutions that address all relevant consequences. This could perhaps be achieved through use of various incentives and a general appeal to consequences. However, getting incentives to work requires political action. But it is part of the contributor's problem that politicians will be equally reluctant to contribute as their constituencies.

From this perspective, the ethics of personal responsibility becomes important. Because of its strong emotional appeal, it might be able to create pressure for political action. But then we have the problem that allowing the trade of emission permits and similar economic instruments is likely to be in conflict with the motivation from personal responsibility, because it is perceived as *not* taking one's responsibility seriously.

Broome (2012: 43–48) makes the suggestion that present emitters compensate themselves for reducing their emissions. They could do so by consuming more and investing less for the future. In theory, this could create a win-win situation, where both the present and future generations will be better off. If the present generation is compensated this way, it may be much easier to solve the contributor's problem, because people would have a self-interested reason to contribute to reducing emissions.

However, from the perspective of the personal duty not to cause harm, this would be a double injustice. First, present emitters are doing the injustice to cause harm to future generations, then they want compensation to address this injustice. But they should rather compensate future generations for the first injustice; instead they commit the new injustice to refrain from this compensation. The conflict between the two perspectives is here taken to its extreme.

As I see it, the only way forward would be to get the two perspectives in better agreement. Regrettably, I see no clear way to achieve that at the moment. But it is an extremely important challenge for the near future.

Notes

1   See Parfit 1984, 56–66 for a more detailed description.
2   Jensen and Bech Flanagan (forthcoming) explores this situation in more depth.

References

Ahmed, S. A., Diffenbaugh, N. S. and Hertel, T. W. 2009. "Climate Volatility Deepens Poverty Vulnerability in Developing Countries." *Environ. Ress. Lett.* 4, 1–8.
Baer, P. 2006. "Adaptation: Who Pays Whom?" In W. Adger, J. Paavola, S. Huq and M. Mace (eds), *Fairness in Adaptation to Climate Change*. Cambridge, MA: MIT Press, 131–153.
Broome, J. 2008. "The Ethics of Climate Change." *Scientific American*, June 2008, 69–73.
Broome, J. 2012. *Climate Matters: Ethics in a Warming World*. New York: Norton.
European Commission 2011. http://ec.europa.eu/dgs/clima/mission/index_en.htm.
Diamond, P. and Hausman, J. D. 1994. "Contingent Valuation: Is Some Number Better than No Number?" *Journal of Economic Perspectives* 8(4), 45–64.
IPPC 2007. IPCC *Fourth Assessment Report: Climate Change 2007*. Geneva: IPCC.

Jensen, K. K. and Bech Flanagan, T. Forthcoming. "Climate Change and Compensation." *Public Reason.*

Nelson, G. E., Rosengrant, M. W, Palazzo, A., Gray, I., Ingersoll, C., Robertson, R., Tokgoz, S., Zhu, T., Sulser, T. B., Ringler, C., Msangi, S. and You, L. 2010. *Food Security, Farming, and Climate Change to 2050: Scenarios, Results, Policy Options.* Washington, DC: International Food Policy Research Institute.

Parfit, D. 1984. *Reasons and Persons.* Oxford: Clarendon.

Sinnott-Armstrong, W. 2005. "It's Not My Fault: Global Warming and Individual Moral Obligations." In W. Sinnott-Armstrong and R. B Howarth (eds), *Perspectives on Climate Change: Science, Economics, Politics, Ethics.* Amsterdam: Elsevier, 285–307.

UN 2012. *The Millennium Development Goals Report 2012.*

UNFCCC 2011. http://unfccc.int/2860.php

WHO 2005. www.who.int/globalchange/news/fsclimandhealth/en/index.html.

2 The liberal tragedy of the commons

The deficiency of democracy in a changing climate

Ivo Wallimann-Helmer

In this chapter, I argue that the normative framework of liberal democracy is one of the sources of the failure of international climate politics. The liberal framework makes it very likely that at least some democracies will not consent to an international agreement to mitigate greenhouse gas emissions. In this situation, the institution of judicial review might be viewed as crucial to overcome the risk of a tragedy of the commons. However, judicial review cannot serve this purpose in the case of climate change and an institutional change of the kind required cannot be derived from within the normative framework of liberal democracy itself.

1. Introduction: the *real* tragedy of the commons

The recent conferences of the parties of the United Nations Framework Convention on Climate Change (UNFCCC) give cause for pessimism that the binding long-term agreements needed to drastically reduce greenhouse gas (GHG) emissions will ever be possible. Stephen M. Gardiner has observed that these negotiations have a decision structure even worse than that in Garret Hardin's tragedy of the commons (Gardiner 2002). Here I argue that one cause for this state of affairs in global climate politics is the normative framework of liberal democracy. This framework makes it unlikely that all nation-states, especially all democracies, will reach an international agreement mitigating GHG emissions. The reason for this pessimistic conclusion is that the liberal framework for democracy tends to reproduce domestically what, on a global level, Stephen Gardiner called the *real* tragedy of the commons.

This chapter is structured as follows. First, I argue that Gardiner's analysis of the global tragedy of the commons is too wide-meshed to consider the domestic decision procedures in democracies necessary to legitimate international policy agreements. Second, I suggest that the normative framework of liberal democracy creates a decision structure likely to lead to a tragedy of the commons. Third, since history seems to contradict this claim, I show why judicial review is crucial to the institutional structure of liberal democracy. However, as the fourth part of this chapter argues, in the case of climate change, a similar mechanism cannot be derived from within the normative framework of liberal democracy. Overall, my analysis will make clear why the liberal normative framework for political decision-making cannot cope adequately with challenges of sustainability such as climate change.

The argument in this chapter, however, is restricted in three respects. First, it provides no defence of the need for an international agreement on mitigating GHG emissions. It simply presumes that such an agreement is necessary to reduce the adverse effects of climate change. Second, it takes for granted Gardiner's analysis of the potentially dilemmatic decision structure concerning climate change. Third, the paper only deals with the ideal of liberal democracy that relies on John Locke's contractualist argument for the need of civil society. Discussion of similar problems arising from the normative ideal of republican democracy must be reserved for another occasion.[1]

2. International agreements and national legitimisation

According to Gardiner, the decision structure in global climate politics is similar to that proposed by Hardin in his tragedy of the commons (Gardiner 2002: 402). A tragedy of the commons occurs when access to a commons is not institutionally or otherwise regulated and all those sharing the commons are rational. In such circumstances, it is rational for all parties involved to preserve their commons for mutual advantage. But it is also in the interest of each individual party to exhaust the commons so as to maximise its own profits. Preserving the commons is in the interest of all parties involved in order to maintain a certain level of welfare. However, it is rational for each individual party to maximise its own profits because, in the absence of mechanisms to avoid maximising behaviour at the cost of the commons, every individual not doing so is at a disadvantage to all other parties potentially maximising their profits (Hardin 1968: 1244). Without mechanisms to regulate access to the commons, the commons will be depleted. However, as Elinor Ostrom and colleagues have shown, if an adequate regulatory framework exists or develops, a tragedy of the commons can always become a simple co-ordination problem (Ostrom 1999, 279).

The structure of Hardin's tragedy also can be applied to pollution, or more exactly to the atmosphere as a common good. It is rational for all to preserve the atmosphere, but because there is no mechanism to control pollution, it is also rational for all individuals to pollute the environment while maximising their own profit (Hardin 1968: 1045). In the case of climate change, Gardiner believes that the *real* tragedy of the commons should not be understood as a dilemma for parties living today but as a dilemma occurring between generations (Gardiner 2002: 404). Gardiner argues, following Ostrom, that this is because a tragedy of the commons among living parties can be overcome if they have the capacity to influence each other's behaviour reciprocally (Gardiner 2002: 394). Such influence can be reached by either social interaction among the parties involved or through institutional design. In the first case, this means that the behaviour of the involved parties changes because they are in regular exchange. In the second case, the institutional framework has to be changed so as to ensure the preservation of the commons (Hampton 1987: 263).

Without a regulatory framework, the risk of a tragedy of the commons is not easily avoided. Since such a regulatory framework does not yet exist for GHG emissions, the decision structure in negotiations on global climate agreements is potentially dilemmatic. Although reducing emissions to mitigate the adverse effects of climate change might contribute to a common good, it is in the interest of nation-states not to enter into such agreements. And, in the absence of a regulatory framework, it is easy to argue that one does not do so because other nation-states may not do so either. Moreover, to overcome a tragedy of the commons at the global level, quite a number of additional structural and contextual obstacles must be overcome than in the case of the management of common goods at a more local level (cf. Axelrod and Keohane 1985; Ostrom 1999: 281f).

However, it is at least imaginable that a subgroup of all nation-states decides to reduce their GHG emissions without a binding international agreement, and their example may put pressure on some other states to adopt mitigating behaviour. This would allow a stepwise change of the dilemmatic situation in global climate politics into a simple co-ordination problem (Gardiner 2002: 408). However, Gardiner argues that climate change should still be treated as if it had a dilemmatic structure. This is for two reasons. First, the effects of not reaching mitigating goals will be catastrophic. Second, a risk of an *inter*generational tragedy of the commons exists (Gardiner 2002: 414). Climate change is an *inter*generational challenge because the most severe consequences of high GHG emissions today will very probably occur in the (far) future. This means that the parties facing the challenges of climate change probably belong to different generations. Since it is hard to see how future generations might have an impact on the behaviour of the generation living now, the circumstances that can turn an *intra*generational tragedy into a simple co-ordination problem cannot arise.

Given that the challenge of climate change involves parties of different generations, a tragedy of the commons is very likely. According to Gardiner, this is what explains the unsatisfactory results of the conferences of the UNFCC. Those negotiating international agreements are living representatives of nation-states, while those most severely affected by climate change will be future generations. Future generations are unable to influence the behaviour of representatives currently negotiating global climate agreements. As a consequence, it is highly probable that representatives of nation-states negotiating currently will not reach a satisfactory international agreement to reduce GHG emissions.

Thus far, I believe Gardiner's analysis is convincing. However, it suffers from a central weakness. It is too wide-meshed to grasp the deeper problem underlying the global climate tragedy. Those negotiating and implementing international agreements are bound by national legitimisation procedures for policy making. It is these procedures that increase the likelihood of the global climate tragedy. Although there is no room in this chapter to defend nation-states' right to self-determination, its pragmatic importance in global climate politics can be demonstrated by introducing David Miller's two-stage model for dealing with the challenge of climate change (Miller 2008: 121). According to this model, the principles for distributing the burdens of emission reductions should first be applied to nation-states. These principles should be fair, because only a fair distribution of burdens makes it likely that subscribing nation-states comply with such an agreement. It should then be up to nation-states to implement those policies for distributing the costs of mitigating GHG emissions that can be legitimised from within. This second stage is necessary because it allows respect for the right to national self-determination and differences in capacity and culture. Miller claims that respecting the right to national self-determination enhances the compliance of subscribing nation-states.

Although Miller wants to preserve national self-determination in applying an international agreement, he does not consider the conditions to legitimate international agreements as such. As Miller presents his model, it presumes that international agreements can be reached by representatives of nation-states without being bound to national legitimisation processes. But, at least in democracies, representatives of such states must be legitimised to negotiate and enter international agreements. Moreover, ratification is needed to legitimise their realisation. In consequence, it is not only the case that international agreements have to respect national self-determination when it comes to their implementation. Establishment and ratification of international agreements also rely on legitimisation processes within nation-states.

These legitimisation processes raise the risk of a tragedy of the commons. The next section discusses the conditions under which political decisions and the agency of liberal democratic nation-states' representatives in international negotiations are legitimate. I suggest that the normative framework of liberal democracy allows for political behaviour that potentially leads to a tragedy of the commons, especially when it comes to the long-term policy decisions required in the case of climate change.

3. The *real* tragedy of the commons in liberal democracy

Following Gardiner's argument, the decision structure concerning international agreements for mitigating GHG emissions may well lead to a tragedy of the commons. Indeed, the *inter*generational challenge of climate change constitutes the *real* tragedy of the commons. Although in my view convincing, Gardiner's analysis does not take into account that the decision structure concerning international agreements applies both to nation-states and their representatives and to legitimisation processes that enable international agreements to be negotiated and ratified. To examine these elements, I introduce Locke's contractualist argument for defending democracy.

The way Locke's contractualist argument for democracy and legitimate political decision making is presented, leads to what Held calls protective or legal democracy (Held 2006: ch. 3 and 201). Two main claims are defended in these two models of democracy. First, political decision making is bound by a fixed bundle of (liberty or human) rights protecting individual citizens from state intervention. Second, policy measures are only legitimate if they are supported by citizens. Therefore, political decisions are only legitimate if they do not impair this bundle of rights and can count on citizens' acceptance. These models of democracy are protective, and their political decision structures are legally bound.

According to Locke, in the state of nature all human beings are equal because they hold a bundle of natural or God-given rights (Locke 1999: II. 6). These rights, together with a natural duty to preserve humanity, would allow humans to live in peace. However, conflict might occur because some humans will affect the individual rights of others or because punishment for such an infringement will be excessive. This is why Locke argues that a civil society is needed to ensure three things: (a) respect for natural or God-given rights; (b) institutions to judge infringements of these rights; and (c) the enforcement of laws protecting these rights (II. 87–88). Thus, entering civil society, humans empower social institutions to secure and enforce the rights given to them in the state of nature. In so doing, they assign to social institutions their natural or God-given right to judge infringements of rights and to execute their enforcement (II. 134). All other rights given in the state of nature still belong to the individual and should be protected by civil society and its institutions. Political authority should be bound by these rights, and legitimate political decision making should stop where these rights begin. These rights indefeasibly constrain political decision making.

Locke's argument for the necessity of civil society allows democracy to be justified for two reasons. First, civil society constitutes a contract among all involved to confer to social institutions their right to judge infringements of natural or God-given rights and their right to enforce these rights. Since the legitimacy of the institutions of civil society is justified by all involved consenting to the transition from the state of nature to civil society, all contracting parties are entitled to control the institutions of civil society (II. 128–131). If civil institutions or their assigned representatives break this contract, it is legitimate for citizens to remove the officials. To guarantee this right, political processes are needed that allow the control and removal of officials, both as members of the legislative assembly and of the executive institutions. Second, such a hypothetical contract establishes a collective body that should be able to decide what directions to take. As such, an agency needs decision structures to choose between options, Locke believes majority vote is necessary because this is the only way to steer a collective body effectively. Hence, he believes that the initial contract justifying civil society also binds civil society to follow majority decisions (II. 95–99).[2] The legitimate coverage of these majority decisions, however, should be constrained by the bundle of natural or God-given rights still remaining after entering civil society. It is these kinds of indefeasible rights that limit the sphere of legitimate policy decisions.

From a modern perspective, it might be questioned whether the bundle of rights constraining legitimate policy decisions is natural or God-given. However, both Lockean arguments justify what is nowadays understood by liberal democracy, as defined by Barry Holden for example:

Liberal democracy is a political system in which (a) the whole people, positively or negatively, make, and are entitled to make the basic determining
decisions on important matters of public policy; and (b) they make, and are
only entitled to make, such decisions in a restricted sphere since the legitimate sphere of public authority is limited.

(1988: 12)

If public or political authority is limited, legitimate political agency must respect
these constraints. These constraints must be respected by political actors because
they define what can be understood as the common good of liberal democratic
societies. This common good consists of securing constraints to state interference. Within the Lockean framework, this means ensuring a bundle of
indefeasible rights, which includes their effective enforcement and institutions
to judge infringement.

However, humans enter civil society only on condition that the bundle of
indefeasible rights is secured. Transition from the state of nature to civil society
must provide this advantage. This shows why citizens in a liberal framework are
often framed as self-interested rational beings. They are understood as self-interested and rational because their own interest in the security of their bundle of
indefeasible rights is the basis for defending the transition from the state of
nature to civil society (Hampton 1997: 81). Consequently, if civil society is
established, self-interested and rational behaviour in political decision making
cannot be legitimately oppressed, since such interests lie at the heart of a normative justification of liberal democracy.

Since self-interested and rational behaviour in political agency is legitimate in
civil society, then the absence of mechanisms to control political agency poses a
risk that citizens might abuse this commons for their own profits. Likewise, there
is a risk that those political actors who might not initially abuse the commons for
their own profits will eventually do so too. They must distrust all others who
might behave in a self-interested and rational way. Such thinking and behaviour
of political actors parallels the situation leading to the tragedy of the commons.
Hence, a Lockean-contractualist defence of liberal democracy by itself cannot
provide a framework for avoiding such a potentially tragic structure.

The risk of a tragedy of the commons increases further when taking Locke's
claim into account that majority vote is necessary for political decision making.
To gain a majority, political actors need to gather as many citizens as possible to
implement those legal regulations that seem to best guarantee the common goal
of the initial contract. In some circumstances, gathering a majority can be more
feasible when contradicting the security of a bundle of indefeasible rights, most
of the time at the cost of a minority. In the absence of mechanisms to control
political agency, it is rational for political actors not only to act in the interest of
the liberal commons but also in a self-interested and rational way. And if no
mechanisms to control political behaviour exist, it is also rational for political
actors to assume that not all other players in the political arena will act to secure
the liberal commons either. Consequently, the need to gather a majority

increases the risk of a tragedy of the commons. Within a liberal framework, aspiration for profit at the cost of the commons is very likely.

Both these arguments can be challenged. In the light of Gardiner's argument that actors in decision processes can influence each other so as to avert the risk of tragedy, these observations seem to be too strongly stated. Reciprocal influence between political actors would allow the transition of a tragedy of the commons into a simple co-ordination problem. Furthermore, and in contrast to my conclusions, actual liberal democracies are not permanently at risk of a tragedy of the commons. According to Jean Hampton, this is because, historically speaking, liberal societies developed parallel to philosophical reflection, what she calls a governing convention (Hampton 1997: 83). A governing convention ensures compliance with political decisions and distribution of powers.[3] Such a convention assigns authorities legitimate power to solve specific social problems (Hampton 1997: 88). Following this view, in the state of nature individuals are not presented with a right to legislative and executive power, which they subsequently assign to civil institutions. Instead, it is a lengthy historical process that leads to civil institutions and commitments with political decisions and distribution of powers flowing from them.

Thus, although legitimate political decision making in liberal democracy might be defended by reference to an initial contract and indefeasible rights, for secure compliance with political decisions, a historically developed governing convention of legitimate political decision-making must be presumed. Given such a convention, the occurrence of a tragedy of the commons is less likely in liberal democracy. If historical processes lead to the development of social norms necessary to secure the common good of liberal society, a potential tragedy of the commons becomes a simple co-ordination problem.

However, this is true only if reciprocal control can actually occur between political actors. Although a governing convention might endure over centuries and influence political actors' behaviour, there is no possibility of reciprocal control between political actors living in the (far) future and those deciding on policy matters today. As the normative framework of liberal democracy must allow for political agency and decisions that infringe upon the liberal commons, and because only the currently living political actors can influence reciprocally and control each other, it is highly likely that political actors today will decide on policy matters in a way that corrodes the liberal commons in the (far) future. In consequence, the Lockean-contractarian framework of liberal democracy still allows for the occurrence of what Gardiner called the *real* tragedy of the commons.

Concerning international agreements on climate change, this argument has three consequences. First, international agreements can only find acceptance in liberal democracies if they are not in conflict with the bundle of rights believed to be indefeasible. Second, such agreements, however fair they might seem from an ethical point of view, can only be adopted by liberal democratic nation-states if they respect their governing convention. Otherwise liberal democracies may either not subscribe to such a contract or not be able to implement it. Third, those bargaining for such agreements have to be empowered by citizens to nego-tiate and implement these agreements. Therefore, in contrast to Miller's two-stage model, although the fairness of international agreements to mitigate GHG emissions might be important in enhancing the compliance of nation-states, such agreements also have to be in accordance with processes of legitimate democratic decision-making. As these processes allow for Gardiner's *real* tragedy of the commons, it is likely that liberal democracies will either not entitle their representatives to negotiate and sign international climate agreements or will not ratify these agreements once they are signed.

4. Judicial review to sustain the liberal commons

At this point, many readers will object that factual history tells against the argu-ment thus far. Liberal democracies tend not to undermine the bundle of indefeasible rights of their citizens, whether they are members of the same or different generations. For several centuries, democracies have remained stable and functioning; they most often do not harm human or other indefeasible rights, and political actors do not behave in a way that undermines this common good of liberal democracy. In what follows, I argue that these points are correct, but only in liberal democracies have institutional mechanisms been developed to control behaviour in political decision making.

In most modern western nation-states, democratic institutions have devel-oped over a long period. Such a lengthy development makes it very plausible that these institutions not only developed because of the influence of philosophical theories but also through the emergence of some kind of governing convention (Hampton 1997: 86). This makes it plausible that Locke's theory has been only one impetus among others for liberal democratic institutions to emerge. Indeed, liberal democratic nation-states have experienced many other influences beyond Locke's theory (Held 2006; Bessette 2011). Liberal democracies would not be as stable as they are if their development had only relied on the Lockean justifica-tion of their institutions. There would have been a permanent risk of a tragedy of the commons, which over the centuries potentially would have led to a corro-sion of the bundle of indefeasible rights. Governing conventions of liberal democracies must have developed mechanisms of control preventing democratic procedures of decision making from the risk of a tragedy in the long run. In my view, these are three institutions: the judiciary or the institution of judicial review, established legal regulations, and conditions of reasonableness.

In modern nation-states, I suggest, the most important mechanism of control is established by the institution of judicial review. As the third main branch of political power in addition to the legislative and executive powers, it allows judgement on all political decisions. Judicial review can decide whether political decisions are in line with the constitution and especially whether they infringe the bundle of indefeasible rights. In so doing, the judiciary is a political institu-tion controlling political agency. If political decisions impair the bundle of indefeasible rights, then they are judged to be illegitimate and can no longer be brought to the political arena. In this way, judicial review serves as a mechanism of control for legitimate political agency in democratic decision making and can avoid the risk of a tragedy of the commons in liberal democracies.[4]

The legitimacy of judicial review can be questioned because the legitimisation of members of these institutions is in conflict with the procedural conditions of legitimate political representation. Judges are often assigned by some members of the elected executive or the legislative assembly but are not elected by citizens themselves (Waldron 2006: 1391). However, although judicial review might be in conflict with the Lockean defence of liberal democracy, it is a necessary part of its institutional realisation and stability. If the risk of a tragedy of the liberal commons is accepted in a liberal democratic framework, then judicial review is a very plausible way to ensure the sustenance of the common good, either for the citizens of one generation or, more importantly, for citizens of different generations. Once established, judicial review serves as a trustee that secures the indefeasible bundle of rights. It allows citizens to claim their rights and to contest political decisions on a legal basis (Lever 2009: 813).[5]

Another mechanism of control for political decision making in liberal democracies is legal regulation going beyond constitutional rights. Whenever a governing convention emerges, it is not only enforced through the constitution but also through further legal regulation. If political programs or political agency are in conflict with such regulations, then these can be judged as illegitimate by institutions upholding legal regulation.[6] In this sense, legal regulations serve as a mechanism of control which can avert the risk of a tragedy. However, this mechanism of control is much weaker than the institution of judicial review, because legitimate political action in democracies has as the central aim of establishing law following democratic procedures. Thus, before judging political agency and decisions to be in conflict with established legal regulation, it has always to be clarified whether these might be appropriate proposals for new legal regulation.

A further mechanism of control for political agency has been defended by deliberative democracy theorists (e.g. Habermas 1999; Cohen 2009). They claim that citizens should respect certain conditions of reasonableness, which include among others the acceptance of the non-coercive enforcement of the best argument and respecting equality among participants in deliberation. Political actors who comply with these conditions of reasonableness will not risk a tragedy of the commons because they will try to abandon self-interested behaviour and aim at advocating the liberal commons to secure the bundle of indefeasible rights. Indeed, the argument thus far underpins the idea that such behaviour of political actors is preferable. In liberal democracies, however, it cannot be legitimately enforced.

Enforcing the conditions of reasonableness would go against the contractualist argument in defence of liberal democracy. It would illegitimately oppress the self-interested and rational behaviour presupposed by the Lockean-contractarian argument for why the establishment of civil society is necessary. In consequence, deliberative democracy theorists cannot defend institutions to enforce the reasonable behaviour of political actors. The only legitimate way to enforce reasonableness in liberal democracies is by elections or by reciprocal social control among political actors. As these mechanisms of control are part of the process of democratic decision making, they cannot have the same power as the judiciary to prevent the risk of a tragedy of the commons.

In consequence, the main instrument to control political agency and policy decisions in the interest of preserving the liberal commons over generations is judicial review. Since judicial review is not part of the process of democratic decision making, it does not bear the same risk of a tragedy of the commons. In contrast, legal regulation and the conditions of reasonableness are much weaker mechanisms for controlling political behaviour. They work only as part of the processes of legitimate political decision making. However, as argued, liberal democratic institutions develop through a long historical process and, consequently, depend on a governing convention. This makes it plausible that political actors will influence each other reciprocally so that they most often comply with the constitution, or in other words with the liberal commons, even without institutional control.

But when it comes to what Gardiner called the *real* tragedy of the commons, institutional regulation that is not part of the political decision process becomes necessary. Members of different generations are not able to control each other's behaviour reciprocally. Future political actors cannot ensure that decisions taken today will secure the liberal commons in the (far) future. Therefore, to avoid a tragedy of the commons *inter*generationally, institutional regulation is needed that cannot be legitimately altered through processes of political decision making. This institutional regulation is provided by judicial review as part of the governing convention of liberal democratic nation-states.

5. The challenge of climate change: A climate judiciary?

The conclusion reached in the last section might provide optimism with regard to the challenge of climate change. If it is possible to avert the *real* tragedy of the commons in liberal democracies by the institution of judicial review, it seems plausible that the same applies when it comes to decisions concerning climate change. However, the argument regarding climate change cannot follow the same line, for two reasons. First, it is not at all clear that mitigating GHG emissions is a liberal commons similar to ensuring the security of the bundle of indefeasible rights. Second, mitigating GHG emissions can be in conflict with at least some rights of the bundle of indefeasible liberal rights. This explains why there is always a risk in liberal democracy of a *real* tragedy of the commons when decisions involving members of different generations are necessary, such as those needed in the case of climate change.

In the previous section, I argued that the institution of judicial review can be defended in a Lockean framework because it is a mechanism necessary to prevent a tragedy of the commons. In the case of climate change, judicial review cannot serve as such a mechanism. To serve as such a mechanism, it would have to be shown that mitigating GHG emissions is part of the bundle of indefeasible rights lying at the core of the liberal normative framework of democracy. Simon Caney has argued that climate change leads to infringements of part of the bundle of indefeasible rights of liberal democracy (Caney 2005: 767). But such an argument does not go far enough. It only makes clear why liberal democracies have good reasons to do something to combat climate change. It does not show that the reduction of GHG emissions is an enforceable right. Reducing GHG emissions is only a means of avoiding an infringement of rights; it is not a liberal right in itself. Although there is wide scientific agreement that mitigating GHG emissions is necessary to combat the adverse effects of climate change, it is also reasonable to argue for technical development that allows for adaptation to such change and reduces its adverse effects. Both mitigating and adapting measures could secure the bundle of indefeasible rights, but the second would put into question the need for an international agreement to reduce GHG emissions.

In liberal democracy, it must be accepted as legitimate for political actors to advance those legal regulations that in their view best serve to secure the bundle of indefeasible rights. This also applies to the question of how to combat the adverse effects of climate change. Since in liberal democracy self-interested and rational political behaviour cannot be judged illegitimate, a tragedy of the commons with regard to climate change is likely. It is likely because, if some political actors opt for policy measures that do not demand reduction of GHG emissions, other political actors might follow suit. Liberal democratic nation-states in such a situation will either not consent to international agreements to reduce GHG emissions or, if their representatives sign such an agreement, it is still possible that it will not be ratified or adequately implemented.

Even worse, enforcing a (drastic) reduction of GHG emissions might call in to question the commons of liberal democracies. Mitigating GHG emissions might lead to an infringement of indefeasible liberty rights because such a policy measure demands a (drastic) change of lifestyle. Thus, scientifically adequate means to combat the adverse effects of climate change might call in to question the bundle of indefeasible rights. This makes it rational for political actors to choose political positions and programmes that result in less harm to individual liberty. Confronted with this challenge, it might be better for political actors to put forward political positions and programmes that are less in conflict with the commons of liberal democracies. This becomes even more rational politically if there is no guarantee that other political actors will not behave similarly. A tragedy of the commons with regard to the need to reduce GHG emissions might be the result.

As Gardiner pointed out, however, such a situation can be modified into a co-ordination problem without a dilemmatic decision structure. If there are enough political actors to reach decisions about an agreement on the necessity to mitigate GHG emissions, then they might also influence the behaviour of other, initially sceptical, political actors. Thus, the situation depends on empirical matters that cannot be decided from a purely theoretical perspective. But, although such decisions are possible, there is a risk that in liberal democracies a tragedy of the commons will occur with regard to the challenges of climate change. This is especially true because climate change is an intergenerational challenge and involves Gardiner's *real* tragedy of the commons. Future genera-tions cannot influence the political agency of those in charge today. And those in charge today might opt for political decisions and programmes in conflict with the long-term policy decisions needed to effectively reduce GHG emissions.

In consequence, it seems that liberal democracy is at risk of not dealing adequately with challenges such as climate change. This situation makes it necessary to explore further how democratic institutions could be changed to be able to take such challenges more seriously without calling in to question the normative underpinnings and the governing conventions developed in liberal democratic nation-states.

One possible institutional change in liberal democracy among others can be installing mechanisms of control that are not part of the process of legitimate political decision making.[7] These mechanisms would be similar to the institution of judicial review and could be called a climate judiciary. Like the institution of judicial review, a climate judiciary would judge political decisions with regard to how well they conform to demands stemming from the challenges of climate change or to demands of sustainability more generally. Members of these institu-tions would be appointed by the legislative or executive institutions as is done for the members of the judiciary. The main question with regard to membership in such an institution is which qualifications should be deemed relevant for becom-ing a member of a climate judiciary, since they cannot simply be individuals with a legal education. Such an education is insufficient to decide whether or not policy decisions conform to demands stemming from the challenges of climate change or more generally, to demands of sustainability. Adequate judgement of these questions, requires some knowledge in the relevant science or some engagement with the interests lying behind these demands.

Inspired by other proposals in green political theory, for the moment I can imagine three possible criteria to qualify as a member of a climate judiciary:[8]

1. Scientists, especially natural scientists, could qualify for such a position because due to their education they are well equipped to understand and judge policy decisions with regard to their sustainability.
2. Perhaps it is enough that potential candidates for a climate judiciary belong to relevant interest groups (e.g. Greenpeace or WWF) or parties acting in the interest of future generations. As members of such groups or parties, they show the required engagement with the challenges of climate change or more generally, with the demands of sustainability.
3. Another way to qualify as a candidate could simply be being young. Those who are young today will have to bear the adverse effects of climate change and unsustainable policy decisions. Since they have a special interest in policy decisions with regard to climate change and the demands of sustain-ability, they qualify as potential candidates for a climate judiciary.

Within the Lockean framework of liberal democracy, the central problem with these proposals for membership in a climate judiciary is that none of these groups of potential candidates is legitimised to take such a role by liberal democratic decision procedures. Scientists are qualified because they have been judged as such by members of the scientific community but not the citizen body. Members of interest groups are only qualified as potential candidates because they vouch for specific political decisions and not because they can be said to be especially competent as members of a climate judiciary. Seeing young political actors as potential candidates for the climate judiciary violates democratic legitimacy, because age is envisaged as a criterion relevant for special power with regard to the political decision making process.

All these proposals conflict with claims about democratic legitimacy because they advance criteria for a special role in political decision-making outside the scope of legitimate power distribution within liberal democracy. It should be all parties contracting to establish civil society who have a say in political decision making. As those consenting to this contract do so irrespective of age, the same applies to age as a criterion of qualification. In consequence, although a climate judiciary might be the solution to overcome a potential tragedy in liberal democracy with regard to demands stemming from climate change or sustainability, it is highly questionable how membership in such an institution should be assigned.

To be sure, this objection also applies to the members of the judiciary. Judges are assigned to their post because they qualify for this role by judicial education or at least some minimal knowledge about the constitution and legal regulation. But such qualification is justified as part of the ideal of liberal democracy itself. To secure the bundle of indefeasible rights, it is necessary that those who judge policy decisions understand their matter. Otherwise the judiciary could not serve its purpose. By contrast, scientific qualification as such is not necessary to secure the bundle of indefeasible rights. Vouching for specific policy decisions as a qualification for a climate judiciary contradicts the initial Lockean justification for democracy. Age is neither necessary nor legitimate to justify a special role to secure the bundle of indefeasible rights.

6. Conclusion: liberal democracy – a deficient ideal in times of climate change

According to the argument in this chapter, there is a risk that at least some liberal democracies will not be able to reach the decisions necessary to mitigate GHG emissions. Such democratic nation-states will either not authorise their leaders to negotiate for international agreements on mitigating GHG emissions or, if these political actors sign such an agreement, there is no guarantee that it will be ratified or adequately implemented. If some nation-states do not support such an agreement, it is likely that others will not do so either. This may, but need not, lead to a tragedy of the commons in international agreements on binding reductions of GHG emissions. Hence, Gardiner is right: the challenge of climate change should be treated as if it were a tragedy of the commons because liberal democracies cannot provide any guarantee that a tragedy of the commons and especially a *real* tragedy of the commons will not occur.

In consequence, facing a pressing challenge like climate change, liberal democracy has to be judged deficient. It bears the risk of not being able to deal adequately with challenges needing long-term policy decisions. The nature of legitimate political decision making stemming from such a vindication of democracy incorporates the risk of a tragedy, or what Gardiner called the *real* tragedy of the commons. Such a tragedy makes it likely that a binding international agreement to reduce GHG emissions will not be reached. This might lead some readers to argue that liberal democracy is a political regime that should be overturned, a position well known in green political theory. However, if it is correct that historically developed governing conventions of liberal democracies have to be respected to reach and to implement international agreements, such an argument proceeds too quickly. Ethical argument concerning climate change has to take seriously the problems of political decision procedures in liberal democratic nation-states, which have here been discussed with regard to a Lockean framework in defence of democracy and to Hampton's idea of a governing convention. Otherwise, acceptance and implementation of an international agreement to mitigate GHG emissions is even less likely.

Notes

I would like to thank Dieter Birnbacher, Anton Leist, Simon Milligan, Johan Rochel, Dominic Roser and Fabian Schuppert for very helpful discussions and feedback. I am grateful to the audiences of the MANCEPT Workshop in Political Theory 2011 in Manchester, the kick-off Workshop 'Rights to a Green Future' in Bucharest and the Colloquium for Political Philosophy at the University of Zurich for the opportunity to present my ideas at an earlier stage of their development. I also would like to acknowledge the generous financial support from Stiftung Mercator Switzerland (http://cms.stiftung-mercator.ch) and the University of Zurich's Research Priority Program in Ethics (URPP Ethics) without which the research for this paper would not have been possible. The work reported on in this publication also has benefited from participation in the Research Networking Programme "Rights to a Green Future" that is financed by the European Science Foundation.

1   See Wallimann-Helmer (2013) for this purpose.
2   For a very helpful discussion of the difficulties with majority decisions as a democratically legitimised procedure of political decision making see Saunders (2010).
3   This theoretical claim gains support from actual history. The emergence of stable and working liberal democracies needs specific historical and social conditions (Ware 1992).
4   In this chapter I try to remain indifferent to the question of whether a strong or weak form of judicial review is necessary to avoid a tragedy of the commons in liberal democracy. According to Waldron, whilst in a system of strong judicial review the court has the right to decline political decisions, in a system of weak judicial review it is only entitled to scrutinise the compatibility of decisions with the constitution (Waldron 2006: 1354).
5   In addition, Lever shows that although processes of legitimisation and accountability for judges are quite different from those for political actors in the legislative and the executive institutions, there are processes which allow judicial review to be seen as a fundamental democratic institution (Lever 2009: 811).
6   In Switzerland, for example, it is possible to bring politicians to court if they voice racist beliefs (Schweizerisches Strafgesetzbuch, Art. 261).

7   Further institutional mechanisms would have to be discussed at another occasion: in green political theory, for example, it is often proposed that non-human nature should have proxy representation in political decision making (e.g. Eckersley 2011). A very long tradition proposes that scientists or wise citizens should have more power than others in political decision making. Most recently, Shearman and Smith made such a proposal because of their analyses of liberal democracy, going in a similar direction as mine (Shearman and Smith 2007). A third category of proposals to be discussed would be to introduce quotas for young political actors or, better, for representatives of future generations to ensure that political decisions take more seriously the interests of future generations (Ekeli 2005; Thompson 2010). For a more fine-grained analysis of youth quotas, see Wallimann-Helmer (forthcoming).

8   See the proposals introduced in preceding note.

References

Axelrod, R. and Keohane, R. 1985. 'Achieving Cooperation under Anarchy: Strategies and Institutions', *World Politics*, 38 (1), 226–254.

Bessette, Murray S. Y. 2011. 'On the Genesis and Nature of Judicial Power', *eidos*, 15, 206–232.

Caney, S. 2005. 'Cosmopolitan Justice, Responsibility, and Global Climate Change', *Leiden Journal of International Law*, 18 (4), 747–775.

Cohen, J. 2009. *Philosophy, Politics, Democracy: Selected Essays*, Cambridge, MA: Harvard University Press.

Eckersley, R. 2011. 'Representing Nature', in Alonso, S., Keane, J. and Merkel, W. (eds), *The Future of Representative Democracy*, Cambridge: Cambridge University Press, 236–257.

Ekeli, K. S. 2005. 'Giving a Voice to Posterity: Deliberative Democracy and Representation of Future People', *Journal of Agricultural and Environmental Ethics*, 18 (5), 429–450.

Gardiner, S. M. 2002. 'The Real Tragedy of the Commons', *Philosophy and Public Affairs*, 30 (4), 387–416.

Habermas, J. 1999. *The Inclusion of the Other: Studies in Political Theory*, Cambridge, MA: MIT Press.

Hampton, J. 1987. 'Free-Rider Problems in the Production of Collective Goods', *Economics and Philosophy*, 3 (2), 245–273.

Hampton, J. 1997. *Political Philosophy*, Dimensions of Philosophy, Boulder, CO: Westview Press.

Hardin, G. 1968. 'The Tragedy of the Commons. The Population Problem Has No Technical Solution: It Requires a Fundamental Extension in Morality', *Science*, 162, 1243–1248.

Held, D. 2006. *Models of Democracy*, 3rd edn, Stanford University Press, Stanford, Calif.

Holden, B. 1988. *Understanding Liberal Democracy*, Oxford: Philip Allan.

Lever, A. 2009. 'Democracy and Judicial Review: Are They Really Incompatible?', *Perspectives on Politics*, 7 (4), 805–822.

Locke, J. 1999. *Two Treatises of Government*, Cambridge: Cambridge University Press.

Miller, D. 2008. 'Global Justice and Climate Change: How Should Responsibilities Be Distributed? Parts I and II', in Peterson, G. (ed.), *The Tanner Lectures on Human Values*, Volume 28, Salt Lake City, UT: University of Utah Press, 117–156.

Ostrom, E. 1999. 'Revisiting the Commons: Local Lessons, Global Challenges', *Science*, 284 (5412), 78–282.

Saunders, B. 2010. 'Why Majority Rule Cannot Be Based only on Procedural Equality', *Ratio Juris*, 23 (1), 113–122.

Shearman, D. and Wyne Smith, J. 2007. *The Climate Change Challenge and the Failure of Democracy*, Westport, CT: Praeger Publishers.

Thompson, D. F. 2010. 'Representing Future Generations: Political Presentism and Democratic Trusteeship', *Critical Review of International Social and Political Philosophy*, 13 (1), 17–37.

Waldron, J. 2006. 'The Core of the Case against Judicial Review', *The Yale Law Journal*, 115 (6), 1346–1406.

Wallimann-Helmer, I. 2013. 'The Republican Tragedy of the Commons: The Inefficiency of Democracy in the Light of Climate Change', *Ancilla Iuris*, 1–14.

Wallimann-Helmer, I. Forthcoming. 'Can Youth Quotas Help Avoid Future Disasters?', in Dimitrijoski, I., Godli, P., Mason, A., Munius, B. and Tremmel, J. (eds) *Youth Quotas: And other Efficient Forms of Youth Participation*, Heidelberg: Springer.

Ware, A. 1992. 'Liberal Democracy: One Form or Many?', *Political Studies*, XL Special Issue, 130–145.

3 Limitations to democratic governance of natural resources

May Thorseth

This chapter argues that sustainability is threatened by lack of coordination of action. This is partly due to lack of relevant knowledge about our own best interests, and partly a result of democratic models of governance when implemented in non-democratic contexts. Economic ways of thinking and moral self-conceptions are increasingly at variance. Three proposals of how a new balance can be attained are discussed: by the role of the public (Dewey), reflective judgment (Kant, Arendt), and deliberative democracy (Dryzek). The discussion is illustrated by the empirical case of institutional obstacles to sustainability drawn from a Chinese context.

1. Introduction

Well-organised coordination of action is presupposed in democratic models of governance. As we shall see in this chapter such coordination may be obstructed when democratic models of governance are implemented in non-democratic contexts. To illustrate this point we shall turn to a concrete case in the latter part of this chapter.

In discussing flaws and shortcomings due to inadequate coordination of action I shall look into four models of analysis. Through these analyses my aim is to propose an alternative focus in our attempt to deal with non-sustainable governance of natural resources. As a beginning we will have a look at Georg Henrik von Wright's civilisation criticism, basically concerned with a lack of balance between economic and ecological development (von Wright 1993). The problem is a serious tension between technological and economic development brought forward independently of sustainable ecological development. Basic to von Wright's model is the anticipation of a moral decline due to uncritical growth and technological fix of all kinds of problems, including existential and moral problems. His theory also serves as a general background for the remaining theoretical analyses.

A second model of analysis is based on a criticism of centric approaches to sustainable development. Both anthropocentric and eco-centric approaches are criticised for reducing environmental issues to a question of prioritising either humans *or* non-human nature. Rather, we should aim for an interactive model in order to establish better coordination between different political spheres (Dryzek 2005).

Third, the role of the public is analysed in view of John Dewey's discussion of the problem of the public (Dewey 1927). According to this view the problem of bad or missing coordination of action is based on lack of methods and procedures for informing the public. This diagnosis applies quite aptly to the Guangdong case discussed here.

Last, reflective judgement (Kant, Arendt) is part of the analysis tool of this chapter. If democracy is to work as intended, i.e. including all relevant perspectives for mankind's own best interests, there is a need for each to overcome their own private and subjective conditions (Arendt 1968). Applied to our context lack of reflective judgment is an obstacle to sustainable development. This is due to absence of viewing natural resources from the perspective of everyone else. A basic point to Kant and Arendt is to make possible intersubjective validity of judgements. In our context this translates to a need for coordination of judgements in the area of governance of natural resources, in order to be sustainable. Thus, sustainable governance is dependent on legitimising of opinions in the public domain.

1.1. Tools of analysis

In this section we shall have a further look at the approaches mentioned above, in order to sketch how each of them contribute to framing the problem of limitations to democratic governance of natural resources. Let us first turn to Georg Henrik von Wright's discussion of unlimited scientific and technological development as one perspective in view. He describes a tension that is partly caused by the technological imperative, i.e. the belief that unlimited technological development and growth is available. In criticising such a belief he points to the escalating technological development emanating from the scientific and industrial revolutions that has brought upon humans a moral decadence. Thus, the belief in unlimited (technological and scientific) development is a threat to our moral development. The point is captured in some well-known myths, in particular the myth of Faust and also the Paradise myth. Briefly, these myths deal with the problem of humananity trying to control all of its environments by the help of science and technology (von Wright 1993). The belief that all kinds of problems are solvable implies a reduction to one standard of measurement, e.g. technological. Thus, existential as well as moral problems are grasped in terms of a quest for technological solutions.

G. H. von Wright's civilisation criticism is partly about reducing developmental issues to one standard of measurement, e.g. scientific and technological. Here I want to link this reductionist line of thought to John Dryzek's criticism of both anthropocentric and eco-centric approaches to sustainability issues. Dryzek wants to substitute any centric approach with a non-centric view, and he argues in favour of an interactive model focussing on the interaction or communication between the different perspectives, e.g. anthropocentric or eco-/bio-centric. The rationale behind this is directly linked to the aim of better coordination between different political spheres.

Thus, treating all kinds of problems according to only one standard (technological progress), or through a one-dimensional focus on either human or non-human nature (anthropocentric vs. ecocentric) as discussed by von Wright and Dryzek respectively are basic points of departure for this chapter. One aspect of the obstacles to sustainable development is here linked to problems concerning coordination of action, which partly also has to do with shortage of information. This is fruitfully discussed by John Dewey as the problem of the public – the lack of a well-informed public (Dewey 1927). In more recent literature this lack can also partly be recognised in terms of Garret Hardin's description of the tragedy of the commons (1968). Here, the problem is basically that rational actions at an individual level are suboptimal at an aggregated – i.e. societal – level. Hardin's famous case is about grassing and farmland. Briefly, this is about depletion of a shared resource by individuals acting independently and rationally according to self-interest, while knowing that depleting the common resource runs contrary to the long-term interests of the group. Still another theoretical source to elucidating obstacles to sustainability is Kant's concept of reflective judgment (Kant 1952). Briefly, the main point in this chapter is the isolating of interests or in Kant's terminology the need for reflective judgment. In order for judgements to obtain validity there is a need for a view from the perspective of everyone else.

Let us just briefly return to von Wright and his understanding of technological progress and moral deterioration. By using some well-known myths, such as the Faust myth, he intends to inform the reader. Faust is a human who attempts to overcome man's imperfect nature, in particular to be non-omniscient. More generally, the problem seems to be humankind's quest for overcoming limits to our very preconditions qua human species, one of them being that we constantly believe that there are technological and finite solutions to fix our imperfect nature. Translated to the area of environmental and natural resource issues there is likewise a quest for finite solutions to the tragedy of the commons. The lack of interaction between human and non-human nature is also sought mended by way of technological solutions. This brings us to a contested distinction within the literature on sustainable development, namely that between eco-centrism and anthropocentrism, to which we shall return in a while.

In following von Wright's line of criticism I shall argue that sustainability should be considered a balance between technological and moral progress. A useful concept for expressing this concern is to avoid 'moral technology' – a concept originating from the Norwegian philosopher Jon Hellesnes (1993). The basic idea is that there are certain problems, in particular existential and moral problems, that do not require a finite solution. As an example, to try to solve the problem of evil by technological means is to raise the question in a wrong context, thereby reducing the problem to an instrumental or technological issue of concern. To try to solve moral problems by way of technology is based on a strong belief that the problem itself is expected to have a scientific solution. By contrast such questions are infinite and as such they need to be part of our continuous moral reflection and concern. In this chapter I shall take as my point of departure that the quest for sustainability belongs to this group of requests, i.e. where we cannot expect to come up with finite solutions that work across the different local contexts worldwide. This also implies a criticism of the way some international rules and regulations are indiscriminately implemented in a huge range of very different local contexts. Agenda 21 is but one such regulatory example, to which we shall turn in the latter part of this paper.

The presumption in von Wright that moral deterioration most likely is the flipside of the coin of technological progress may also be considered part of an incompatibility between (liberal) democracy and sustainability. At an individual level sustainable politics implies a need for putting constraints on people's consumption choices, while at a societal level there seems to be a likewise conflict between liberal democracy and sustainable politics. In order to realise sustainability politics at a societal level there seems to be a need for constraints on scientific and technological progress.[1]

One obvious example is to be found in information technology, and may appear to represent a solution to Dewey's problem of the publics, i.e. the lack of methods and procedures for informing the public.[2] However, despite the improvement of methods there are no clear indicators that people become better informed due to improvements of methods alone.[3]

Another example of technological progress is any kind of general and context insensitive governance by way of global institutional regulations, e.g. Agenda 21.[4] Briefly, the problem consists in technologies being developed at a distance from the particular contexts for which they are developed and to which they apply. As a consequence they are thus turned into a 'one size fits all' technology. In Section 4 we shall discuss a case in point.

In the literature on sustainable development the distinction between eco-centrism and anthropocentrism applies to the question of scope and extension of our concern on environmental issues: whether human and non-human nature, or only human nature should be our point of departure. The latter distinction is partly connected to the technological/moral relationship to the extent an anthropocentric approach may imply an instrumental attitude towards non-human nature. This is, however, a separate debate. Here I shall only briefly mention John Dryzek's scepticism to both of these perspectives (Dryzek 2005). His main point is the one-sided focus on only one interest – e.g. eco-/bio-centric – rather than the relation or communication between them. This is discussed in further details under Section 3.

For the purpose of this chapter I shall focus on the institutional obstacles following from a strong belief in moral technology with respect to the quest for sustainable institutions. The quest for technological fix has to be balanced against the risk of moral deterioration in order to gain sustainable governance and institutions.

In the following I examine the quest for such a balance from three perspectives: (a) the problem of the public (Dewey 1927); (b) reflective judgement/broadened way of thinking (Kant, Arendt); and (c) deliberative democracy (Dryzek 1995). Additional to discussing sustainability within this theoretical framework I also bring in an empirical case of institutional obstacles to sustainability, drawn from a Chinese context.

2. Theoretical framework

2.1. Dewey and the problem of the public

First we shall have a look at John Dewey's understanding of lack of information and coordination of action resulting from it. He referred to this as 'the problem of the public'. In the first half of the twentieth century he identified an eclipse of the public, and a need to convert the 'Great Society' into a 'Great Community'.

> Till the Great Society is converted into a Great Community, the public will remain in eclipse. Communication alone can create a great community. Our Babel is not one of tongues, but of the signs and symbols without which shared experience is impossible.
>
> (Dewey 1927: 142)

Due to political complexity he recognises on the one hand a need for a better-informed public, on the other a need for legislators and policy makers to become better informed of the experiences of the public.

> The essential need ... is the improvement of the methods and conditions of debate, discussion and persuasion. That is the problem of the public.
>
> (208)[5]

New information technologies of our time partly intend to facilitate resolutions to the problems identified by Dewey and by many other philosophers and political thinkers before him.[6] How could we ensure that both political policy makers and the public are well informed, and what methods are at our disposal? Part of this discussion is about modes of communication, among others, whether rhetoric and storytelling are legitimate forms of communication in deliberation (Dryzek 2001).[7]

The problem of the public is highly relevant to our context, as well. Faced with sustainability problems of global scope, we need to coordinate actions at local, national and transnational levels. We do struggle at least as much with this coordination today as when Dewey wrote his book in 1927. One challenge is directly related to feasibility of coordinating communication across the different organisational levels, a challenge that can to a certain extent be improved by better communication technologies, e.g. ICT. Trying to solve the problem of the public solely by improving the communication technologies is, of course, to miss the point. The real problem is only partly a technological one. The main obstacles, I shall argue, rather have to do with the unevenly distributed capabilities and preferences for taking an interest in the tragedy of the commons, i.e. the tragedy of open-access regimes (Woods 2010: 83). The tragedy itself in particular relates to sustainability of global ecosystems, in providing resources, assimilating waste products and biodiversity. The tragedy itself cannot be resolved purely by technological means. The problem of achieving better-informed publics is also a quest for forming people's preferences in the right direction. Thus, even if our communication systems are being improved we still have only met one necessary, but far from sufficient condition for decreasing the tragedy. The problem of free will is but one obstacle here, as any restrictions on people's free will as consumers would counter basic liberal values being embraced by most people in liberal democracies.

The lack of coordination is partly seen as a (information) technological problem that Dewey described in terms of lack of such technologies. However, the problem of lack of well-informed publics also relates to the tragedy of the commons as described by Hardin (1968). This is, however, not simply a problem of scarcity of resources and the problem of (individual) free will, but even as much a communicative problem of coordination in order to achieve better-informed publics.

Rather than pursuing the free will problem here I shall concentrate on the problem of the public as it comes to the fore in the sustainability context. One basic conflict acknowledged by most authors is the one between economic and ecological values: any free market is inconsistent with ecological sustainability. There is, however, one basic division line stemming from conflicting views of eco-centrism and anthropocentrism, having to do with the community of moral concern. Put very briefly, the main question is whether we should include non-human nature as well as human nature when dealing with questions of sustainability. My view, based on von Wright and Hellesnes, is that an anthropocentric approach by definition includes non-human nature, as well. Thus, any discussion of human rights and duties, inter- and intra-generational justice etc. presupposes that the community of moral concern implies some kind of interaction between human and non-human nature. This further implies that speaking in terms of rights as opposed to duties is futile, as it does not make sense to ascribe neither duties nor rights to any independent 'bodies' of 'non-human nature'. The interconnection between humans and non-human nature is already presupposed when discussing at the level of rights and duties.

2.2. Reflective judgement and broadened ways of thinking: Kant and Arendt

In dealing with obstacles relating to human capabilities of coordination, we shall here look into Kant's conceptual scheme of judgements, by focussing on reflective judgements. Kant distinguishes between two different kinds of judgements: either they are determinant, as when something particular is subsumed under universal laws, or, by contrast, '[i]f only the particular is given and the universal has to be found for it, then the judgment is simply *reflective*' (Kant 1952: Introduction IV, 18). The purpose of reflective judgement is not to determine anything, rather, it is to give itself a law. Hence, validity is gained through reflection of something particular as opposed to subsuming something under universal laws. This is partly because judgement, which is the topic of investigation in his third *Critique*, is about empirical contingencies and not about universal laws of nature or final ends of freedom. Judgement is one among three cognitive faculties, the other two being theoretical and speculative reason (along with sensibility and understanding) in the first *Critique*, and pure practical reason in the second *Critique*. Kant's own focal point in his treatment of judgement is taste and the sublime, and applies first and foremost to art, as distinguished from nature (pure reason) and freedom (practical reason). As such, judgement primarily concerns the aesthetic domain of feelings of pleasure and displeasure, as opposed to the faculties of cognition and desire. As such, pleasure and displeasure can never make claims to objective necessity or a priori validity.

> As with all empirical judgments, [pleasure or displeasure] is, consequently, unable to announce objective necessity or lay claim to a *priori* validity ... [J]udgment of taste in fact only lays claim ... to be valid for every one ... [O]ne who feels pleasure in simple reflection on the form of an object ... rightly lays claim to the agreement of everyone, although this judgment is empirical.
>
> (Kant 1952: VII, 32)

The ground of this pleasure is found, according to Kant, in the universal, even if subjective, condition of reflective judgement. One essential point is to be noted here: the judgement receives its validity from the anticipated agreement with every judging person.

The validity of judgements depends on the judging, and it is not valid for those who do not judge. Hannah Arendt puts this point forth in emphasising that the claim to validity presupposes communication between self and others. Hence, a judgement's claim to validity can never extend further than the public realm of those who are members of it (Arendt 1968: 221). There are in particular two aspects concerning validity that should be noted here. One concerns the relation between the particular and the universal, whereas the other has to do with the public aspect of judgement. Any particular judgement is based on contingent and finite appeals that nevertheless may transcend the subjective conditions of the particular judgment. The potential for transcending the purely subjective condition is due to the communicative aspect of all judgements. Hence, reflective judgement is deeply founded in communication. For Kant himself reflective judgement is supposed to lie outside the political domain, whereas both Arendt and later Sheila Benhabib have argued that it should rightfully be extended to the faculties of politics and morality as well (Arendt 1968; Benhabib 1992).

To answer this challenge, we shall first have a look at Kant's own account. He introduces the concept *sensus communis* i.e. a public sense and a critical faculty that takes account of the mode of representation in everyone else. This faculty is the power to make judgements for the purpose of public appeal, thereby avoiding the illusion that private and personal conditions are taken for objective.

> This is accomplished by weighing the judgment ... with the ... possible judgments of others, and by putting ourselves in the position of every one else ... [abstracting] ... from the limitations that contingently affect our own estimate.
>
> (Kant 1952: §40:294)

Sensus communis emphasises the importance of looking at the world at large in order to transcend one's own private and subjective conditions. In different terms we could here speak of a global as opposed to local worldviews. In the context of sustainability issues such a perspective is essential, in particular on the background of the uneven distribution with respect to (governance of) natural resources around the world, not least between developed and developing countries. Reflective judgment is a way of bringing judgments of the local under a global perspective as 'everyone else' extends to the remaining world.

Kant's way of thinking in the place of everyone else is called 'enlarged thinking' by Arendt. The power of judgement rests on a potential agreement with others. Judgements derive their validity from this potential agreement. According to Arendt:

> This means, on the one hand, that such judgment must liberate itself from the 'subjective private conditions', that is, from the idiosyncrasies which naturally determine the outlook of each individual in his privacy and are legitimate as long as they are only privately held opinions, but are not fit to enter the market place, and lack all validity in the public realm.
>
> (Arendt 1968: 220)

Sensus communis may thus be compared to the procedure of universalisation in the categorical imperative that in a similar way appeals to a public sense through universalisation.

The potential agreement with others along with the liberation from private subjective conditions is what makes possible intersubjective validity of judgements. This is the kind of coordination that is requested in our context, as it is not only a question of an aggregation of different judgments, but rather a coordination of judgements in order for them to gain validity. The kind of communication at work in judgment is a different kind of relation between the particular and the universal. In Sheila Benhabib's words: 'Judgment is not the faculty of subsuming a particular under a universal but the faculty of contextualizing the universal such that it comes to bear upon the particular' (Benhabib 1992: 132). I understand the 'contextualizing of the universal' that Benhabib talks about as a claim to demonstrate how the universal appeal works in each particular context. As an example, a claim directed towards the authorities to make exceptions for some particular group of citizens may contextualise the universal by demonstrating how the particular case relates to other similar cases. Otherwise, contextualising the universal might appeal to others' imagination of putting themselves in the particular circumstances of others. Both Arendt and Benhabib agree on Kant's account of reflective judgement as far as the validity procedure for particular judgements are concerned. However, as we have seen, the kind of intersubjective validity that is derived should not only be restricted to the aesthetic domain of taste. The main reason is that the intersubjective appeal in all judgement anticipates communication with others. Even if a person is alone in making up her mind, there is an anticipated communication with others with whom one must finally come to some agreement (Arendt 1968: 220).

The extension of reflective judgment to the public domain of reason in general is vital to the argument of this chapter. One reason is that legitimising opinions in the public domain requires approval of other participants in the discourses and disputes going on. This might be interpreted either as agreement that an opinion is reasonable, or as actual agreement with some other's opinion. The main point here is the kind of approval contained in Habermas' theory that public opinion is moving towards increasingly stronger validity of public opinion rather than claiming actual agreement of opinions. Validity is then conceived as an ongoing legitimising process whose ultimate arbiter is public reason itself. This will be treated more thoroughly in the next paragraph.

2.3. Enlarged thinking in public reasoning

As seen in the preceding paragraph, reflective judgement and enlarged thinking should not be restricted to the aesthetic domain, but can be extended to the domain of public reason. A key question is whether the claim 'to think from the standpoint of everyone else' in Kant's third *Critique* should be interpreted as making an appeal to context, which is assumed in Arendt's extension of reflective judgement to the public faculty. Validity in the Kantian model is grounded in the universal communicability of particular judgements. Thus, it might be argued that the emphasis is still on universality rather than particularity conceived as context. Universality is, however, based on a public sense that is possible to share with others only to the extent that it is communicable and may gain universal validity. Thus, I think it makes good sense to interpret particularity in Kant's account of judgements as an appeal to the context of particular judgements, on topics concerning reason just as well as judgement. In other words, I see no good reason why reflective judgement should not apply to all of our cognitive faculties: understanding, judgement and reason. At a metaphysical level the traditional dividing line between Kant's claim on universal communicability and Aristotle's appeal to exemplary quality of judgement may be important in some respects. I would, however, argue that these metaphysical assumptions are of less importance to much of the modern debate on public reason. With Benhabib, rather than discussing the old metaphysical controversies between Aristotle and Kant, we should pay more attention to the question 'whether a universalist moral standpoint must be formalistic, aprioristic and context insensitive or whether moral universalism can be reconciled with contextual sensitivity' (Benhabib 1992: 134). I think it is important to interpret Kant's claim on universality as always context sensitive in a certain respect: to think from the standpoint of anyone will, by necessity, always be context dependent since the action that is the object of debate will always take place in some particular context.

What is at stake is still the relation between the particular and the universal, and how the former derives validity by relating to the latter. In contemporary debate on deliberative democracy this is a core question. Habermas, as an example, has argued that discourse must make an appeal to universal validity claims in order to be legitimate, while some of his critics have argued that the contextual conditions of communication are ignored in his model (Habermas 1996; Young 2000). The importance of transcending the merely private subjective conditions, however, appears to be recognised by both. Rather, what is contested concerns the role of the particular: as constituent and necessary of all kinds of judgement, or as contextual limitations of legitimate communication in public deliberation. In the following we shall explore the relevance of Kant's faculties of cognition and maxims of common human understanding to public reason in deliberation.

A main concern in Kant is to explain the grounds and limits of human reason. In doing so, according to Onora O'Neill, he holds practical use of reason to be the more fundamental (O'Neill 1989: 29). Practical use of reason is fundamental by enabling us to act autonomously, i.e. not to be ruled by external forces. The only limit to this freedom is the categorical imperative or the universalisation principle. Likewise, we have connected reflective judgement to public reason by way of publicisability of particular judgements. This point is fundamental to understanding why public use of reason is of such importance.[8] Basically, it is due to Kant's claim that the public use of reason should always be free. In order for our public use of reason to be free we must look upon acts of communication as the proper objects of toleration. The reason is that toleration is seen as a response to communication. This is a more profound concept of toleration as compared to viewing utterances by others as mere expressions. The basic point is that communication rather than expression is required in public reason. Part of the claim to make public use of reason builds on the maxims of common understanding: (1) to think for oneself; (2) to think from the standpoint of everyone else, i.e. enlarged thought; and (3) always to think consistently (Kant 1952: §40, 294). The first is the maxim of understanding, the second the maxim of judging, and the third the maxim of reason. All of these maxims of public reason are more profound than any other use of reason, and they are standards for addressing 'the world at large' (O'Neill 1989: 48). In addressing the world at large reason accepts no external authority. 'External authority' in Kant here means any source that is not found in the judging subjects themselves. In our context it is reasonable to interpret different kinds of abstract rules and regulations as external authorities to the degree that they have not been qualified by consent from the subjects upon whom they operate. Thus, reflective judgement runs counter to external authorities that are implemented from outside of the context in question. We shall return to a case in point in a while.

Reflective judgement, or enlarged thinking is public use of reason. According to Kant it is this use of reason that is at work in judgements on particular situations, derived from the human capacity for reflective judgement. Thus, we see how reflective judgement and enlarged thinking in Kant is basic to any other form of communication. This is the important point to be drawn from his model for validation in the public faculty, and it is particularly interesting because it gives an account of how reflection of particular situations and conditions can make a claim to validity. This holds true as far as the appeals put forth address a universal audience. By contrast, addressing only a restricted audience cannot make claim to something that is universally communicable. Still, private uses of reason may be legitimate for certain purposes. The important point to be made, however, is that '[t]here are no good reasons for tolerating any private uses of reason that damage public uses of reason' (O'Neill 1989: 49).

Thus, arguing with Kant, it would be legitimate to accept uses of reason that do not address the world at large – perhaps even by accepting external authorities – as long as they serve public reason.[9]

Based on reflective judgement and the quest for public use of reason we are now in a position to argue that public debate on sustainability is about the kind of goods that are vulnerable due to being threatened by the tragedy of the commons. If we accept this premise we can make a move forward to discuss how to broaden our thoughts on sustainable progress. For this purpose we shall bring a concrete case into our discussion in Section 3 of this chapter. Before getting there we shall first introduce a deliberative model of public reasoning.

2.4. Deliberative models of public reasoning

In 'Political and ecological communication' John Dryzek criticises both eco-centric and anthropocentric approaches in environmental debates. Eco-centrism – or biocentrism – implies that intrinsic values are located in nature, in absence of human interests. Still, even though eco-centrism does give priority to ecological values it need not necessarily rule out human interests being 'sheltered under the eco-centric umbrella' (Dryzek, 1995: 16). Dryzek argues against Robyn Eckersley (1992) that the problem is the centrism involved in both eco- and anthropocentrism. Speaking with Hellesnes, the criticism could also be framed as an instance of reducing all kinds of problems to one overarching dimension. The same criticism applies to anthropocentrism, as well, as the human nature in this approach is being exalted to the measure of all nature. In order to avoid any such 'centrism' Dryzek finds 'interaction' to be a more apt term (Dryzek 1995: 16–17). He argues from the perspective of deliberative democracy, the key argument being that 'democracy can exist not only among humans, but also in human dealings with the natural world' (17). He emphasises the need for a more egalitarian interchange at the human/natural boundary. Thus, ecological democratisation is seen as 'a matter of more effective integration of political and ecological communication' (ibid.).

The less metaphysical upshot of this argument seems to be his pointing to the problem of isolating interests. To the extent that, for example, an anthropocentric approach implies an attitude of domination and instrumentalisation of non-human nature this argument seems sound. Likewise, with respect to ecocentrism, several problems seem to follow from subordinating human interests under those of non-human nature, basically having to do with democracy and freedom of choice. Dryzek's emphasis on interaction does, however, raise another problem: how to interact with bodies devoid of subjectivity. Dryzek argues that this model of communicative rationality very well may be extended to agents like nature, who are devoid of subjectivity. He thereby introduces a concept of agency that applies to nature without subjectivity: 'we should treat signals emanating from the natural world with the same respect we accord signals emanating from human subjects' (Dryzek 1995: 19). His vision of a non-anthropocentric democracy thus involves communicative rationality extended to non-human nature, thus including ecological signals.

Against Dryzek I shall argue that we need not extend deliberative democracy in this direction, as we obviously run into lots of problems about metaphysics, as well as blurring Habermas' concept of communicative rationality. Several arguments have been put forth against Habermas' model of communicative rationality, one of them being that it does not to a sufficient degree include disempowered people. One line of criticism is to argue in favour of communicative rationality while extending rational communication to allow for further forms of communication. This huge debate however is not our main focus here. Instead, I shall conclude this paragraph by sketching another strategy for how to make democratic deliberation contribute to improve handling of the problem of the better use of public reason in dealing with questions of sustainability.

The potential for deliberative models to annihilate the distinction between human and non-human world should not be based on stretching communicative agency to non-human nature. Basically it seems superfluous. If we take on board Dewey's analysis of the problem of the public, the main problem is the lack of broadened ways of thinking. This lack is more likely to stem from flaws of human interaction in the first place. This flaw partly depends on insufficiencies of institutional governance as well as of informal communication flows partly operating outside traditional institutions. In the next part of the chapter we shall have a closer look at both, starting with some clarifications of institutions.

3. Institutional obstacles to public use of reason

The interactive model of green or ecological democracy envisaged by Dryzek is partly a response to institutional obstacles: how to coordinate the numerous and crosscutting loci of political authority (Dryzek 1995: 23). As already mentioned in Section 1 his main point is to criticise 'centrisms' because they imply privileging of one level of political organisation (local, national, global). Rather, we should think of coordination in terms of different public spheres existing apart from political authority, for example like Solidarity in Poland in the 1980s.

Further witnesses are found in contemporary examples of new social movements concerning ecology, peace, and green movements – movements that do not seek entry into the state through electoral politics.

One reason why electoral or representative democracy fails in coordinating actions towards sustainability has to do with boundaries and jurisdictions. The main reason is that many of the urgent issues are unbounded and variable in the sense that they transcend boundaries of geographical jurisdictions: e.g. fisheries regulation in China most likely requires action that transcends Chinese jurisdiction.

The upshot of Dryzek's argument is that the concept of institutions for sustainable development is much broader than that of institutions dedicated to sustainable development. This amounts to a quest for sources different from standard political institutions in the efforts towards sustainability. In the next section we shall have a brief look at one case illustrating the institutional obstacles of our focus here.

4. A case in point: China's fisheries policy

The case in point (Ferraro and Brans 2012) is about rapid economic growth followed by strong exploitation of fisheries resources in the Guangdong province in southern China, relating to both the fish stock and marine environmental deterioration. One obvious tension here is rather general as it points to the conflict between environmental protection and economic development. The case in point demonstrates how this conflict merges at a local level, due to a range of institutional obstacles. One remarkable conflict is about diverging objectives both at an inter- and intra-level of organisations. Briefly speaking, the conflict prevails between the national State Oceanic Administration (SOA) and the Fisheries Management Bureau (FMB), i.e. the national and the subnational levels. Whereas the former acts as 'the ruler of the sea' the latter acts as 'the servants of the fishers' (Ferraro and Brans 2012: 41). The conflict is thus about protection on the one hand, and increasing economic growth on the other. According to Agenda 21 and other international regulations there are some international conventions to be implemented at the local levels in different countries. However, when these objectives are implemented at local levels responsibility is often delegated to the subordinate level, which in the Guangdong case is the provincial level regulated by FMB. Several obstacles are at work: the policy implementation is: (1) captured by informal patron-client type relationships (local governmental level); (2) management responsibility is transferred to FMB who owns a huge fishing company; and (3) FMB is responsible for their own budget.

This case demonstrates how fiscal decentralisation leads to bureaucratic fragmentation and vertical specialization: those who are responsible for environmental protection have no direct say in the implementation of the protection policies, which are governed by those who also have ownership interests in the fisheries production. In the Guangdong case there is even a further complication having to do with a certain division at the central level, resulting in fisheries management and environmental protection remaining separate competencies. The reason is that the Ministry of Agriculture (MOA) governs two main branches divided between fisheries and marine protection. Now, this case most likely demonstrates more than an average amount of institutional obstacles. Additionally, as pointed out above in the Guangdong case, the authors found the 'ruler' and the 'ruled' to coexist in the same agency, i.e. the Federal Management Bureau being responsible for policy implementation and also being the owners of an important fishing company.

The Guangdong case serves as an illustration of institutional obstacles to sustainability, mainly having to do with the lack of adequate coordination of action. This flaw could be described in different terms, in line with the theoretical frames presented above. For the one, it is partly a demonstration of the problem of the public to the extent that the coordination of action on the local level is corrupted, partly due to lack of well-informed actors and institutions. Second, there is also lack of public use of reason, as the capability of reflective judgment within the relevant institutions in this particular case is impaired. Third, there is also clearly an institutional obstacle having to do with the strong belief in one technological model applied indiscriminately also to contexts where it does not work, i.e. acting according to general international rules and regulations according to Agenda 21.

5. Conclusion

Several problems of insufficient or inadequate coordination of action have been discussed in connection with the Guangdong fisheries' case. One main problem relates to problems of delegating governance to sublevels without safeguarding communication between the global, national and local levels of governance. This problem has been identified as a challenge to implementation of local Agenda 21, whose aim is to enhance sustainability, to empower people through participation and to create ownership to the local project. These goals sound good as long as they are considered apart from concrete contexts. However, as shown through the implementation in the Guangdong case, the local conditions are apparently not consistent with these aims. This is proved by lack of enhanced sustainability. Rather, overfishing and pollution of the environments are not reduced despite implementation of Agenda 21. Further, empowerment of people through participation seems to have little to do with concern for the environment, and a whole lot to do with safeguarding of nutrition and income. In this particular case there are several reasons why the environmental responsibility is evaporating. Some have to do with patron/client relationships at the local level, thus preventing natural resources and environments to be governed along democratic lines.

The main point of the authors of the Guangdong case was to show how Agenda 21 and other international regulations often work poorly at the level of policy implementation. The objective of this chapter, however, has been not only to illustrate how overlap of authorities and double accountability may complicate the political process. Having identified some serious flaws in the coordination of democratic institutions at different levels of jurisdiction, I also wanted to question whether, deliberative-ecological democracy as suggested by Dryzek for example, may offer a viable alternative to the current institutional systems. There is of course no unequivocal answer. Still, there is solid documentation of the need for looking in a different direction as coordination of formal agencies regulating sustainability policies obviously does not work, at least not in developing and non-democratic countries.

Some of the problems we found in the Guangdong fisheries case have to do with the absence of alternative sources to nutrition and livelihood. In this particular case one may ask whether responsible fisheries is an achievable objective at all. As long as there is lack of reflective judgement, and the problem of the public persists, I'm afraid the answer is negative. I think it goes without further argument that the international organisations' capacity for solving the problem institutionally is doomed to fail as long as actions at the global, national and local levels are poorly coordinated. In the Guangdong case there are certain values at conflict that obviously prevent efficient coordination of action, as we have seen. The most obvious conflicting values have been observed as the double role of owners and controllers co-residing in the same body. The Federal Management Bureau is both responsible for policy implementation while also being the owners of an important fishing company.

Another procedural aspect of poor coordination of action is that the proof of success is measured by reporting procedures that most often depend on the local agencies reporting to the superior levels of government. Thus, the proof of success is manifested in a report on, for example Good Governance Handbook (GGH) and Local Agenda 21 being successfully implemented without any environmental improvements actually being reported. This is the 'free rider' problem reported by Fonseca et al. (2012), resulting from only procedural gains being reported, rather than substantive progress.

What is needed is on the one hand to realise that the current institutional set-up of governance towards sustainability is insufficient at best. Additionally, there is a quest for improvement of both coordinating methods (Dewey), but also improvement of a broadened way of thinking. For this purpose I believe deliberative/ecological democracy can work as an antidote against the false belief that we can solve the economic/ecological imbalance by way of coordinating scales of governing institutions only. The problems we face regarding the incompatible objectives of environmental protection and economic growth are not only questions of solving the problem by way of either distributive or restorative strategies towards justice. Rather, we need to pay more attention to the lack of coordination between formal and informal institutions. For this purpose I believe the deliberative democratic ideal, which is to improve public use of reason, is generally a good point of departure.

Part of the problem discussed above is a challenge to democratic governance. While governance of natural resources surely ought to be considered a global enterprise, there is still a strong belief among the public in delegating responsibility to local levels of governance. As we have seen in the particular case discussed here, we also have to face problems due to lack of formal and informal institutions capable of taking on this responsibility. To put it briefly: no one would question a local community prioritising nutrition over sustainable development if that choice has to be made.

Notes

This chapter is a further developed and revised version of Thorseth (2014).

1   This problem is developed in another forthcoming chapter by the author. Here I shall only give some more contents to 'technological progress'.
2   Dewey's problem of the public is presented in 2.1 below.
3   This is discussed in Thorseth 2006.
4   See http://sustainabledevelopment.un.org/content/documents/Agenda21.pdf. The core of Agenda 21 may be summarised in three points: (1) enhance sustainability; (2) empower people through participation; and (3) create ownership to the local project.
5   Quoted in Coleman and Gøtze 2001,11.
6   This problem is closely related to the ideal of enlightenment found in Kant and many other Western liberal thinkers.
7   The term 'rhetoric' is here considered to be a constituent part of deliberation, because participants – especially lay deliberators – have no alternative but to make character judgements about experts (*ethos*). This holds true whenever experts reach contradictory conclusions (see Dryzek 2001: 53). *Pathos* is equally important for reaching a particular audience, without which the argument would fall to deaf ears (52). The standard definition of rhetoric stems from Aristotle, it is 'the faculty of observing in any given case the available means of persuasion' (Aristotle 2004: 1.2.).
8   The distinction between public and private use of reason demarcates the difference between *sensus communis* and *sensus privatus* (O'Neill 1989: 45). The former is identified with enlarged thinking, addressing an unrestricted audience, while the latter is restricted, for instance, by filling the roles of clergy, officers and civil servants.
9   It is disputed whether public reason should be seen as a gradual process towards more enlightenment, which concerns the relation between the first and the third maxims of *sensus communis*: the maxim to think for oneself and the maxim to think consistently. If it is conceived in developmental terms, then we may envisage an ongoing process towards better understanding that can only be judged along the developmental line.

References

Arendt, H. 1968. 'Crisis in Culture', in *Between Past and Future: Eight Exercises in Political Thought*. New York: Meridian.

Aristotle. 2004. *The Art of Rhetoric*, H. C. Lawson-Tancred (trans.). London: Penguin Classics.

Benhabib, S. 1992. *Situating the Self*. Cambridge: Polity Press.

Brown, L. 1978. *The Twenty-Ninth Day: Accommodating Human Needs and Numbers to the Earth's Resources*. New York: Norton.

Coleman, S. and Gøtze, J. 2001. *Bowling Together: Online Public Engagement in Policy Deliberation*, Hansard Society. Available at www.catedras.fsoc.uba.ar/rusailh/

Unidad%207/Coleman%20and%20Gotze%20Bowling%20Together,%20online%20
public%20engagement%20in%20policy%20deliberation.pdf

Dewey, J. 1927. *The Public and its Problems*. New York: Henry Holt & Co.

Dryzek, J. 1995. 'Political and Ecological Communication', *Environmental Politics*, 4(4), 13–30.

Dryzek, J. 2001. *Deliberative Democracy and Beyond: Liberals, Critics, Contestations*. Oxford: Oxford University Press.

Dryzek, J. 2005. *The Politics of the Earth: Environmental Discourses*. Oxford: Oxford University Press.

Eckersley, R. 1992. *Environmentalism and Political Theory: Toward an Ecocentric Approach*. London: UCL Press.

Fishkin, J. 1997. *Voice of the People*. New Haven, Conn.: Yale University Press.

Ferraro, G. and Brans, M. 2012. 'Trade-offs Between Environmental Protection and Economic Development in China's Fisheries Policy: A Political Analysis on the Adoption and Implementation of the Fisheries Law 2000', *Natural Resources Forum*, 36, 38–49.

Fonseca, F., Bursztyn, M. and Allen, B. 2012. 'Trivializing Sustainability: Environmental Governance and Rhetorical Free-Riders in the Brazilian Amazon', *Natural Resources Forum* 36, 28–37.

Habermas, J. 1984. *The Theory of Communicative Action*. Boston: Beacon Press.

Habermas, J. 1990. *Moral Consciousness and Communicative Ethics*. Cambridge, Mass.: MIT Press.

Habermas, J. 1996. *Between Facts and Norms*. Cambridge, Mass.: MIT Press.

Hardin, G. 1968. 'The Tragedy of the Commons: The Population Problem has no Technical Solution: It Requires a Fundamental Extension of Morality', *Science*, 162, 1243–1248.

Hellesnes, J. 1993. 'Etikk-satsing? Om moralteknologi, diskursetikk og kvardagssokratisk verksemd', *Norsk filosofisk tidsskrift*.

Kant, I. 1952. *The Critique of Judgment*, J. M. Meredith (trans.). Oxford: Clarendon.

Kant, I. 1991. *An Answer to the Question: 'What is Enlightenment?'* H.B. Nisbet (trans.), in *Kant's Political Writings*, Hans Reiss (ed.). Cambridge: Cambridge University Press.

O'Neill, O. 1989. *Constructions of Reason: Explorations of Kant's Practical Philosophy*. Cambridge: Cambridge University Press.

Thorseth, M. 2006. 'Worldwide Deliberation and Public Use of Reason Online', *Ethics and Information Technology*, 8(4), 243–252.

Thorseth, M. 2014. 'Institutional Obstacles to Sustainable Development of Natural Resources: A Deliberative Approach', *UNIVERSITAS: Monthly Review of Philosophy and Culture (ISSN 1015-8383)*, 63–84.

Woods, K. 2010. *Human Rights and Environmental Sustainability*. Cheltenham: Edward Elgar.

von Wright, G. H. 1993. *Vitenskapen og fornuften* (The Myth of Progress). Oslo: Cappelen.

Young, I. M. 1998. 'Inclusive Political Communication: Greetings, Rhetoric and Storytelling in the Context of Political Argument'. Paper presented at the Annual Meeting of the American Political Science Association, Boston.

Young, I. M. 2000. *Inclusion and Democracy*. Oxford: Oxford University Press.

4 Is democracy an obstacle to ecological change?

Bernward Gesang

For the transition to a future-oriented society the present type of democratic government is in many ways dysfunctional. The main incentives for politicians in democratic systems are conservation of power-base and re-election. Both incentives are only partially compatible with ecological policies that adequately take into account the interests of future people. This dilemma could be solved, however, by institutional changes short of constitutional reform, e.g. by the introduction of Future Councils or ombudspersons at the European level. The pending reform process in Europe holds the prospect of creating a climate in which citizens and politicians are open to institutional innovations.

1. Introduction

The first report from the Club of Rome published in 1971 (Meadows *et al.* 1972) warned of the existential crisis facing humanity. This warning has since been repeatedly confirmed by climatologists and the regularly published reports from the Club of Rome (Randers 2012) alike. Greenhouse gas emissions, the use of land and resources, food production, the global population, and industrial production are all growing at unyielding rates, posing a threat to us all. The earth is a system with finite resources and capacities to absorb waste. If the global population continues to grow at current rates, we will ultimately reach the limits of this system.

In recent years, a new dimension of climate change has emerged that will drastically exacerbate the situation. For a long time, the earth, soils and oceans have acted as sinks for CO_2 und methane. However, the danger exists that increasing temperatures will cause the stored CO_2 or methane to be released into the atmosphere. Members of the Hadley Centre (Cox *et al.* 2000) and other climatologists believe that an increase in the Earth's temperature by more than two degrees centigrade would cause us to exceed tipping points. This would create a self-perpetuating momentum: exceeding the first tipping point would lead to the release of additional CO_2 and methane, which would trigger the next tipping point, causing yet again the further release of such gases, and so on. The message is simple: *if we exceed an increase of two degrees, the result could be an increase of six degrees or more.* While feedback effects are commonly known, this hypothesis by the Hadley Centre lists just one possibility and should be considered in earnest as a *worst case* scenario.[1]

The existence of humanity itself is at stake, as humans will no longer be able to survive on this planet at such high temperatures. However, have humans not always developed some sort of new technology out of necessity, one which allows us to overcome obstacles whenever they arise (cf. Simon 1981)? But how often will we be saved by such technological wonders? We can ask ourselves, at least, whether we are acting in a responsible manner when we allow problems after problems to arise in the mere hope that we will always find a technological solution to them. The ways in which we deal with nuclear power, climate change, water scarcity, green genetic engineering and economic growth given the ecological limits to this growth are all comparable to writing a cheque without the funds to back it up. And we do so to make a wager that we will be able to solve these problems at some point with technologies yet to be developed. In none of these wagers can we allow ourselves to fail, for the stakes are far too high (Jonas 1979). As early as the 1950s, the problem of cooling technology was believed to have been solved by the use of chlorofluorocarbons. This 'solution', however, caused even more problems (for example, a hole in the ozone layer) than it solved. There is a danger that technological solutions in complex ecological systems can initially appear to have a positive effect, yet ultimately lead to a poor and thus 'dialectical' effect.

In this respect, we are reminded of the Tanaland Study (Dörner and Reither 1978) in which young development aid workers are deployed to an imaginary, virtual developing country. The technologies implemented, however, resulted in utter ruin for the country, as they had a dialectical effect. These virtual technologies included the drilling of wells, which, in turn, eventually caused the water table to sink, resulting in an insufficient water supply for the country. The idea was to carry out the measures as a series of 'linear' causal chains (A is followed by B, which is followed by C and then D); however, in reality the implementation proved to be a complex system of reciprocal effects. What we can learn from this is that we should first find feasible technological solutions for future problems and then avoid this kind of dialectical effect. The notion that such solutions will be found in all of the aforementioned problem areas is certainly a bold claim.

Conclusion: the problems are almost overwhelming, yet exigent, and we must urgently consider how we are going to solve them.

2. Policy failure by politicians

The proposed therapies include regulating the growth of the global population, a worldwide system for emissions trading, expanding the availability and use of renewable energies, and many more. Many informed people have been preaching these remedies for decades; however, binding agreements on limiting the effects of climate change or the growth of the global population have failed thus far. Why is this? What kinds of obstacles lie in the way of such a great transformation?

In the search for solutions, we must turn our attention to our political institutions. Politicians in office cannot issue decrees for citizens to follow that would cause fear and impose restrictions on them, for citizens may punish these politicians by voting them out of office. This is one of many reasons that leads us to the following insight: we must also subject our hitherto successful democratic structures themselves to a diagnosis and therapy if humanity is to be saved. In the following section, I will provide several arguments as to why policies have failed on the part of politicians and then apply some of these to citizens as well.

(1)

Democracy can be described as a form of government that is characterised by a large *problem of qualification*.[2] This can be initially applied to politicians, that is, the Reagans, Bushes and Berlusconis of the world, as well as politicians who belong to the Tea Party, all of whom gain power through democratic means, only to cause an enormous amount of damage once in office. For example, Ronald Reagan simply ignored the 'Global 2000' study initiated by President Carter and helped to create our current crisis with his political 'business as usual' approach. But this also applies to other leaders who do not understand, or choose to not understand, the threat posed by these ecological problems when they give the economy the highest priority. Even the Obama administration, as members of the Democratic Party, and the US Congress, the majority of which was controlled by the same party, consciously allowed the negotiations during the Copenhagen Summit to fail based on a prior agreement with China, as was claimed by people involved in the negotiations.[3]

In the age of modern technology, the effects humans can have on nature have increased enormously. A linear mentality is no longer sufficient; the new method must involve thinking and working together 'as networks' (see the Tanaland Study above), as it is very difficult to predict how ecosystems will react to human interference. Politicians often do not master this complex way of thinking, one which takes feedback loops into consideration.

(2)

The *incentives for politicians* in a democratic system are maintaining power and securing re-election. Neither of these can really be attained by implementing environmentally friendly policies. Politicians usually act in ways that enable them to pursue these incentives, for they also want to ensure their own interests. Decisions are made based on the prospect of re-election and therefore usually have a short-term focus. Future generations are not today's voters and therefore can neither punish nor reward politicians by voting them out or back into office. Incentives in democracy follow a detailed plan of maintaining power from one legislative period to the next, but the benefits from ecological policies, of course, only become discernible many years later. It is in this respect that T. Stein points out that 'the essence of the ecological problem does not correspond to the time-frame of democratic power' (Stein 1998: 135).[4]

(3)

In addition, many politicians describe the mandate given to them by their clientele – i.e. those who elected them – as to represent them, if necessary, by *going against the common interest*. Only when this 'clientele' is that of the national electorate and this common interest becomes a global and timeless one will it become a majority position supported by politicians. It is then counterproductive to place obstacles in front of themselves and their clientele in the form of structures that limit the execution of power.

However, this understanding of the common good cannot be morally justified. Future living beings have the same importance and value as do current beings, and the well-being of people in Africa is as important as the well-being of those in industrialised countries (cf. Gesang 2011). It makes sense, of course, for practical reasons, that politicians feel *particularly* obligated to their own countries, as they can much more effectively dedicate their efforts to specific regions rather than to the entire world. But this does *not* mean that politicians are not morally bound to the interests of citizens from other countries that are affected by the very decisions these politicians make. The very definition of 'moral' describes it as a form of behaviour that takes into consideration *to an equal extent* the interests or rights of all those affected by it. Usually, the problem of fulfilling obligations of varying degrees can be easily solved in this context: Future generations of industrialised countries will also experience the adverse effects of rising temperatures in the atmosphere and a fragmented social fabric in the world. As such, it is usually enough to simply add the future generations of their own country to the current voters to whom politicians feel particularly obligated, in order to justify more than simply a clientele policy. Just as politicians must take into consideration the interests of those citizens in their own country who did not vote for them, they should also keep in mind the interests of the generations who will live in their country in the future.

(4)

Another factor is the *influence of lobbyists on policy making*. Democracy is de facto an interplay of voters and elite politicians. Voters can vote the elite out of office, and the elite themselves can make decisions relatively independently from voters during the legislative period. The secret of democracy lies in the notion of yielding power neither to a majority nor to a minority, but rather to depend on the interplay between both groups. In addition to this, organisations such as trade unions, employers' associations, organised representatives of industry, and other lobbyist groups exert their influence on both voters and the political elite. Most often, leaders of lobbyist groups are not elected by registered voters, but rather merely by 'lobby-members'. The practice of policy making usually involves compromises agreed upon by political representatives and representatives of lobbyist groups. In reality, the various organisations and interest groups now sit down with politicians at the same table to negotiate and barter, with the objective of reaching a compromise.

Several theorists see this development as a new form of democracy in which the reciprocal control of power that is inherent to democracy primarily takes place in conflict and in the mutual limitations inflicted by these organisations (Winter 1995: 146). In such a form of democracy, the organisations become the true representatives of the people, as they are assumed to be organised entities in which each citizen is represented. The organisations represent certain interests, for example, those of employed workers, and they try to assert these interests over all other interests. The result is: *it is not the most important interest rather than the best organised interest that wins out.* Many interests, such as the interests of future generations, the third world or homeless people, are not organised and lose out in this system, which discredits lobbyism. The fact that individuals nowadays have to make do with this current system dominated by lobbyists, while, at the same time, attempting to organise unorganised interests as a new form of lobbyists is a completely different story.

R. Bahro is cited as stating: 'Until now, our parliamentary system of democracy continuously prevents truly essential things from even making it to the negotiating table' (Bahro 1987: 481; cf. Guehenno 1994: 40–45). In our current system, it is impossible for the common good to even have a voice. The common interest does not have a lobbyist to represent it and usually takes second place to the prevailing majority.

The notion of majority rule used to make decisions in democracy is also justified by the promise that the minority will itself become the majority in the future and be able to change the relationships put in place at one time by the previous majority. However, given the irreversible destruction currently taking place, such hope is no longer tenable (Stein 1998: 191). As such, there is reason enough to believe that not everything in a democracy should be subject to the majority principle; what is much more important is the fact that irreplaceable natural resources need to be preserved.

(5)

The last factor to be mentioned here is the *lack of a concentration of power.* Power in a system of democracy is often fragmented and separated in such way that there is often not enough of it concentrated in one area to change course (Stein 1998: 165). The sphere of influence is extremely small; governments and their oppositions, once their roles have been switched, often are forced to continue the same policies out of an 'inherent necessity'. There are, of course, many sound historical reasons for this kind of mistrust among advocates of democracy towards the concentration of power; however, the situation has now drastically changed. The present day and age can no longer be compared to earlier times. Such a concentration of power as we have seen it develop in line with technology requires powerful political control, and such control might be no longer possible in our system of democracy.

Based on the aforementioned factors, the following deficiencies on the part of politicians can be described:

1.   A lack of knowledge and a lack of qualification: *Qualification argument.*
2.   Incentives within the system to reach populist decisions for the short term: *Incorrect incentives.*
3.   An incorrect, truncated understanding of the common good limited to one's own country and in the era in which we live: *Incorrect understanding of the common good.*
4.   Dependency on lobbyists: *Lobbyism.*
5.   Power structures that are fragmented too often: *Lack of concentration of power.*

3. Policy failure by citizens

Item (1) and, to a certain extent, items (2) and (4) can also be applied to citizens, as they are also overwhelmed by the complexity of decisions to be made in this day and age. What is more, citizens are not trained to think in terms of systems. They also often look to fulfil *their own short-term interests* in a system of democracy, for example, fewer taxes, fewer regulations and less unemployment. Fulfilling these interests is their objective, to the detriment of the environment. It is misleading to believe that the electorate would know what the common good is, let alone pursue it, while we blame politicians and lobbyists for thwarting efforts to attain this. The electorate is often less interested in global problems, such as poverty in developing countries. What does interest citizens, however, is whether they will have to pay a few more euros in taxes or whether their families can take advantage of some sort of tax benefits. For example, some studies show that only four per cent of Germans are willing to pay more to protect the environment.[5] *The electorate and politicians both have an interest in externalising the costs of today's policies,* that is, postponing them for future generations to deal with (cf. Stein 1998: 136).

The lobbyist system reflects the interests of many citizens. Otherwise, they would hardly organise themselves in entities that are obligated to undermine the common good (for example, in mass organisations such as trade unions) with the objective of ensuring individual interests. Making sacrifices does not allow us to secure a majority in politics (cf. Jonas 1979: 269; Bahro 1987: 330, 355), for only those measures that provide more rights or goods to the current electorate or their dependents allow us to do so (cf. Kielmannsegg 1980: 79). Citizens support lobbyism, that is, the diagnosis that our problems are based merely on a lack of information on the part of citizens who would otherwise make correct decisions if they were only informed falls short of the mark.[6] The interests of the majority are an essential part of the problem (cf. Gesang 2000).

We are accustomed to recognising the aforementioned weaknesses (as individual undesirable developments) and accepting this as the price of democracy, however, this price can only be afforded by a healthy planet, and our Earth is seriously ill. If we were to only consider the common interest in such a way that there would be no greater conflicting individual interest, this would then kill a significant portion of the global population. We must quickly change our lifestyles, and this can simply not be achieved quickly enough by merely proposing endless compromises with the economy.

The usual defence of democracy that does not deny the existence of the aforementioned malfunctions in the political system, yet argues that these neither dominate the entire system nor are irreparable is correct; however, in this sense, *democracy then needs the correct repairs*. Winston Churchill was also correct when he stated: 'It has been said that democracy is the worst form of government, except all those other forms that have been tried from time to time', for there is no alternative to democracy in sight. But we cannot just leave it at that. We have to be open to reforms of our democratic system, particularly as we hold this form of government in high esteem and want to maintain it.

4. New political institutions: referenda, grassroots democracy

Our current democratic structures are not able to solve the ecological crisis. As it is set up now, our system is oriented too much towards short-term solutions; it is too egoistical and too populist. Under the current system of government, how can we expect a great transformation to happen that will enable humanity to continue to survive?

Democracy as we know it is not up for debate. There are no alternatives and only democracy possesses the *potential for self-criticism* required to learn from our mistakes. Only if a larger section of the global population were to realise and accept the necessity for change could they be moved to make sacrifices in the medium term. A global dictatorship acting against the will of the majority of the world's population would, however, require instruments of suppression of gigantic proportions. It would have to exert most of its efforts on merely maintaining its power, so that it would not be able to even focus its efforts on the actual tasks at hand (Stein 1998: 217). We could therefore simply give up, or we could switch our attention to creating new democratic institutions that would balance out the aforementioned deficits.

One possible form of therapy would be to pave the way for more direct democracy by expanding the practice of referenda and plebiscites. Proponents of this position point out that allowing citizens directly to make decisions increases their interest in politics, establishes a high level of sympathy for the common good, compels them to be better informed and prevents them from ignoring the political process. Citizens who have become well-informed by accessing the internet, the argument goes, would then make better decisions than politicians who only answer to lobbyists and are concerned about their own retention of power (Precht 2010).

This form of therapy, however, will not solve our ecological problems once and for all (cf. Rux 1999: Section III. 2, a). Of course, direct participation by citizens will help to eliminate a few of our ecological problems that are based on a lack of information and ignorance. The prerequisite for this is, however, to have responsible citizens take a very close look at the problems before making a decision. However, there are limits set by the *qualification argument*, for managing complex ecosystems cannot be learned autodidactically simply by surfing the internet. Moreover, the objectives laid out by direct democracy are primarily immediate objectives in the immediate vicinity (for example, preventing the construction of a wind turbine next door, if need be), if the argument of incorrect incentives of short-term interests shall apply here and we have empirical evidence for this (Bonoli and Häusermann 2009). The problems of future generations 100 years from now are hardly of interest to citizens today. Switzerland is an example of a country with a high degree of direct democracy, but in no way is it an ecological or moral paragon, mainly due to the fact that citizens have given the banks free rein since the citizens benefit enormously from them.

Of course, an increased degree of grassroots democracy also brings advantages: ecological problems based on a lack of knowledge or ignorance can be reduced. In addition, citizens are spurred by elements of direct democracy to identify with and play a more active role in the political system. This development would resist the 'internal decay' of democracy that we are currently experiencing. To implement the advantages of grassroots democracy while avoiding its disadvantages, we must connect grassroots democracy with an institutional safeguard for future interests, which would allow grassroots democracy to be implemented without harming future generations. Establishing advocates for future generations in an institutional manner, as proposed in the following sections, is a prerequisite for a successful form of grassroots democracy. First, because this idea takes the entire basis of concerned people into consideration, including the voices of citizens who are not yet with us and who would otherwise not be heard. Second, because such an incorrect trend in the mentalities of citizens – for example, considering short-term individual interests as the sole standard – can be corrected. The healing powers of grassroots democracy can be implemented after an institution to protect the interests of future generations has been set up.

5. New political institutions: future councils

For years now, 'future councils' have been discussed as a new form of institution.[7] These councils are seen as a kind of third chamber in the parliamentary system. They are made up of citizens who have garnered particular public attention through their work in pursuing a sustainable lifestyle. The most ideal situation would be a council that is made up of well-known academics, artists, authors, journalists, etc. Members of such a council could be nominated by environmental associations, universities, journalist associations, etc. and directly elected by citizens for a single mandated period of 8 to 10 years. Such council members would be committed environmentalists who, as advocates for the future, are appointed with the objective of introducing the interests of future generations into the current legislative process. They would then have the right to introduce legislative initiatives and referenda, gather information, and make it available to the public; they would also be given the rights to a suspensive or extensive veto for any laws that pertain to sustainable development. If more countries were to have such an institution, then climate change would not advance so quickly, especially if such institutions were more than just an advisory council, of which we currently have enough.[8] A future council or an ombudsperson (see below) without authority would be a disservice to the cause. At any rate, such councils would be legitimated by democratic structures if they were elected by citizens. The benefits would come from the fact that experts could receive more clout. In addition, the work done by the advocates of the future, the long mandated periods and the independence of the candidates could all help to eliminate incorrect incentives and short-term interests. An independent chamber is less susceptible to influence from lobbyists, and such a chamber would have an obligation to develop a correct understanding of the common good and would give greater attention and power to the interests of future generations.

But politicians, of course, are neither willing to give up their power nor to amend the constitution in such a way. However, they could be forced if a referendum could be held – perhaps even at the European level. In this respect, minority positions could exercise an enormous amount of pressure, similar to the way in which joint stock companies are placed under pressure by their stakeholders. For example, with the support of a mere 11 per cent of eligible voters, PIRC, a critical shareholders association in the United States, was able to bring the Shell Group to its knees (Kahlenborn 1997: 66). By organising an effective media campaign in favour of future councils and referenda, it would be possible to force politicians to accommodate these issues if they want to maintain their chances of re-election. It is equally effective to try to convince young members of parliament across party lines to pursue a committed policy that would benefit their own future (Tremmel 2005: 12). Such initiatives should be implemented at an international level.

If all else fails, a future council could be established on the level of NGOs. Its role would be to take a position on current policy making, by adopting and recording alternative measures parallel to actual policies. It would then be possible over time to document how a given policy would be differentiated with or without the involvement of a future council, and this could then lead to increased publicity and acceptance for the institution.

What arguments are there against such a proposal?

(1) Ecodictatorship – legitimisation

Are these nothing else but arguments in favour of a dictatorial instrument in disguise? Is there not a threat of an 'expertocracy', a domination by academia? The responses to these two questions are as follows: a future council will only be created if many citizens want such a council and exert enough pressure to make it happen. In addition, only such an institution enables a grassroots democracy, as it incorporates the voices of those who otherwise would never be heard. Only with such an institution will future generations have a voice in current policy making, and grassroots democracy is the opposite of dictatorship. Those who support the idea of a future council can also argue that grassroots democracy is capable of activating the electorate. The only difference is that they would argue grassroots democracy does not solve all problems, rather that it is an institutional enhancement.

A future council would have a democratic structure. It would be made up of elected and therefore democratically legitimate representatives; it should also become a constitutional political institution. It would be bound to precisely formulated thematic limits to questions of sustainable development (ecology, solid state finances, sustainable education?) and be subject to legal controls just as any other constitutional body.

Does not everyone in a democracy have a right to equal representation, and would this right not be infringed upon by a particular representation of future generations? Such a line of argument can be followed if we disregard the empirical evidence that such equal representation does not work due to anthropological barriers. Making 'lobbyists for the future' just as strong as current lobbyists requires a form of 'reverse discrimination', in other words, an institutional preference of future generations. It is true that the vexed lobby system has not been abandoned and the problem of sustainable development has not yet been fully solved, as it must be pursued by the entire political spectrum. This is, however, an obstacle that can be overcome. From a utilitarian perspective, the overall level of happiness will increase by giving preference to the future generations, and the following case shows how the principle of equality can be endangered by insisting on it: if sustainable development is not secured, democracy itself will be in peril, for if the future continues to be dominated by migration, war and catastrophes, the foundation for democracy and its principle of equality will be in extreme danger. This is why other forms of normative ethics can consider the values of 'procedural equality' and 'the lives of numerous living beings in the future' in a similar way as a utilitarian would, for it is questionable whether equality is diminished due to reserve discrimination, but it is obvious that this kind of discrimination is of enormous benefit for future generations. We can also examine the plausibility of this benefit by looking at the level of equality in the future that will increase if we practice reverse discrimination. This last argument is of no use for other minorities who might also require an ombudsperson to represent their interests.

We must admit, however, that a future council could also be susceptible to a misuse of power. The suggested procedure of nominating and electing its members does not eliminate the possibility that individuals or even certain groups could manage to gain power or even misuse this power. As the division of power remains intact, the risk here is not any greater or smaller than with any other institution. Even our parliaments and governments are susceptible to the misuse of power. However, it would not be plausible to assume that a future council could be an institution that is particularly vulnerable to such misuse of power. A constitution similar to the Russian constitution, in which the president enjoys a wide range of authority, is much more prone to dictatorial misuse. Dictatorships often begin in the executive office. A future council would have no or very little direct influence on such an office (see below).

(2) Blockade of politics

Many people might think that the aforementioned authority of a future council would be too great. For example, most laws in the economic sector could be affected by a possible range of caveats. Regulated and effective policy making would not be possible with a future council. Much more, there would be a fear that constitutional bodies would simply impede one another. The power of a veto could lead to a situation in which hardly any more laws would be passed at all. The future council would only lead to an unfathomable legislative logjam.

First, it is correct to say that the majority of conventional economic laws could possibly be rejected by a future council, for this would be its very purpose, as the council should promote sustainable economic policies. The conventionally 'regulated' policies have led us to the brink of disaster. A future council would initiate a change of direction. Despite this, the potential of such an institution to act as a blockade should be taken very seriously. The very essence of policy making depends on the ability to exercise rights. However, there is no reason to fear that a future council would eliminate this ability to exercise rights in policy making. We should not assume that, after establishing such a council, we would only see a permanent wave of vetoes etc. The practice of policy making is usually different. Politicians are pragmatic enough to avoid the necessity of a veto by proposing laws that are capable of finding a consensus. A brief look at the situation in the United States shows that the president's power of veto is hardly ever used to block legislation passed by Congress. It rarely comes to this; instead the parties involved seek to find a compromise. Indeed, we would expect to see changes in the platforms of conventional political parties after establishing a future council, since a party platform that prevents cooperation with the future council from the outset would eliminate this party's ability to govern.

(3) Little power to shape policy

One shortcoming of a future council would certainly be that it would have little power to shape policy (Stein 1998: 165). The council could introduce legislative initiatives; however it would mainly act as an instrument of prevention rather than implementation. However, as mentioned above, one can hope that the party platforms would be adapted to accommodate the work of a future council. In addition, it could also be planned to have the council send a representative to the executive office to help shape policy, for example, as a minister of the environment. However, a future council or any other such institution acting in its role is not the panacea for the future, even if a council would be an important step in the right direction.

6. New political institutions: ombudspersons

Another proposal is to appoint an ombudsperson as an 'advocate for the interests of future generation'.[9] Such an ombudsperson already exists in Hungary, and similar positions have been in place in Israel and other countries. The objectives of such an advocate are similar to those of a future council. They can range from simple awareness-raising programs for the general public to delaying legislation (suspensive veto) or an outright power of veto. Until now, such advocates have been appointed by parliament or the government, and also removed by them. This procedure would mean that greater control is given to the parliament, and established politicians might be more willing to create such an institution, as they would not have to relinquish as much of their power as with an elected future council. However, all aforementioned methods for appointing an ombudsperson would also be possible for future councils.

As many institutions in our democracy cannot claim to have a direct democratic legitimisation, such an office would not be an exception by any means. An example in Germany is the lower house of parliament, the Bundesrat, which is not elected directly by the people; in Europe there is the European Central Bank, the European Commission and numerous other institutions that have been legitimated through appointment by governments and/or parliaments (Rux 1999: Section III. 2. c). All of these institutions can be equally controlled, and none of them is a haven from the misuse of power.

As compared with elected future councils, the prospective increased enforceability is coupled with the reduced effectiveness of such an advocate. If such an advocate is appointed by the parliament, he or she will hardly be able to exercise a radical opposition to the majority of parliament. Much more, he or she would probably be a deserving politician from the governing party's own faction, thereby bringing his or her neutrality into question. At the same time, the ability quickly to remove such an advocate does not make the position into a particularly independent entity. However, preventive measures could be implemented, for example, by requiring a two-thirds majority in parliament to remove the advocate. Otherwise, the same supervisory authorities as with the future council could be implemented: clearly defined areas of responsibility for the institution laid down in the constitution and the ability to lodge a complaint if these are breached.

If the advocate could be directly elected by the citizens of a country, however, the aforementioned dependencies would no longer be an issue. If an individual were appointed as an ombudsperson in this way, his or her influence and ability to act could even be greater than those of an entire elected chamber. In this respect, an ombudsperson could be more effective than a future council. It should be pointed out that an ombudsperson actually would be an office where citizens could enter complaints about policy making. This would allow for greater public participation in politics, but this has limits. The ombudsperson serves the interests of future generations. Of course, he or she can act on the basis of information provided by current citizens; however, he or she would only represent their interests if they can be combined with the interests of future generations. Otherwise, there could be a considerable conflict of interests between future and current generations, and in these conflicts the Ombudsperson would definitely have to take the side of the future generations. Indeed, the Ombudsperson can help to shape policy to make it more transparent and in touch with the electorate, and he or she could incorporate and address issues important to local citizens' movements; however, this would only be possible if the interests of both future and current citizens are identical.

Ultimately, it does not really matter whether there are calls for a future council or, rather, an individual advocate for the future. Both models present great similarities. Most of the time, when NGOs etc. refer to ombudspersons, they mean the type of advocate in place in Hungary or their other well-known forms. The question of neutrality is, then, its Achilles' heel. However, an advocate of the future will certainly not be able to implement much damage in current decision committees. In the worst case, the result would be an ineffective new institution that provides established politicians with the ability to greenwash their policies. However, it is worth taking this risk.

7. Generational justice as a national policy objective?

A line of argument could also be pursued that would, instead of calling for new institutions, seek to incorporate generational justice or, at least, the consideration of the interests of future generations into the constitution as a national policy objective and then wait for complaints about legislation that demonstrate an unfair bias towards current generations.[10] This is certainly an interesting option that could be attained together with new democratic institutions. It is not necessarily true that this option offers several advantages in terms of enforceability, as even here politicians have to practice self-restraint. If we are to understand this instrument as an alternative to new institutions that has to cope with 'dreadful advisory boards', as J. Tremmel sees them, then several shortcomings need to be fixed:

1. We can point out that the 'national policy objective of environmental protection' in Germany has not led to any major changes, although a national policy objective can be abrogated by arguing that other policy objectives take precedence (Rux 1999: Section B, 2. c).
2. There is no guarantee that a complaint will be registered against a poorly drafted law. Individual interests of persons or associations submitting the complaint could be affected by the law in such a way that a potential plaintiff could be put at a disadvantage by merely entering the complaint. This could hardly happen, for example, to an ombudsperson who thwarts pending legislation, for he or she holds a position that is financially secure.
3. An Ombudsperson or a council could raise awareness among the general public before a law is passed, for example, by organising media campaigns, etc. When reaching a decision, a judge is obligated to explain the reasons

behind his or her opinion. Citizens would then have to research such explanations themselves if this information is not made readily available by the media. No one would be there to start a campaign or initiate a debate.

4. After a complaint is brought before a court, the judges would have to reach a decision in controversial cases, but, contrary to council members or ombudspersons, they are not experts. They could, of course, seek the opinions of experts in the field, yet second-hand knowledge is always more susceptible to error than first-hand expertise.
5. The image of the courts suffers if they have to intervene too much in policy making.

8. Outlook: Europe

Precisely at a time when Europe is experiencing an institutional crisis, initiatives should be started to introduce future councils or Ombudspersons as a new institution at the European level. We are currently experiencing proof of the fact Europe cannot work as a purely monetary union. We need a unified system of European policy making, and a future council or an ombudsperson could be a decisive factor in such a system. The pending reform process in Europe should create a climate in which citizens and politicians are open to innovations in our institutions. If changes are to be made nonetheless, then we should ensure that we protect the interests of future generations at the same time. It is prudent to start with a European future council etc., and then follow up with equivalent councils at the national level.

At any rate, the following should be said for Europeans who do not want to give up in the face of the overwhelming problems: an institutional reform of European democracy is the front on which we have to fight. To close with the words of the political scientist T. Stein: 'It is not risky to implement constitutional reforms motivated by ecological polices; what is risky to not do it at all' (Stein 1998: 165).

Notes

1   For more on the spectrum of feedback effects, see Friedlingstein *et al.* 2006.
2   This argument is based on Plato in Politeia: Plato 1997.
3   Available online (German): www.spiegel.de/wissenschaft/mensch/ 0,1518,733230,00.html. Retrieved: 23 December 2010.
4   cf. also BUND *et al.* 1997, p.379f. or more recently, Thompson 2010 and Tremmel 2005.
5   Available online (German): www.acs.allianz.com/downloasds/zwei_grad_studie_ final_strategiebericht.pdf. Retrieved: 17 February 2010.
6   This is how Geißler describes these problems (Geißler 2012). Stein contradicts him by stating that the electorate is often oriented towards their own interests (homo oeconomicus) (1998: 150–164).
7   For a sophisticated and legally elaborated draft of such an amendment of the German Basic Law see Rux 2003.
8   Tremmel refers to 'dreadful advisory boards' (2005: 6).

9 As Tremmel correctly points out, we should speak of successive and future generations as to include the generations that have already been born. For reasons of simplicity, however, I will adhere to the common term used (Tremmel 2005: 7).

10 For example, Tremmel calls for this (2005: 6).

References

Bahro, R. 1987. *Logik der Rettung*. Stuttgart/Vienna.

Bonoli, G. and Häusermann, S. 2009. 'Who wants what from the welfare state? Socio-structural cleavages in distributional politics: evidence from Swiss referendum votes', in J. Tremmel (ed.), *A Young Generation under Pressure?* Berlin/Heidelberg, 211–231.

BUND, et al. (eds) 1997. *Zukunftsfähiges Deutschland*. Basel, Boston et al.

Cox, P.M., Betts, R.A., et al. 2000. 'Acceleration of global warming due to carbon-cycle feedbacks in a coupled climate model'. *Nature* 408, 184–187.

Dörner, D. and Reither, F. 1978. 'Über das Problemlösen in sehr komplexen Realitätsbereichen'. *Zeitschrift für experimentelle und angewandte Psychologie* XXV (4), 527.

Friedlingstein, P. et al. 2006. 'Climate – carbon cycle feedback analysis: results from the C4MIP model intercomparison'. *Journal of Climate* 19 (14), 3337–3353.

Geißler, H. 2012. *Sapere Aude! Warum wir eine neue Aufklärung brauchen*. Berlin.

Gesang, B. 2000. *Aktien oder Apokalypse: Wege aus der globalen Ökokrise*. Paderborn.

Gesang, B. 2011. *Klimaethik*. Berlin.

Guehenno, J.-M. 1994. *Das Ende der Demokratie*. Munich.

Jonas, H. 1979. *Das Prinzip Verantwortung*. Frankfurt am Main.

Kahlenborn, W. 1997. 'Stimmen für die Natur'. *Politische Ökologie* 53, 65–66.

Kielmannsegg, P. G. 1980. *Nachdenken über Demokratie*. Stuttgart.

Meadows, D. H. et al. 1972. *The Limits to Growth*. Washington.

Plato 1997. *Complete Works*, Cooper J. M. (ed.). Indianapolis/Cambridge.

Precht, R. D. 2010. *Die Kunst kein Egoist zu sein*. Munich.

Randers, J. 2012. *2052: A Global Forecast for the Next Forty Years*. White River Junction, VT.

Rux, J. 1999. 'Intertemporale Strukturprobleme der Demokratie', in M. Bertschi et al. (eds) *Freiheit und Recht*. Stuttgart, 301–333.

Rux, J. 2003. 'Der ökologische Rat – Ein Vorschlag zur Änderung des Grundgesetzes mit Begründung', in Stiftung für die Rechte der zukünftigen Generationen (ed.), *Handbuch Generationengerechtigkeit*. Munich, 471–490.

Simon, J. L. 1981. *The Ultimate Ressource*. Princeton, NJ.

Stein, T. 1998. *Demokratie und Verfassung an den Grenzen des Wachstums*. Opladen.

Thompson, D. F. 2010. 'Representing future generations: political presentism and democratic trusteeship'. *Critical Review of International Social and Political Philosophy*, 13 (1), 17–37.

Tremmel, J. 2005. 'Verankerung von Generationengerechtigkeit in der Verfassung'. Available at: http://library.fes.de/pdf-files/akademie/online/03594.pdf (retrieved 5th September 2012).

von Winter, T. 1995. 'Interessenverbände im gesellschaftlichen Wandel', in T. Jäger and D. Hoffmann (eds), *Demokratie in der Krise? Zukunft der Demokratie*. Opladen, 145–168.

Part 2

Aspects of transition

5   Climate justice in the straitjacket of feasibility

Dominic Roser

There is a consensus that current climate policy falls short of the demands of justice. Feasibility constraints are often taken to be responsible for this failure. This chapter examines the structure of feasibility constraints and cautions against envisioning them as too constraining a straitjacket. Four pitfalls are pointed out: drawing a false picture of the feasible set; failing to acknowledge that feasibility constraints hold for certain agents and time spans; treating constraints rooted in one's own motivation the same way as other feasibility constraints; and failing to exploit all opportunities for decreasing injustice within the feasible set.

1. Introduction

In some areas of political philosophy, debates revolve around the justifiability of the status quo. In other areas, debates are conducted against the backdrop of a consensus that the status quo is unjustifiable. Climate change belongs to the latter category. The lack of a strong global mitigation effort puts the human rights of future generations excessively at risk (cf. Caney 2009), and if the current unwillingness for just burden-sharing continues the socio-economic human rights of presently living people in developing countries also might well be at serious risk. It is often suggested that feasibility constraints are responsible for this failing: We seem unable and unwilling to pursue climate justice more ambitiously.

This chapter takes a closer look at feasibility constraints, their structure and their uses in the public discourse on climate change. I argue that these constraints are less confining than it may seem at first sight. The four sections identify various mistakes in feasibility-related reasoning, each of which unnecessarily paralyses climate action. Section 2 notes the temptation to give a false picture of the feasible set. Section 3 discusses the failure to make claims about feasibility relative to agents and time. Sections 4–6 question whether an agent's own motivation should count as a feasibility constraint. Section 7 brings in a slightly different perspective: while the previous sections warn of *abusing* feasibility talk, Section 7 warns of missing out on opportunities to *use* up the full space within the feasible set.

Feasibility is ubiquitously referred to in climate debates, sometimes also in the form of related expressions such as practicability or realism. For example, Fankhauser (1995: 133) claims that the allocation of emission rights 'should be both fair and feasible', Metz (2000: 125) notes that 'for practical solutions [to climate change] equity has also to be balanced with [efficiency and] political feasibility', and the IPCC says that there is 'a broad consensus in the literature that a successful agreement will have to be environmentally effective and cost-effective, incorporate distributional considerations and equity and be institutionally feasible' (IPCC 2007a: 748). Some of these statements insinuate that it is a *desideratum* that feasible policies be implemented – a desideratum that has to be balanced with other desiderata such as justice, efficiency or environmental integrity. This is misleading, however. While normative considerations such as justice, efficiency or environmental integrity determine the *goal* of climate policy, feasibility considerations operate on a different level. Feasibility *constrains* the space within which we can pursue these goals. There is no point in saying that we ought to aim at enacting feasible climate policies: if a certain climate policy is unfeasible, this already tells us that it is not put into practice and if it is feasible, this tells us nothing about whether it ought to be enacted. Staying within the feasible set is thus not a desideratum in its own right.[1]

A more appropriate picture of how feasibility interweaves with desirability goes as follows: the normative exercise of finding out what we ought to do relies, first, on evaluating and ranking the options according to normative criteria (in this chapter the primary criterion will be justice) and, second, on the descriptive exercise of finding out which options are ruled out by feasibility constraints. The *basic injunction* then says:

Choose the least unjust option from the feasible set.

The 'least unjust' part is the normative puzzle piece and the 'feasible set' part is the descriptive puzzle piece. Put together, they yield action-guidance. This 'basic injunction' is meant to express in broad brush manner a certain widely shared view on how normative and descriptive considerations add up to yield prescriptions for choice (cf. for example Swift 2008: 369). The wording of this injunction is only a starting point. One aim of this chapter is to show how it has to be amended.

Two preliminary remarks: first, I speak of 'least unjust' rather than 'most just'. Both expressions might well express the same idea, but the former seems preferable to me, primarily for rhetorical reasons: it impedes complacency by highlighting that feasibility constraints currently make us choose among a set that includes only unjust options. I also use 'least unjust' to acknowledge that there may be a threshold of justice beyond which no options are 'more just' than others (i.e. many conceptions of justice are satiable (cf. Raz 1986: 235–6)), even if some of the just outcomes are morally better than others in some other respect. Second, I assume that feasibility constraints only affect which option we ought to *choose* (i.e. 'ought implies can') but do not affect how we ought to *evaluate options* according to justice or other normative criteria. It is a conceptual possibility that the feasible set includes only unjust options either because it is a conceptual possibility that there are unjust state of affairs without anybody having done anything wrong (cf. Gheus 2013) or because the choice of options depends on both past and present decisions with past decisions having excluded all just options from the currently feasible set (cf. also Lawford-Smith 2013b: 665).

2. Mistake 1: distorting portrayals of the feasible set

Because the 'basic injunction' tells us that choice prescriptions do not only rely on normative premises but also on premises about feasibility, agents who want to influence society's response to climate change do not only have the option of influencing beliefs about justice and increasing the motivation to act in accordance with these beliefs, but they also have the option of revising popular beliefs about the contours of the feasible set. For example, business lobbyists often consider it easier to inculcate the belief that a renewable energy transformation is unfeasible rather than discrediting the view that such a transformation is required. And since both beliefs are necessary for the conclusion that we ought to opt for it, lobbyists focus on the belief that is easier to manipulate. Of course, the temptation to distort must not necessarily have a conservative bent but can also go in the other direction: portraying the unfeasible as feasible. If politicians manage to instil a belief that climate mitigation and economic growth are jointly feasible, this can convince voters to support mitigation policies who otherwise would not.

Painting a distorted picture of the feasible set is facilitated by the difficulty of acquiring evidence about the shape of feasibility constraints. And where evidence would actually be accessible, it is often not made use of. Even in the academic literature, references to feasibility often go without empirical support. This is particularly surprising given that those who do actually invoke feasibility considerations let them do a lot of the work in arriving at the ultimate normative conclusions. Peter Singer spends many pages on examining moral reasons for various positions in the climate justice debate but, at the end of the day, one of the two reasons that lead him to support the equal per capita emission proposal one is its suitability as a political compromise (2002, 43). Boldly asserting its suitability as a political compromise would seem to need better empirical support than pointing to its simplicity. Posner and Weisbach are another example for the disproportion between the argumentative weight that feasibility constraints have to carry and the dearth of empirical backing offered for the precise shape they assume these constraints to have. Without any serious effort to give supporting evidence, they make the simplified, unconvincing, and ambiguous (Caney 2014) assumption that only treaties that make all states better off are feasible (Posner and Weisbach 2010: 6). Another example is the reasoning employed in the budget approach of the German WBGU (2009: 25). The report deems it politically difficult to distribute emissions equally across the globe over the time span from 1990 to 2050. Therefore, it is suggested to forego backward-looking considerations and to focus on equalising emissions over the time span from 2010 to 2050. While few need to be convinced that equalising emissions from 1990 onwards is politically infeasible, many would surely ask for evidence regarding the feasibility of equalising from 2010 onwards. Choosing 2010 rather than 1990 might well have been driven by the results the researchers aimed at rather than their best guesses about significant differences in political feasibility between those two dates.[2]

Distorting and abusing feasibility constraints is aided by the fact that the structure of feasibility constraints and their role in practical deliberation are more intricate than it seems at first sight. The potential for smuggling unstated normative views into the political debate via the Trojan horse of superficially descriptive feasibility claims is greatly facilitated by the subtleties of feasibility claims.

In order to give substance to this assertion, it is helpful to break feasibility statements down into different parts:

> Option O is feasible with probability P for agents A at time T due to determinants D

This is a modified version of the insightful analysis in Gilabert and Lawford-Smith (2012). In this section I make some cursory remarks about 'Option O' and 'with probability P'. The aspects 'for agents A' and 'at time T' will be discussed in section 3 and 'due to determinants D' will be discussed in Sections 4–6. Taken together, these brief remarks aim to highlight how the intricacies of the concept of feasibility open the door for agents to publicly tailor seemingly empirically grounded feasibility claims such that their preferred practical conclusions come out of the equation.

'Option O ...'

Feasibility talk is made difficult by the fact that the options we refer to as feasible or unfeasible can be different types of objects, in particular: (i) outcomes (say, 2° warming); (ii) actions and policies (say, reducing emissions by 20%); or (iii) combining the two previous suggestions, actions and policies that bring about a certain outcome (say, achieving climate stability by relying primarily on carbon capture and storage). A particularly delicate issue consists in linking the feasibility of an action to willing or trying to perform the action (Gilabert and Lawford-Smith 2012: 817; Estlund 2011: 212).

'... with probability P ...'

Meinshausen *et al.* (2009) claim that there is a 75 per cent chance of staying below 2° if anthropogenic CO_2 emissions are limited to 1000 Gt between 2000 and 2050. Statements of this type raise an interesting question: is it appropriate to claim that it *is* feasible to limit temperature increase to 2°C by limiting emissions to 1000 Gt? Or should we rather make the radical claim that 'achieving 2°C by limiting emissions to 1000 Gt' is *not* in the feasible set since its being in the feasible set would imply that we can make it happen at will – simply by choosing to do so? Or should we be even more radical and claim that feasibility statements *do not apply* at all in cases of uncertainty?[3] One of the comparatively less implausible ways of treating such cases takes feasibility statements to apply but to stand in need of being complemented by probabilities.

The claim 'O is feasible with a certain probability' is often made with the help of a shortcut expression: it is claimed that O is 'highly feasible' or 'hardly feasible'. Such *gradual* feasibility claims are very common (see for example the references to a '*most* feasible' climate policy in Frankel (2005), Stott (2008) and Lorenzoni and Pidgeon (2006)). However, taken literally, such gradual feasibility claims would seem perplexing. Feasibility is close in meaning to possibility, which is a binary notion: something is either possible or not. Also, the idea of a 'feasible set' is more straightforward when feasibility is understood as a 0/1-notion rather than a scalar notion. An easy way to resist a gradual interpretation of feasibility (cf. e.g. Lawford-Smith 2013a: 255) interprets them as shortcuts for the more precise claim that O is feasible (or not) in a binary way but that there is uncertainty as to whether it is so. The gradual claim about the *probability* of O being feasible is thus collapsed into a gradual claim about the *feasibility* of O.[4] Note that understanding gradual feasibility claims as shortcuts for probabilistic claims about binary feasibility statements allows for gradual claims even in cases when feasibility constraints are rooted purely in laws of logic or nature (which seems to me an advantage over the suggestion in Gilabert and Lawford-Smith (2012: 813)).[5]

Importantly, the fact that feasibility statements come with probabilities means that we have to amend the basic injunction ('choose the least unjust option from the feasible set') by adding probabilities into the equation. We have to make space for the fact that an option that is feasible with much higher probability than another option might be preferable to the latter even if the latter is slightly more just. We ought to choose options that strike an optimal balance between the degree of injustice and the probability of feasibility. For example: a geo-engineering technology that minimises the exposure of future generations to catastrophic risk to the same extent as an emission reduction policy might use fewer resources from present generations (and thus count as less unjust) but have a smaller probability of being feasible and thus be overall less choiceworthy. In that sense, the wording that I criticised in the introduction about a balance that has to be struck between justice and feasibility is not necessarily off the mark if it is understood as a shortcut for the balance that has to be struck between the degree of injustice of a certain option and the probability of its being feasible. It is a very difficult question how an optimal balance between the probability of feasibility and the degree of injustice has to be struck, especially for those who are not willing to simply resort to expected utility type reasoning. For rights theorists, a certain probability of giving someone less than she has a right to is not straightforwardly counterbalanced by giving that person (or, *a fortiori*, someone else) an equal probability of receiving more than she has a right to.

To sum up, the first common mistake consists in spreading an inaccurate and overly narrow picture of the feasible set, often without empirical support, and doing so in order to rule out certain options from consideration. Manipulating beliefs about feasible options is facilitated by the subtleties involved in the concept of feasibility. The next two sections turn to further aspects of the structure of feasibility claims. Besides pointing out other mistakes on which exaggerated claims about the stifling nature of feasibility constraints rest, this also serves to underline the asserted intricacy of the concept.

3. Mistake 2: refraining from relativising feasibility claims

'... for agents A ...']

The feasible set is obviously relative to agents. Whereas reaching the target of limiting temperature increase to 2° is unfeasible for me or for the European Union, it is not unfeasible for humanity. Refraining from a precise specification of the agent or arbitrarily disregarding those sets of agents for whom an option would be feasible are two strategies of abusing feasibility considerations for pushing a certain agenda.

In the case of sets of agents, there are often exaggerated claims about how the feasibility of an option depends on how the set of agents is internally organised (cf. also Lawford-Smith 2013a: 247). For example, it might be said to be feasible for *Belgium* to cut the amount of car travel in half within a decade because Belgium is internally well organised: there is a government that can coordinate, incentivise and enforce the actions of Belgians. In contrast, it might be said to be unfeasible for all *French-speaking persons* of the world to cut car travel in half within a decade because there is no central decision-making mechanism for all French-speakers. I believe the latter claim to be false. In a trivial sense, the set of French-speaking persons *could* cut car travel in half within a decade – each agent within this set would simply have to do so. Claiming that this is unfeasible diverts attention from the truly relevant differences between Belgium and the set of all French-speaking persons. The set of agents that constitutes Belgium includes a small subset of agents (*viz.* the agents in the Belgian government) for whom it is possible – without exerting tremendous effort – to make the whole set of agents cut car travel in half. In the case of French-speaking persons, there is no such subset. Also, in the Belgian case there is a subset of agents that is legitimised to affect the actions of the whole set of agents. These two (plus probably further) factors may imply that if Belgians do not cut their car travel in half, there have been duties on the part of some or all Belgians that have not been lived up to, whereas the same may not be true in the case of French-speakers. The potential exculpation of French-speakers rests, however, not on a simple unfeasibility for French-speakers to cut their car travel in half. Doing so *is* within their feasible set and if there should be no duty for them to do so (whereas there should be one for Belgium), this must be justified in more complex ways than by a reference to unfeasibility, for example by reference to an overdemandingness clause, by reference to the unfair distribution of burdens that occurs in the absence of a central decision-making procedure, or by reference to individual lifestyle changes being an inefficient means for reaching the relevant environmental goals if there is no coordinating authority.[6]

'... at time T ...'

Feasibility claims are relative to time. While some of the determinants of feasibility constraints are static (e.g. laws of logic) other determinants change over time. Among the latter some change without human interference (e.g. solar activity) while others can be affected at will (e.g. the amount of accessible fossil fuels).[7]

In practice, many feasibility claims are not accompanied by a statement disclosing from what starting date to what end date they hold. If an 'expiry date' is attached at all, rough descriptions such as 'short-run' and 'long-run' are usually deemed sufficient. Implicitly, feasibility constraints are often taken as static, which should invite scepticism as to whether this is anything else but an attempt to justify the status quo. This scepticism is for example appropriate when we dismiss an anti-consumerist revolution of the hearts and minds as a serious climate mitigation strategy as quickly as we usually do simply on account of assuming materialist self-interest to be a stable trait of human psychology.

The fact that the feasible set can change over time invites us to revise the basic injunction ('choose the least unjust option from the feasible set'). If option A is slightly *less just* than option B *today* but has the benefit of increasing the feasible set *tomorrow* significantly, then A might well be the option we ought to choose. Rather than simply relying on the injunction to choose the least unjust option from the feasible set, we ought to choose the option that strikes an 'optimal' balance between the two considerations of (i) decreasing the degree of injustice at various points of time, and (ii) increasing the feasible set at various points of time in relevant ways. Such balancing is no easy matter. While it is obvious for utilitarians how to make such trade-offs, other theorists, such as human rights theorists, face larger challenges as they do not allow in straightforward ways for increasing injustice for some for the sake of decreasing injustice for others. One particular challenge is that striking a balance between different points of time is partly an issue of making trade-offs within the lifespans of persons and partly an issue of making trade-offs between persons of different generations.

Such balancing was typically done explicitly by supporters of the Kyoto protocol: many evaluated its direct success in terms of mitigating climate change – and thus decreasing injustice towards future generations – to be small but they evaluated its indirect success in terms of getting international cooperation running – and thus increasing the feasible set of policies available in the future – favourably. One special way of affecting the future feasible set relies on the fact that feasibility claims can work as self-fulfilling prophecies. For example, pursuing geoengineering on the basis of a belief in the infeasibility of significant emission reductions in turn decreases the probability of the feasibility of significant emission reductions in the future. Sometimes, merely bringing feasibility up as a point on the agenda affects future feasibility, for example by dampening enthusiasm for action.

The temporal dimension of feasibility statements includes issues of accessibility and stability (cf. also Cohen (2009) or Buchanan (2004)). In a highly stylised manner, accessibility can be conceptualised as follows: first, a just outcome for period T_2 is determined (typically an outcome that is already known to be feasible were it not for the constraints rooted specifically in how history plays out). Second, it is examined whether there is an outcome at t_1, representing the points of time in a transitional historical period, that make the just outcome in the second period feasible and which then has to be evaluated according to, possibly minimal, criteria of justice. If no such transition can be found, a less ambitious goal has to be set for the second period. 'Contraction and Convergence' can be interpreted along these lines. Criticisms of an eco-dictatorship as a means for ensuring environmental protection rely on the fact that the transition to protection does not measure up to minimal standards of justice and legitimacy. We can look at stability in a similarly stylised manner: first, a just outcome for t_2 is determined. Second, it is examined whether choosing this outcome affects the feasible set at t_3, representing the points of time belonging to the 'long term', in such a way that the probability of the just outcome being in the feasible set is high not only at t_2 but also at t_3. The stability issue surfaces for example with respect to techno-fixes for single environmental problems such as climate change: while it may be granted that techno-fixes offer an accessible path to an outcome in the medium term that is to be evaluated positively, this outcome, it might be argued, is not stable. Techno-fixes (and the general mindset in which they are embedded) in turn cause new environmental problems after having solved one specific issue.

Note, in terms of a side remark, that there would be a way of framing deliberation under feasibility constraints that avoids the complexities introduced by the time dependence of the feasible set: rather than claiming that certain outcomes or actions are feasible over a certain time span we could claim that certain *courses of history* are feasible (where courses of history are sets of actions and outcomes across all points of time). The simple injunction to choose the least unjust option – the options would then be courses of history – from the feasible set could then be salvaged. Even if this would make for more straightforward choice prescriptions, thinking in terms of complete histories would be too much for human computing abilities. The best we can do is to break down the choice situation to a limited number of vague time spans.

Summing up, feasibility statements must be relativised to agents and time spans. If we tacitly or explicitly only take a restricted set of agents or points of time into account, we inflate the threat of infeasibility.

4. Mistake 3: conflating motivational and genuine feasibility constraints

'... due to determinants D'

This section cautions against treating one's own motivation as a root of feasibility constraints in the same way as other roots of feasibility constraints, such as natural laws or history. The section starts off from the last aspect of the analysis of feasibility claims: feasibility constraints have multiple factors that determine their shape. Some of these determinants are themselves rooted in further determinants (for example, present political institutions are a determinant of feasibility constraints and this determinant is itself determined by past human decisions which in turn are rooted in past human motivation). 'Ultimate' determinants for feasibility constraints might be classified as follows:

1. Determinants which are *unaffected* by human motivation such as laws of logic and nature, certain physical facts and constants, etc.
2. Determinants which are *affected* by human motivation
   a. *Past* human motivation
   b. *Present and future* human motivation
      I. The motivation of *others*
      II. The agent's *own* motivation

Some remarks on the distinction between one's own motivation and the motivation of others are appropriate. Feasibility constraints rooted in the motivation of others could be labelled 'social feasibility constraints'. The motivation of others is relevant insofar as it leads to actions of others that shape the feasible set of options for the agent whose choice is under consideration. Depending on what type of agents we look at, these social feasibility constraints have very different appearances. For example, nations take into account how other nations respond to unilateral action on climate policy, advocacy NGOs take into account whether individual citizens are more effectively moved by rational or emotional appeals, and individual voters take into account whether enough parties and individual opinion leaders support the conservative candidate to give him a realistic chance to steal the seat from the green candidate.

Feasibility constraints rooted in one's *own* motivation could be labelled 'own-motivational feasibility constraints' or, shorter, 'motivational feasibility constraints'. Together with social feasibility constraints they are the primary factors responsible for what is often labelled 'economic' or 'political' or 'psychological' feasibility. Economic, political, and psychological unfeasibility usually indicates only that the burdens are not *accepted* as a matter of fact – without implication that they are not *acceptable* in a moral sense or that it is not *possible* to accept them. Usually, it indicates an unwillingness to accept them rather than an inability.

Note that motivational feasibility constraints indirectly also apply to *sets of agents*. For a set of agents, the constraints resulting from the motivational setup of individuals is mediated by institutions and mechanisms (such as democracy and markets) that aggregate individual behaviour (which is rooted in individual motivation) into aggregate outcomes. Even if this is not as straightforward as in the case of individual agents, it allows us to make sense of talk of the motivation of a set of agents, such as talk of the political will of a nation. Note, however, that in the case of sets of agents, it can be difficult to distinguish between social and motivational feasibility constraints, i.e. to distinguish when it is the willingness of *other* agents and when it is the set of agents' *own* willingness that sets a limit on what is feasible. In order to illustrate, assume that a carbon-intensive industry sends a team of lobbyists to government officials. The individuals in both groups might all – say, in their capacity as social scientists – agree that companies typically react to incentives and that a carbon tax would thus have the effect of companies relocating their production to jurisdictions without a carbon tax. However, if the lobbyists cite this fact in their talk with the officials, they are the mouthpiece of a set of agents (the industry) citing its own *motivational* feasibility constraint (its unwillingness to bear the cost of the tax). In contrast, if the government officials cite the very same fact, they are the mouthpiece of a set of agents (the government) citing a *social* feasibility constraint on the government's set of options. Also, if the lobbyists pushed the government to forego the introduction of the tax and if the individuals in this team would have to defend their hard line to their green friends at the end of the work day they could perfectly well claim that if they did not do so, they would lose their lobbyist's job to someone else. This is best interpreted as a *social* feasibility constraint on the *lobbyists*: the industry's stance is a constraint on their personal actions. However, if the lobbyists push the government to forego the tax and tell the government that they have no alternative to pushing them since they would otherwise lose the backing of the industry association that sent them, there is a temptation for them as individuals to dress this up as a social feasibility constraint as well. This, however, is misleading: in that case, they are most naturally interpreted as referring to a *motivational* feasibility constraint of the *industry* for which the lobbyists speak. Thus, depending on context, the very same fact (that companies relocate in response to a tax) can be employed in practical reasoning both as a motivational and a social feasibility constraint. At least in the case of sets of agents, it is not always immediately obvious which type of constraint is at stake. This intricacy can be abused by sets of agents, for example, when a nation tries to justify its inaction on climate change to other nations by letting its government portray the democratic support of its voters as a *social* feasibility constraint, whereas a more adequate picture of the situation conceives of the government and the voter base as two subsets of the relevant set of agents: the nation – which then has to try to justify its inaction by reference to its *motivational* feasibility constraint.

There is a fundamental difference between motivational feasibility constraints, on the one hand, and all other feasibility constraints, on the other hand. The fundamental difference between the two is that, at any given point in time, current motivational feasibility constraints are under the *control* of the agent in question while feasibility constraints rooted in the current motivation of others, in history, in natural laws and in logical consistency are *given*.

A paradigmatic case of motivational feasibility constraints is the resistance to incur economic costs for the sake of emission reductions. In 2010, the environmental committee of the Swiss National Council deemed emission reductions of 30 per cent until 2020 to be 'unbearable' for the economy.[8] The US Senate's 1997 Byrd-Hagel Resolution (passed with a vote of 95–0) states that the USA should not be a signatory to any agreement regarding the UNFCCC which 'would result in serious harm to the economy of the United States'. The wording of the resolution does not frame it as an inability or impossibility issue, but rather as something that the USA is simply not agreeing to do: it is not a case of '*can't do*', but rather a case of '*won't do*'. Obviously, the USA *can* incur serious harm to the economy and, obviously, Switzerland *is* able to bear the costs of 30 per cent emission reductions. Refraining from bearing these costs is the 'plain vanilla' case of more or less deliberately limiting the amount of self-interest one is willing to sacrifice for the sake of justice. It is the case we are all phenomenologically familiar with from everyday life: we think we ought to take the bicycle rather than the car but we do not feel like it and thus decide not to do so. It is not a *given* constraint but rather a *chosen* constraint.

While common usage of language subsumes not only constraints rooted in the motivation of others, in history, in natural and logical laws under the heading of feasibility but also motivational constraints, I suggest that the former have a much stronger claim to capture the core idea of feasibility. I thus suggest subsuming all of the former under the label of 'genuine' feasibility constraints (denoting what we *cannot* do) and distinguish them from 'motivational' feasibility constraints (denoting what we are *not willing* to do). By using the label 'genuine' for the former, I implicitly question whether motivational feasibility constraints should labelled *feasibility* constraints at all. Compliance with current usage speaks for sticking with this convention but the misleading language should not serve to hide the fact that motivational and genuine feasibility constraints are two very different animals and thus also ought to enter our practical deliberation very differently (cf. Lawford-Smith 2013a: 256–7; Caney 2014). Motivational constraints are typically simply expressions of human selfishness – thoroughly *common* selfishness to be sure, but selfishness nonetheless. We should treat them as such, acknowledge their ubiquity and not conflate them with genuine feasibility constraints. A large share of the constraints mentioned under the heading of feasibility might well not be what I call genuine feasibility constraints. Motivation seems to be the more serious bottleneck. Given that 'ought' implies 'can', reframing a lack of motivation to do O as an inability to do O is a tempting escape from a duty to do O. This move, however, must be resisted and distinguishing between motivational and genuine feasibility constraints helps us to do so.

5. Two objections

Some will disagree with the stark contrast I have drawn here between genuine and motivational feasibility constraints. Often, motivation (sometimes under the heading of 'human psychology' or 'human nature') is mentioned without hesitation as a root of feasibility constraints on the same level as laws of nature and logic (cf. for example, Buchanan 2004: 61; Zuolo 2012: 7). Two objections to my strong distinction between motivational and genuine feasibility constraints stand out. First, one could count motivationally difficult options as similarly 'genuinely' infeasible on the basis that this has the welcome effect of protecting us from an excessively rigorous morality. Second, one could doubt whether our motivation is truly under our control in all cases, such as cases of addiction or compulsion.

Proponents of the first objection worry about excessive 'moral weightlifting'. One strategy for blocking off overly demanding moral requirements consists of conceiving such harsh demands as unfeasible in such a genuine sense that 'ought' implies 'can' applies to them. These supposed demands would then trivially fail to be true demands. However, this strategy of 'repackaging' the burdensome as the genuinely unfeasible is a misleading approach to the topic of overdemandingness. While the set of motivationally unfeasible policies certainly overlaps with the set of overdemanding policies, the two do not coincide. The set of motivationally unfeasible policies is generally larger than the latter. Even if the overdemandingness and the unfeasibility of a supposed moral requirement are both rooted in the same fact – the weighty sacrifices implied by the supposed requirement – and even if they should both lead to the same conclusion – the supposed demand not constituting a true demand at all – it still serves clarity to treat the issues separately. While motivational unfeasibility covers *any* actions and policies that agents refrain from doing because they find them burdensome, overdemandingness constraints only come into play as a result of actions and policies that burden agents in certain ways, such as when the harshness of a proposed course of action thwarts the sanity and integrity of an agent or when it conflicts with agent-centered prerogatives to pursue personal projects. The shape of the motivationally feasible set is chosen by the agent while the shape of the 'overdemanding set' is given by normative considerations.[9] Trivially, these must not coincide and, typically, they do not coincide: human motivation clashes with demands of justice at much earlier points than where plausible overdemandingness clauses start to kick in. Such clauses protect us primarily (if at all) from morality seriously curtailing our personal space and primarily (if at all) when there are no countervailing, weighty considerations at stake, such as climate change induced human rights violations. This point gains relevance when we note that seriously reducing emissions might not yield larger burdens than keeping economic growth over the next decades 0.1 per cent lower than in it would otherwise be (IPCC 2007b: Table SPM.7) or collecting a 1.5 per cent per annum wealth tax on the richest 1 per cent of the global population (Bell 2011: 119). Also, most burdens would not have to be actively and voluntarily taken up by individuals but would rather be imposed on them through political measures, which is less challenging. While it is plausible that these burdens overstrain current political will, it is much less plausible to consider these burdens as sufficiently harsh to make overdemandingness concerns relevant.[10]

A second objection to my stark contrast between motivational and genuine feasibility constraints questions whether humans are always *able* to control their motivation. If humans are unable to do so, then it is less controversial to subsume motivational constraints under the heading of genuine feasibility constraints. This would be relevant for the case of climate change if the frequently heard suggestion that we are 'addicted' to fossil fuels implied a genuine inability to reduce emissions. It is, however, questionable whether such claims should be understood literally. First, it is not straightforward to apply the concept of addiction, weakness of the will, and compulsion to *sets of agents*. The disanalogy is also noted by Suranovic (2013) in his comparison of cigarette and fossil fuel addiction. Second, it is dubious whether the idea of addiction is not only interesting in theory but applicable to the case at hand. The reluctance to move away from fossil fuels has much less to do with compulsion-like behaviour and much more with simple economic self-interest. This is particularly so if emission reductions are implemented by political means rather than by voluntary measures. Also, if there are elements of addiction to be discerned, it is rather an addiction to the *lifestyles* that are *currently* tied to extensive carbon emissions. Thus, even if the addiction should be genuine, emission reductions could be implemented by severing the link between the lifestyle and the emissions.[11]

These two objections thus raise interesting points but they do not refute the claim that there are cases of motivational feasibility constraints that do not amount to genuine feasibility constraints. The distinction is important because reasoning under motivational feasibility constraints should take a different form from reasoning under genuine feasibility constraints.

6. Practical reasoning under motivational feasibility constraints

The basic injunction tells us to choose the least unjust option from the feasible set. This injunction had to be modified in Sections 2 and 3 to take note of the fact that feasibility statements are relative to time and come with likelihoods attached. When we bring motivational feasibility constraints into the picture, the injunction is undermined in more fundamental ways. In the face of motivational constraints, three reactions seem appropriate.[12]

First, motivational constraints differ from genuine constraints because at any given time they are not *given*. Therefore, insofar as climate policy is constrained by the agent's choice to limit the extent of burdens he is willing to bear, considerations of justice do not primarily require the agent to choose the least unjust option from the constrained set. Rather, the first and foremost injunction is simply *to forego the constraint*.

Second, experience teaches us that lack of motivation and thus *moral failure* is a persistent feature of human life. In reaction to flouting the duty to forego motivational constraints (a 'first order' duty), certain moral and non-moral 'second order' responses are appropriate. Such responses consist of *acknowledging* failure, coming to terms with *guilt*, seeking a type of *reconciliation* with the imperfections of the current world that does *not include complacency*,[13] and expressing *remorse* towards the wronged (insofar as this is coherently possible while holding on to one's motivational constraints).

Third, one important second-order response to one's motivational limitations consists of at least choosing the least unjust option from the motivationally constrained set of options. Some care is needed in making this injunction – an analogue of the basic injunction from the introduction – precise. Assume that a country faces three policy options where option A yields a 30% emission reduction at the cost of 3‰ of GDP, option B yields 20% at the cost of 2‰, and option C 10% at the cost of 1‰. Assume that A is the only just option and assume that the country decides – based on its lack of motivation – not to bear costs exceeding 2‰ of GDP, i.e. to limit the choice set to options B and C. It would be wrong to simply use the wording from the basic injunction, i.e. to say that the country ought to choose the least unjust option from the motivationally constrained set (i.e. option B). What the country ought to choose, after all, is simply option A, the just option. A more accurate phrasing of the idea states that when choosing between option B and C, the country ought to choose B. Further correct wordings include that the country acts less unjustly when choosing B rather than C or that the country ought never to choose C when B is available.[14]

Summing up, we can note that – even if not always easily distinguishable – motivational feasibility constraints are importantly different from genuine feasibility constraints, and their widespread clash with demands of climate justice cannot be made to disappear by reference to overdemandingness clauses or by assimilating them to addiction to fossil fuels. The injunction never to choose a more unjust over a less unjust option from the feasible set holds for both types of constraints; in the case of motivational constraints this injunction should, however, not distract from the primary duty to refrain from constraining the set of options in the first place. As motivational constraints are not a given at any point of time, it is a mistake – the third of the four mistakes discussed in this chapter – to conceive of them as a limiting factor in the same way as genuine feasibility constraints.

7. Mistake 4: missing out on free lunches

The injunction to choose the least unjust option when choosing among feasible options comes with a natural follow-up injunction: a duty to spend time and energy on *identifying* the least unjust option in the feasible set. Even if we can change genuine feasibility constraints over time and even if we can forego motivational feasibility constraints in the present, there is also reason to identify ways for squeezing as much justice as possible out of whatever feasible set one currently takes as fixed. We can always look for opportunities to decrease injustice within the bounds of feasibility. These are 'free lunches' in terms of justice: agents can act *less unjustly* (that's the 'lunch' aspect) *without* first expanding current feasibility constraints (that's the 'free' aspect). As a joke among economists goes, there can never be a dollar bill on the ground because if there were, someone would already have picked it up. But as we all know, there actually are dollar bills on the ground. This proves that humans do not manage to spot and 'pick up' all free lunches in terms of self-interest; and thus, we also need not expect them to have exploited all opportunities for free lunches in terms of justice.

Alas, discovering these opportunities can be difficult. One has to bring together two pieces of knowledge in order to notice them. First, a normative piece of knowledge: what counts as gradual progress on justice relative to where we are 'here and now'? This is an exercise in non-ideal political philosophy and it consists of knowing the shape of the moral landscape around the status quo. Second, a descriptive piece of knowledge: what are the precise contours of the feasible set around the status quo? Some authors portray such choice situations analogously to how economists portray ordinary consumption decisions (cf. Cohen 2003: 244–5; Baumgärtner *et al.* 2012; Stemplowska and Hamlin 2012). The indifference curves (the curved lines in the Figure 5.1) represent options that are equally unjust and the budget (the area below the straight line) represents the feasible set. The horizontal axis represents, *for example*, global emission reductions and the vertical axis represents, *for example*, the (negative) Gini coefficient (an inequality measure) of per capita emissions. Moving from point A – the status quo – to point B is a graphical representation of exploiting a free lunch: Points A and B are both feasible but point B is less unjust.

The disanalogy to simple consumption decisions is that, in practice, there are not only two factors that determine how unjust a certain climate policy is and whether it is in the feasible set. Rather, there are a host of determinants of justice and feasibility and these factors interact in innumerable complex ways. These factors include amongst many others the global and intergenerational distribution of costs, the attention given to worst-case scenarios, decision procedures in global climate negotiations, or the specific policy instruments chosen for implementation. Graphically, this would amount to an n-dimensional graph where the analogues of the indifference curves and the budget line would be rippled and

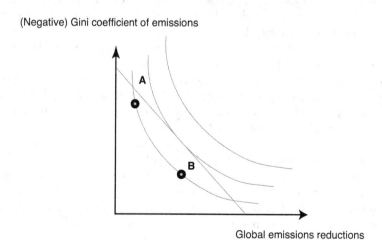

Figure 5.1 The analogy between the policy decision and the consumption decision

irregular rather than nice and smooth. Given this complexity, it is an art rather than a mechanical application of simple principles to know the shape of the indifference curves and the feasible set in the vicinity of point A. Our theories of justice have not been purpose-built for identifying the shape of the justice indifference curves in the non-ideal territory and this is especially true for certain approaches, such as non-consequentialist or value-pluralist theories. Also, our scientific theories are much too coarse-grained to make an intuitive grasp super-fluous when it comes to identifying the shape of the feasible set around point A. In practice, approximations for the constraints that climate policy faces often rely heavily on the one-dimensional measure of economic costs that agents are willing to bear (see for example Bosetti and Frankel (2012), or Barrett and Toman (2010: 67)). But, of course, one and the same amount of economic costs can be compatible or incompatible with feasibility depending on how these costs are framed, what they are used for, on whom they fall, etc. In order to spot 'free lunches' one has to know these constraints with more precision.

Given that having a better idea of the contours of the feasible set is one of the most promising means of making progress on justice, and given how little evidence is offered by those who actually make assumptions about its shape, this seems to be a promising area of research.[15] In order to leave this less abstract, I offer some – highly tentative – suggestions of what might be free lunches for current climate policy, i.e. changes that would allow a smart policy architect to decrease the degree of injustice without first having to increase the feasible set. One example consists of making use of the fact that foregone gains are perceived as less burdensome than losses of equal size (cf. Kahneman *et al.* 1991). Thus, climate policy measures have a greater chance of being compatible with human motivation if they reduce the rate of growth ahead rather than incurring subtrac-tions from present endowments (even if these subtractions would be more than compensated for by additional future growth). Also, people discount the future. While this is usually considered deplorable by those who want to further the cause of climate justice, it can also be put to good use by 'tricking' ourselves into accepting larger mitigation costs by shifting these costs somewhat into the future (or to specific points of the future such as the immediate aftermath of a major storm). A further example: verbal framings of the choice situation have an effect on whether a given amount of costs is feasible (Thaler and Sunstein 2009). This can be witnessed in attempts to brand costly mitigation measures as job creation or energy independence measures or by highlighting any voluntary aspects of otherwise coercive measures. Similarly, costs that are indirect and therefore less visible (such as terms of trade effects of climate policy or economic losses due to technical standards) are compatible with motivational constraints to a larger extent than costs that can be easily and transparently linked to climate policy (such as taxes or costs of emission permits). A further example: default options are more readily chosen even if the non-default option is equally costly and switching is not costly (Thaler and Sunstein 2009). If airlines would, for exam-ple, make voluntary emissions offsetting the default option for their customers, people might well offset their emissions to a higher degree than now. A trivial example includes exhausting no-regret options. According to McKinsey and Company (2009), there are a number of emission reduction measures that would not only fail to yield any costs but would rather yield a side benefit. A further proposal that has been discussed is the idea of preventing climate change but doing so at the expense of future generations (see for example Rendall 2011). The distribution of costs can also be deliberately tailored such that those parts of society that have less tight motivational constraints – or less means for insisting on them – carry a larger share of the costs than those who are particularly opposed – or have particularly good means for making themselves heard – to complying with a just share of the costs. Many of these proposals might be considered manipulative, exploitative of the irrational biases of humans, or as introducing new injustices, at least if they are not democratically self-imposed. While this has to be examined on a case-by-case basis it must also be remembered that all these proposals are meant to apply only in situations where we act unjustly and where there are loopholes to make us act less so. They are not meant to make people act supererogatorily or act better in their self-interest.

8. Conclusion

Political philosophy that aims at practical relevance is well advised to seriously engage with feasibility constraints. Climate change is the perfect test case for this engagement as it is an area where justice and feasibility clash especially hard. This chapter discussed the structure of feasibility constraints and cautioned against envisioning feasibility as too constraining a straitjacket. In particular, it highlighted four mistakes that make the pursuit of climate justice seem unnecessarily constrained by feasibility: first, drawing a false picture of the feasible set, either deliberately or due to a lack of evidence; second, failing to acknowledge that feasibility constraints hold for certain agents and time spans; third, treating constraints rooted in one's own motivation the same way as one treats other feasibility constraints: as given; fourth, failing to exploit all opportunities for decreasing injustice within the feasible set.

Notes

This chapter draws a lot on joint work done with Clare Heyward and Lukas Meyer. Helpful comments on parts and earlier versions of this paper from Simon Caney, Jaakko Kuosmanen, Holly Lawford-Smith, Felix Pinkert, and participants in workshops in Graz, Berlin, Reykjavik and Zurich are gratefully acknowledged. The work reported on in this publication has benefited from participation in the research networking programme Rights to a Green Future, financed by the European Science Foundation, the Human Rights for Future Generations Programme of the Oxford Martin School, the project Response of the Austrian Climate Research Programme and the URPP Ethics of the University of Zurich.

1   Note, however, that it is a different and sensible question to ask whether we ought to advocate only feasible policies (Cowen 2007: 8). This is a sensible question because publicly talking about currently unfeasible policies may turn them into feasible policies of the future.

2   An example of a positive exception is Pickering *et al.* (2012) who carefully discuss the assumptions they make about the shape of the feasible set.

3   In this chapter, I use the notion of uncertainty and the idea of options coming with a certain probability in a very broad sense: It does not only include the case where options have – or can justifiably be assigned – precise probabilities but the more general case where options can be more or less certain even if the corresponding probabilities are unascertainable, or if ascertainable, only in extremely crude terms.

4   Another way to understand our common use of gradual feasibility statements is to acknowledge a strict cut-off point between feasible and unfeasible options but to note that options can be closer or further away from the cut-off point. Those that are further away – in the sense that physically, motivationally, etc. a lot would have to change for them to switch from being unfeasible to being feasible – then count as 'highly' unfeasible. This would make sense of gradual feasibility talk without reference to probabilities.

       A further way to make sense of gradual feasibility statements is to understand them as shortcuts for expressing the temporal aspect of feasibility claims: 'Highly feasible' policies would then be policies that can be implemented in the short term.

5   As a side remark, it should be noted that technological feasibility can be interpreted such that it is closely linked to the probabilistic aspect of feasibility statements. This is so because the concept of technology and probability both have an epistemic interpretation. On one understanding, technology is a certain type of knowledge, roughly, practically applicable knowledge of certain means for solving problems. Probability, on the other hand, also has an epistemic interpretation: if achieving 2° is probable, this can mean that there are good grounds for believing that 2° will be achieved. Thus, to give an example, if cheap and large scale carbon capture and storage is claimed to be technologically feasible this can be translated into the claim that we will know how to capture and store carbon cheaply on a large scale; this in turn implies, that there are good grounds for believing this to be feasible which can be translated into the claim that there is a high probability that it is feasible.

6   The lack of a central coordinating mechanism is, however, relevant for the probability of feasibility in those cases where achieving a certain outcome requires a specific combination of individual actions which complement each other: Even if performing the required action is perfectly feasible for each individual agent taken separately if each agent were to know what her task is, the probability of achieving the outcome without coordination can, of course, be very low in these cases.

7   This is tiny deviation from Gilabert and Lawford-Smith (2012) who seem to distinguish only between constraints that are not subject to dynamic variation and constraints that are malleable whereas there seem to be constraints that are unmalleable but still changing over time.

8   *Neue Zürcher Zeitung*, 4 March 2010, 12.

9   A different take on this issue assumes ability to be partly normative already on conceptual grounds (cf. Seidel 2011: 909).

10   Admittedly, in case not all agents cooperate in the common effort to protect the climate and in case one believes that the remaining agents have a duty to 'take up the slack' left over by the non-compliers, the climate duties of these slack takers might actually become very demanding. This is even more so if we operate with a broader understanding of costs which includes non-economic burdens (such as obstacles to maintaining relationships on account of curbing mobility or the liberty lost to freely choose leisure activities) and if we take into account that costs will inevitably not be distributed evenly and include unemployment and particular hardships for some.

11   An intermediate option would be to conceive of motivation as *partly* under our control, with addictions, compulsions, and generally motivation constraining us to a

certain *degree* (cf. Lawford-Smith 2013b: 660). This would yield a gradual distinction between motivational and genuine feasibility constraints.

12 The first and the second bear some resemblance to the first and second response in Lichtenberg (2010: 130).

13 Getting accustomed to injustice is one of the dangers if we follow the – otherwise sensible – injunction to search for the least unjust option within the motivationally constrained set. Consider the Copenhagen Consensus: it asked experts about the optimal use of an additional 50 billion US dollars provided by governments. Focusing on this question can *distract* from the fact that governments should provide more than an additional 50 billion US dollars. The danger is also present in Posner and Weisbach's (2010) *Climate Change Justice*. After passionately arguing for taking into account that real world governments need incentives to participate in a climate treaty, the acknowledged background fact that this need for incentives is not morally justified fades out from view during the book (at times even raising the suspicion whether Posner and Weisbach really do regard it as questionable at all). On adapting to injustice, see also Gilabert (2012: 53).

14 For contributions to the wider debate on how to take one's own failings into account in practical deliberation see for example the discussion on Professor Procrastinate (Jackson and Pargetter 1986) or Lawford-Smith (2013b: 654-5).

15 For a positive example of searching for unexploited motivationally feasible options, see Birnbacher (2009).

References

Barrett, S. and Toman, M. 2010. 'Contrasting Future Paths for an Evolving Global Climate Regime', *Global Policy* 1(1).

Baumgärtner, S., Glotzbach, S., Hober, N., Quaas, M. and Stumpf, K. 2012. 'Economic Analysis of Trade-Offs Between Justices', *Intergenerational Justice Review* 1/2012, 4–9.

Bell, D. 2011. 'Does Anthropogenic Climate Change Violate Human Rights?' *Critical Review of International Social and Political Philosophy* 14(2), 99–124.

Birnbacher, D. 2009. 'What Motivates us to Care for the (Distant) Future?' in, Axel Gosseries and Lukas H. Meyer (eds), *Intergenerational Justice*. Oxford: Oxford University Press, 273–300.

Bosetti, V. and Frankel, J. 2012. 'Politically Feasible Emissions Targets to Attain 460 ppm CO_2 Concentrations', *Review of Environmental Econnomics and Policy* 6(1), 86–109.

Buchanan, A. 2004. *Justice, Legitimacy, and Self-Determination*. Oxford: Oxford University Press.

Caney, S. 2009. 'Climate Change, Human Rights and Moral Thresholds', in Stephen Humphreys (ed.), *Human Rights and Climate Change*. Cambridge: Cambridge University Press, 69–90.

Caney, S. 2014. 'Two Kinds of Climate Justice: Avoiding Harm and Sharing Burdens', *Journal of Political Philosophy* 22(2), 125–149.

Cohen, G. 2003. 'Facts and Principles', *Philosophy and Public Affairs* 31(3), 211–245.

Cohen, G. 2009. *Why not Socialism?* Princeton: Princeton University Press.

Estlund, D. 2011. 'Human Nature and the Limits (If Any) of Political Philosophy', *Philosophy and Public Affairs* 39(3), 207–237.

Fankhauser, S. 1995. *Valuing Climate Change: the Economics of the Greenhouse*. London: Earthscan.

Frankel, J. 2005. 'You're Getting Warmer: The Most Feasible Path for Addressing Global Climate Change Does Run Through Kyoto', in John Maxwell and Rafael Reuveny (eds),*Trade and Environment: Theory and Policy in the Context of EU Enlargement and Transition Economies*. Cheltenham: Edward Elgar, 37–55.

Gheaus, A. 2013. 'The Feasibility Constraint on The Concept of Justice', *The Philosophical Quarterly* 63.252, 445–464.

Gilabert, P. 2012. 'Comparative Assessments of Justice, Political Feasibility, and Ideal Theory', *Ethical Theory and Moral Practice* 15(1), 39–56.

Gilabert, P. and Lawford-Smith, H. 2012. 'Political Feasibility: A Conceptual Exploration', *Political Studies* 60, 809–825.

IPCC 2007a. *Mitigation. Contribution of Working Group III to the Fourth Assessment Report of the Intergovernmental Panel on Climate Change*. Cambridge: Cambridge University Press.

IPCC 2007b. *Climate Change 2007: Synthesis Report. Contribution of Working Groups I, II, and III to the Fourth Assessment Report of the Intergovernmental Panel on Climate Change*. Geneva: IPCC.

Jackson, F. and Pargetter, R. 1986. 'Oughts, Options, and Actualism', *The Philosophical Review* 95 (2), 233–255.

Kahneman, D., Knetsch, J. and Thaler, R. 1991. 'The Endowment Effect, Loss Aversion, and Status Quo Bias', *Journal of Economic Perspectives* 5(1), 193–206.

Lawford-Smith, H. 2013a. 'Understanding Political Feasibility', *The Journal of Political Philosophy* 21(3), 243–259.

Lawford-Smith, H. 2013b. 'Non-Ideal Accessibility", *Ethical Theory and Moral Practice* 16, 1–17.

Lichtenberg, J. 2010. 'Oughts and Cans: Badness, Wrongness, and the Limits of Ethical Theory', *Philosophical Topics* 38, 123–142.

Lorenzoni, I. and Pidgeon, N. 2006. 'Public Views on Climate Change: European and USA perspectives', *Climatic Change* 77(1–2), 73–95.

McKinsey & Company. 2009. 'Pathways to a Low-Carbon Economy: Version 2 of the Global Greenhouse Gas Abatement Cost Curve'. Available at: www.mckinsey.com/client_service/sustainability/latest_thinking/pathways_to_a_low_carbon_economy (accessed 23 November 2013).

Meinshausen, M., Meinshausen, N., Hare, W., Raper, S., Friele, K., Knutti, R., Frame, D. and Myles, A. 2009. 'Greenhouse-gas Emission Targets for Limiting Global Warming to 2 °C', *Nature* 458, 1158–1162.

Metz, B. 2000. 'International Equity in Climate Change Policy', *Integrated Assessment* 1, 111–126.

Pickering, J., Vanderheiden, S. and Seumas, M. 2012. '"If equity's in, we're out": Scope for Fairness in the Next Global Climate Agreement', *Ethics and International Affairs* 26(4), 423–443.

Posner, E. and Weisbach, D. 2010. *Climate Change Justice*. Princeton: Princeton University Press.

Raz, J. 1986. *The Morality of Freedom*. Oxford: Oxford University Press.

Rendall, M. 2011. 'Climate Change and the Threat of Disaster: The Moral Case for Taking Out Insurance at Our Grandchildren's Expense', *Political Studies* 59(4), 884–899.

Seidel, C. 2011. 'Personale Autonomie als praktische Autorität', *Deutsche Zeitschrift für Philosophie* 59: 6, 897–915.

Singer, P. 2002. *One World: The Ethics of Globalization*. New Haven: Yale University Press.

Stemplowska, Z. and Hamlin, A. 2012. 'Theory, Ideal Theory and the Theory of Ideals', *Political Studies Review* 10.1, 48–62.

Stott, R. 2006. 'Contraction and Convergence: Healthy Response to Climate Change', *British Medical Journal* 332, 1385–1387.

Suranovic, S. 2013. 'Fossil Fuel Addiction and the Implications for Climate Change Policy', *Global Environmental Change* 23(3), 598–608.

Swift, A. 2008. 'The Value of Philosophy in Nonideal Circumstances', *Social Theory and Practice* 34(3), 363–387.

Thaler, R. and C. Sunstein. 2009. *Nudge: Improving Decisions about Health, Wealth, and Happiness.* New Haven: Yale University Press.

Tyler, C. 2007. 'The Importance of Defining the Feasible Set', *Economics and Philosophy* 23, 1–14.

WBGU. 2009. 'Solving the Climate Dilemma: The Budget Approach'. Available at: www.wbgu.de/fileadmin/templates/dateien/veroeffentlichungen/sondergutachten/sn2009/wbgu_sn2009_en.pdf (accessed 23 November 2013).

Zuolo. 2012. 'Being Realistic Without Realism: Feasibility and Efficacy in Normative Political Theories', *Centro Einaudi, Laboratorio di politica comparata e filosofia pubblica Working Paper* 3.

6 Climate justice, motivation and harm

Kerri Woods

The dominant approach to climate justice is thoroughly liberal in orientation and relies on widely held notions of harm and responsibility to justify duties. Notions of harm and coercion are held to be potentially available to motivate compliance with these duties. This chapter defends the claim that this way of characterizing climate justice relies on a notion of harm that is at odds with conventional understandings of the concept, and that the character of the duties prescribed is thereby obscured. This presents a double-edged problem for the vital task of motivating climate justice.

> If we fail to make the cuts required within the next couple of decades it is no exaggeration to say that we, the particular cohort of people alive now, will have failed to do justice to the whole human race. For shame.
>
> McKinnon 2011: 211

> It's fanciful to suppose that such 'deep' cuts in emissions can be achieved without impacting on people's lives and lifestyles.
>
> Jackson *et al.*[1]

1. Introduction

The cuts referred to here are cuts in greenhouse gas (GHG) emissions sufficient to prevent catastrophic climate change (McKinnon) or to comply with the 2008 UK Climate Change Act (Jackson *et.al.*). The 'we' referred to are people in rich countries most able to bear costs. 'We' are sometimes called the 'advantaged' (Caney 2010a), 'the global elite' (Cripps 2011a), 'the richer and more powerful members of the current generation' (Bell 2011), 'those who are rich by global standards' (Jamieson 2005), or more inventively, 'post-cosmopolitan citizens' (Dobson 2003). Claims about the resources commanded by 'the richest 1 per cent' relative to either the costs of climate change, or to the resources commanded by poorer people, are frequently found in this literature.

It is most likely the case that 'we' have at best a couple of decades to change our lives or face dire consequences, though it is also true that environmental theorists have been here before: growing environmental consciousness in the late

1960s and early 1970s heralded a wave of environmental literature critiquing conventional moral and political thought, some of it permeated with dire warnings about the consequences of continuing to accept dominant liberal ideas about autonomy and individualism.[2] What is interestingly different about responses to anthropogenic climate change is the eagerness of many theorists to draw on resources *within* liberal political philosophy to articulate just solutions.[3]

Though the liberal approach is constructive in important ways, I argue here that something is being missed, or rather obscured, in much of the current literature on climate change justice. The *character* of what climate justice demands of those held to bear related duties has bearing on the substantive shape of a (shared) life. McKinnon's claim (above) is that theorists of climate justice have paid insufficient attention to the problem of motivation. This seems right to me, but it also seems that some of the justificatory architecture employed in debates about climate justice rooted in liberalism are ill-suited to redressing this deficit. Indeed, by invoking harm as the central moral concept, climate justice theorists ultimately frustrate the motivational project that McKinnon helpfully raises.

2. A just distribution of duties: not who, but why?

The literature on climate change justice has grown considerably since Stephen Gardiner noted it was rather thinner than it ought to be, only a few years ago (Gardiner 2004).[4] Much of the debate has focused on the question of what would be a just distribution of the related burdens, or, who should bear the costs of mitigation and adaptation that are necessitated by anthropogenic climate change? In fact, the question of who should bear these burdens is substantially agreed upon; rich(er) people in Western countries are generally held to be liable.[5] What is generally lacking is a full explanation of why this particular cohort should be the relevant duty bearers. In this section I look at two approaches that have been influential (and that have sometimes been combined); ability to pay and polluter pays. The broad sketches that I offer will not do justice to the detail of some of the more careful accounts that have been advanced, but I hope they suffice to give a flavour of the arguments and to set the parameters of the discussion to follow.[6]

2.1. Ability to pay

We cannot ask the question of whether or not at all to pay costs generated by climate justice. Simon Caney makes the point that costs will be borne one way or another: if no action is taken then the costs of adapting to climate change will be borne in the future.[7] These costs would be borne by all in the future, but would hit hardest the poorest in the world, in terms of more erratic weather and severe weather events, higher food prices, more diffusely spread tropical diseases and ultimately more premature deaths associated with these events. This would be a very high cost, and its inequitable distribution would be profoundly unjust. It follows, on Caney's view, that the costs ought to be redistributed so as to be borne by others, ideally as mitigation costs, since acting now is necessary for the measures to be preventative rather than adaptive, and since it is much less of an injustice for the rich, who can bear these costs, to do so, than for them to fall on poor persons unable to bear the costs without suffering threats to a minimum standard of well-being. 'The most advantaged are most able to pay the price without sacrificing any reasonable interests: therefore, they are under a duty to do so' (Caney 2010a: 215).

As a justificatory move, this seems very quick indeed. We might say that it is simply a matter of luck that the responsibility for dealing with climate change falls on the rich today because they have the ability to bear the cost. This ability to pay (ATP) strategy owes much to the thinking animating Peter Singer's (1972) 'principle of sacrifice'.[8] A profound injustice currently looks certain to fall on A, who is poor, unless B, who is rich, bears costs to prevent the injustice. This action can be demanded of B *because* she is rich and *because* A is poor. Thus, so the story goes, B has the capacity to prevent or amend the injustice.

Note that, seen in this light, B is no longer an innocent bystander, but will be *harming* A, if she shirks the responsibility. Thus, a moral relationship arises between A and B, one which disconnects remedial responsibility from causal responsibility, but still implicitly includes the notion that one party will be harmed and another will be responsible for this, not via their action, but via their inaction – their failure to rescue.

It may be uncontroversial to hold that 'the rich' are more able to bear the costs than the poor, and thus the burden ought to fall on them (the rich) given that it will fall somewhere; how that translates into obligations to be borne by rich *individuals* is less clear when we see those individuals in social and political contexts characterized by multiple injustices, as any rich individual surely is. The ATP thesis looks simple when applied to one injustice, but as an action-guiding principle more generally it does look vulnerable to concerns about demandingness – arguments that have been well-rehearsed already in responses to Singer's thesis. To avoid these issues, we either want a reason why climate justice is a special problem where this principle applies, even if it does not always apply to all cases of injustice, or a means of protecting the rich individual from excessive demands.[9]

On the first of these, I have suggested that climate change certainly is an urgent problem, perhaps more pressing than many, but not all, others that might make demands on individual agents. To say more than this is to enter into invidious debates about the relative moral urgency of a host of social problems. On the second, two strategies appear in the literature. The first of these is to hold that the individual agent's obligations only extend as far as 'mimicking duties'; that is, she honours those obligations she would have under a fair cooperative scheme that allocated a portion of the costs of climate justice to all those bearing remedial responsibility (Murphy 1993).[10]

The second is to avoid the question of individual obligations at all. Some of the same difficulties in terms of choosing which injustices should be addressed might persist, but one might hold that the depth of collective pockets, especially where they belong to 'the global elite', 'the richest 1%', etc., could in principle fund prevention of, or compensation for, all serious injustices. On this argument, precisely which individuals fall within the identified group, and what their share of the burden would be, is a matter of policy to be worked out, but the *moral* argument establishing the justice of allocating the burdens of climate justice substantially to this group can be defended independently of these details.

I agree that there is much to be gained from thinking about climate change justice in collective terms, and that political action is certainly necessary. However, this move is unsatisfactory as a means of silencing further questions. Individuals need to know what they ought to do, here and now, in the absence of adequate political leadership and in the absence of adequate cooperative schemes to allocate burdens and ensure effective compliance, and, as Walter Sinnott-Armstrong (2005) points out, the answers to these questions are not simply derivable from an account of collective duties. Even if climate justice is properly a collective matter, there will nevertheless be legitimate and important questions unanswered by a collective approach. So we need to continue our inquiry.

2.2. Polluter pays

The claim that individuals from richer states bear a greater share of the remedial responsibility for climate change because they bear a greater share of the causal responsibility has strong intuitive appeal. The typical resident in developed countries today has a much larger carbon footprint than her counterpart in developing countries. Inspired by this, several scholars have proposed that a polluter pays principle (PPP) should determine the distribution of duties with respect to climate justice (e.g. Shue 1999; Neumeyer 2000). There are many variants of PPP, but they each hold that the agent responsible for a particular instance of pollution should bear the costs of its clean-up, either in terms of mitigation or adaptation. Unlike ATP, this reflects conventional intuitions about moral responsibility, cause and effect; all other things being equal,[11] we typically imagine that an agent who causes harm should be the agent who is liable for the costs of remedy (though, as we noted above, ATP has been woven in to a story about harm as well).

PPP allows us to allocate responsibility for GHG emissions produced by persons alive today who were not 'excusably ignorant' of the environmental impacts of their actions.[12] There is some debate as to whether or not we can or should expect to be able to calculate with accuracy an individual's carbon footprint and their proportionate share of the costs, e.g. via carbon offsetting schemes.[13] My own view is that even if it were possible to accurately assess one's exact carbon footprint and to arrive at a reasonably accurate figure of the costs of compensating the planet and/or future generations for the ecological costs thereby incurred (which is doubtful), there are good reasons to resist this as a way of thinking about climate justice, not least because the actual impacts of our individual carbon footprints will always be contingent on the impacts of others.

The idea of an individual calculation suggests that we can parcel up our environmental impacts, and presupposes some sort of fair share measure and wide-spread compliance. But the impacts of climate change, and the causes, are distributed across space, time, and are the cumulative result of multiple actions by multiple uncoordinated agents, whose individual actions make little, if any, perceptible difference from the point of view of the agent. This is a facet of a profoundly changed moral landscape in comparison to the circumstances in which many of the canonical texts of (liberal) political philosophy were written (Attfield 2009). Derek Parfit has put this well:

> Until this century, most of mankind lived in small communities. What each did could affect only a few others. But conditions have now changed. Each of us can now, in countless ways, affect countless other people … For the sake of small benefits to ourselves, or our families, we may deny others much greater total benefits, or impose on others much greater total harms.
>
> Parfit 1987: 86

Again, it is rarely our individual actions that cause these harms or frustrate these benefits. In contrast, the analogies that theorists have used to explicate the wrongness of anthropogenic climate change have typically focussed on individual and deliberate actions. Think of Robert Elliot's (1988) idea of a booby-trapped time capsule, or Caney's (2010b) metaphor of a sabotaged bridge. Elliot imagines a time capsule that is booby-trapped at time t, such that, when a person opens the time capsule at t+80, the person is injured. This demonstrates that the person setting the booby trap was wrong to do so, even if the injured party was not yet born when the booby trap was set. The underlying claim is that future generations can be harmed by current actions. In Caney's bridge case, he draws an analogy between climate change and the act of a saboteur who damages a bridge that people drive across. The sabotage causes the bridge to collapse, resulting in the deaths of several people beneath it. Insofar as we recognize that a person ought not to commit the harmful act in the sabotage case, then it follows that persons ought not to engage in acts that will cause harmful climate change, since these similarly threaten fundamental rights.

But climate change is not a deliberate act of sabotage by one agent; rather, it is the cumulative result of many uncoordinated acts that individually would not cause harm to other persons. It is therefore much more like a bridge that has been overused by lots of otherwise moral and law-abiding motorists, whose individual actions alone are not harmful, but whose cumulative impacts unwittingly cross a critical threshold. The saboteur, like the booby-trapper, purposefully commits one act, for which she is solely responsible, and the intent of which is to cause harm. Those responsible for climate change commit multiple acts, with at best limited coordination,[14] whose purposes are multiple, and it seems implausible to suggest that causing climate change is the *intention* of any of them.

The target of the argument from harm is in part a rejoinder to Parfit's (1984) much-discussed non-identity problem; Caney and Elliot, and others pursuing this line of argument, aim to demonstrate that future persons can be harmed by action (or inaction) now, and that consequently future persons have a claim to be protected. But in presenting the wrongness of climate change via analogies that are significantly disanalogous to the conditions we face, they expose both the complications of thinking about climate change in terms of individual acts of harm, and the limitations of what have hitherto been our most reliable ways of approaching moral problems. As Dale Jamieson observes:

> A paradigm moral problem is one in which an individual acting intentionally harms another individual; both the individual and the harm are identifiable; and the individuals and the harm are closely related in time and space.
>
> Jamieson 2007: 475

In the case of climate change, in contrast, what we confront is a moral problem where multiple individuals act in multiple ways without the intention of causing harm, where the resulting impacts are individually imperceptible and accrue in aggregate, incrementally, over considerable spans of time and space. Thus, a determinate allocation of duties based on an individualist PPP is unrealistic. Anthropogenic climate change is an irreducibly collective endeavour. The same is true of the project of achieving climate justice.

This set of problems explains the attention climate justice theorists have begun to pay to the concept of collective responsibility. Elizabeth Cripps (2011a), for example, argues for a reinterpretation of Mill's harm principle wherein collective responsibility for harm creates legitimate grounds for coercing the collective responsible, either by restricting their liberty in order to prevent future harm, or by creating a scheme that allocates enforceable compensatory duties. Her aim is to defend a plausible strategy for pursuing climate justice whilst retaining liberalism's 'core individualism – its focus on the individual as the unit of moral value' (2011a: 172).

This seems to me a promising approach, not least because it allows scope for the thought that while the individual may be the ultimate unit of moral concern from a liberal point of view, there are some things that we – that is, human beings – do, that are irreducibly collective.[15] At the same time, it gives us reasons to think that there can be legitimate grounds (i.e. grounds considered legitimate within a liberal framework) for coercing people to comply with the distribution necessary for climate justice on account of their belonging (in some sense) to the collective causally responsible for climate change. Having the tool of legitimate coercion available may go a considerable distance to addressing the problem McKinnon identified, with which we began, namely, the paucity of the evident motivation on the part of 'we', 'the global elite', etc., to shoulder the necessary burdens with respect to climate justice. Because the idea of collective responsibility for harm allows us to hang on to the conventional thought that remedial responsibility is intimately connected to causal responsibility, it arguably gives a simpler, cleaner justification of the distribution of the burdens that climate justice entails than is offered in the ATP approach.

To sum up the argument so far: both the ATP argument and the PPP approach point us towards a view of climate justice as a collective moral problem, though this leaves important questions unanswered. Combined, they may provide a satisfactory justificatory argument in defence of the favourite distribution of burdens in climate justice as seen by the majority of theorists in the field. However, we should not be too hasty in thinking that the motivation problem is thereby resolved. For there is more to say about the concept of harm that is in play here, and about the relationship between individuals and collectives, which will have implications for the question of motivation.

3. More on why: harm, shame and the collective virtues of living well

> Successful justifying reasons must be fit to motivate people to act for these reasons; they must be action-guiding. Justifying reasons must be motivationally adequate because political justification is a practical activity.
>
> McKinnon 2011: 205

The next question to confront, then, is whether the justifying reasons, PPP and ATP, are fit to motivate. But we also need to think about how motivation plays out in collective terms. These are partly empirical questions – will agents be motivated by these principles, or by claims advanced in the terms set by these principles? As such, it may be difficult, in the abstract, to say conclusively, X principle is fit or not. But there is a valuable contribution for political philosophy to make here: we can clarify the moral concepts that are implicitly or explicitly invoked in the justifying reasons, and we can say something about how those concepts fit with the wider claims being made and the assumptions about agents and agency at work in the argument.

The dominant moral concept at work in both the ATP and the PPP arguments is the concept of harm. This is explicit in the PPP approach; an agent (or unintentional collective of agents) acts in a way that causes harm, and it is this that generates the obligation to stop the harming act and to compensate. It is also implicit in the ATP argument. The burdens of climate justice are to fall on the rich, and not the poor, because the rich are most able to bear the burdens, they therefore have the power to choose to prevent a harm befalling others.[16]

Thus, the injunction not to cause harm does a lot of work in driving climate justice. There are obvious benefits to this. That we should not cause avoidable harm to others is one of the most basic and widely accepted moral intuitions. It tracks an individualist logic to the extent that it is based in respect for persons (thus it coheres with dominant liberal ideas). It also depends upon widely held intuitions about individual agency, cause and effect; that the capacity for agency brings with it responsibilities, or at any rate culpability for the consequences of actions, on the part of free and rational beings. The thought that we would be culpable for our actions not as individuals, but as members of a collective, particularly an unconscious and unchosen collective, is more controversial. But the question that I want to draw out here is whether relying on the concept of harm here is action-guiding, and what the idea of harm communicates about the content of the duties associated with climate justice.

First, then, to the question of whether the injunction not to cause harm is action-guiding. For it to be so, we need to be able to identify which behaviour is harmful. But there seems to be a degree of elasticity in what is meant by harm in the literature on climate change. Let us say that current persons are under a duty not to harm future persons. In the case of the booby-trapper discussed above, it was readily intelligible to say that the booby-trapper's actions were harmful. Setting a trap designed to cause injury to another would be plausibly ruled out by a principle that holds that causing (avoidable) harm is wrong. But, as noted above, most of the activity that generates GHG emissions is not of this character. As Margaret Moore puts it:

> The problem arises not because of my actions, but because millions of people like me, live a *lifestyle* that involves greenhouse gas emissions, and it is our uncoordinated individual action, which, together, cause harm to the environment.
>
> Moore 2008: 504 (emphasis added)

Does driving to work, for example, harm future persons? Well, yes, if (enough) others do so; no, if not. So we need to know what others will do before we can be clear about the extent and content of our own obligations – whether or not an action is harmful is contingent on the behaviour of others.

Another point to be teased out here is the slippage between 'harm' and 'avoidable harm' in the preceding discussion. We need not get into discussions of trolley problems to realise that there is a moral difference between causing harm wantonly, causing harm negligently but avoidably, and causing harm unavoidably in the context of pursuing some goal (the value of which may make a further difference to the culpability of the agent(s)). Caney writes that, 'my version of the PPP asserts that people are entitled to those emissions necessary for them to attain a decent standard of living' (2011: 544). On this account it seems that actions that generate GHG emissions up to a decent standard of living are not harmful, whereas *the same* actions that generate GHG emissions beyond this level *are* harmful.[17]

These harmful actions are plausible examples of what Judith Lichtenberg (2010) calls 'the new harms', where one is guilty of harming countless unknown others simply by living a life – by the pernicious consequences attendant upon the coffee one drinks, the electricity one uses, the employers' pension scheme one has auto-enrolled in, and so on. Seen in these terms, harm is pervasive, and the failure to rescue unknown others from these harms is an injustice perpetrated by almost all of the global elite, thoughtlessly, every day. Lichtenberg is rightly sceptical about the intelligibility of the claim that one ought not to cause harm if harm is understood in so pervasive a manner. In this case, the clear motivating potential of claims about harm lose their purchase.

In an authoritative analysis of the concept of harm, Joel Feinberg discusses similar cases of environmental harms where the impact is cumulative and the causal responsibility diffuse:

> In these contexts, no prior standard of wrongfulness exists. There is nothing inherently wrongful or right-violating in the activity of driving an automobile, generating electricity, or refining copper. These activities can be meaningfully condemned only as violations of an authoritative scheme of allocative priorities.
>
> Feinberg 1984: 230

If this is right, then we are returned once again to the collective dimension of the problem. To say that persons ought not to harm future generations is not in itself action-guiding, because we need to know what others will do to know what might be harmful, and if we are to avoid harm, that others will cooperate in our efforts. In the disanalogous analogies discussed above, obligations are clear when individual, purposive actions are at stake. Presenting the problem of climate justice in these terms obscures the scale and complexity of what it is that climate justice demands. I do not mean to suggest that we do not have reliable evidence and a fairly sophisticated understanding of what will exacerbate climate change – we certainly do. But when we say that agents of climate justice ought to stop harming future generations, or avoid harming future generations, what we mean is not that they ought (not) to do one simple thing, or few identifiable things, and pay some kind of reparation. What we mean is considerably more complex and variable. It is not (just) that agents have to stop flying, or stop driving, or change their domestic energy suppliers, or become vegetarians, or accept the redistribution of 1 per cent of GDP to a climate change adaptation fund.[18] Rather, agents ultimately have to live sustainably, and that requires agents to think about the ecological footprint of the food they eat, the clothes they wear, the goods they consume, the jobs they are employed in and much more besides.[19]

What makes this enormously challenging, and all the more so within a liberal framework that typically respects individual autonomy and a separation between the public and the private sphere, is that it ultimately implies giving some thought to the question of what it is to live well, or, to live a good life, *together*.[20] Recall that Moore noted that what for Caney would be denoted excess emissions are part of a 'lifestyle'. It is not distinct action(s) that generates climate change; it is *a way of living* that does so, a way of living pursued by a critical mass of individuals that produces more GHG emissions than are necessary for a decent standard of living.[21]

Constructing the argument about climate justice in terms of harm is constructive to the extent that it allows theorists of climate justice to draw on an intuitive connection between causal and remedial responsibility that is deeply rooted in our conventional moral thought. But it also ties us to a moral architecture that obscures where the problem lies: the problem rests not in a set of discrete actions that can be objectively identified as harmful, but in multiple patterns of actions that add up to a way of life that is pursued by significant numbers of people. Continuing to present anthropogenic climate change in terms of harm implies a moral calculus of harmful actions, compensation and penalties. So we might think that what we have to do, if we want to fly somewhere, is pay the penalty of carbon offsetting. But if we say that the problem is a way of life, then we have to reassess more comprehensively how we will go about achieving our goals, and indeed we might begin to reassess some of those goals as well.[22] Moreover, we have to begin a collective conversation about this.

If a collective harm principle guides us to any action, it first and foremost guides us to think of ourselves as moral agents in a collective sense. Put another way, climate justice demands that we accept something Aristotle held to be self-evident; humans are social animals. Whether we are so by nature is a moot point; today our use of technology makes us so.[23] This accounts for the popularity, amongst climate justice theorists, of duties to establish a structure for managing the allocation of benefits and burdens via a fair cooperative scheme (e.g. Bell 2011; Cripps 2011a). What this suggests is that, being, as we are, ecologically embedded agents who have developed technologies that have impacts that are long-term, diffuse, and can compound exponentially, we harm future generations by acting as individuals, rather than as members of collectives.

But this is not the end of the story; we have only moved the problem back one step. Now agents are duty-bound to create a fair allocative scheme that will regulate behaviour, thereby introducing opportunities for coercive structures to address the motivational lacuna that plagues climate justice. The obligation to do so arises because only by doing so will the individual (and the collective) be able to honour their duty not to harm future persons. But the actions that generate the harm are not wrongful independently of their being determined excessive under an allocative scheme.

The concept of harm is doing a lot of work here, and is being used in ways that stretch the conventional moral weight and motivational power on which theorists of climate justice presumably hope to rely. In practice, what climate justice demands is that we recognize that our conceptions of the good life are importantly wrong or ill-founded, insofar as they license a collective way of life that is beyond the planet's ecological means (and, indeed, foster myopia with respect to the necessarily collective dimension of our lives). On the basis of that judgment, agents of climate justice must make multiple, coordinated, more or less small, more or less costly reassessments and adjustments to the practice of living together as ecologically embedded beings. The disanalogous analogies that have been used to draw out the wrongfulness of climate change obscure rather than clarify this point. They highlight determinate harmful actions, rather than innocuous actions that become harmful in the context of a particular collective pattern of living.

The notion of a collective green good life was a favourite theme of environmental ethicists before the turn to liberalism emerged in green thought.[24] One plausible explanation for the turn away from what we might call these more comprehensive approaches to environmental justice is that they were thought not to be motivating for agents deeply shaped by liberal political institutions.[25] So, let us return to the issue of motivation.

The argument from harm, particularly within the PPP approach, is intended to make available motivational resources such as shame and guilt. The duty to create an authoritative allocative scheme brings with it the possibility of legitimate coercion to achieve compliance with the just distribution prescribed. But we should note that, in the context of liberal democracies, coercive policies require popular support if they are to succeed. In social rather than legal terms, the appeal of an argument from harm is surely tied to the motivational power of shame and guilt; certainly, it is here that McKinnon (2011) finds resources for tackling the problem of motivation. If causing harm is shameful, and shame is a powerful motivator, then presenting the argument for climate justice in terms of harm makes strategic sense. But it is conceptually difficult to connect the totality of a lifestyle with harm and shame.[26]

The comprehensiveness of the practice of climate justice may well be better captured in a moral idiom that registers the virtues of living well, understood to mean living sustainably, rather than the injunction not to harm. The language of virtues and vices sits somewhat uncomfortably in a moral landscape dominated by talk of rights, entitlements, distributive shares, harm and liability.[27] But it is one that environmental ethicists have long found hospitable,[28] and that a minority of climate ethicists are beginning to explore (e.g. Jamieson 2007).

Less comprehensively, we might note the potential in 'nudge' policies and practices to respond to the collective dimension of climate justice. There is a wealth of literature in social psychology suggesting that individuals in liberal democracies are much more likely to act in particular ways if the choices that they face are framed so as to nudge them towards the desired action (see *inter alia* Thaler and Sunstein 2009). There is certainly some potential here (setting aside concerns about paternalism), but we should note that the underlying ideological dispositions have a huge bearing on an individual's responsiveness to such nudges. That being the case, a more fundamental shift towards endorsing principles of climate justice, and environmental sustainability more broadly, remains important.

The point, then, is not that we all have to become paragons of virtue (environmental or otherwise); rather, that the idea of what it is to lead a good life must be challenged and revised such that carbon-heavy lifestyles are seen to be vicious (or unjust), and further, this has to be a shared conception of a good life. That is the case not only because the agent responsible for climate justice is a collective one, but also because shared conceptions of the good influence behaviour (and receptiveness to nudges). Without them, shame as a motivating lever will never get purchase amongst members of a collective.[29] There is an inherently reciprocal and social structure to shame. In contrast to guilt, which can be internal, shame depends for its operation on the (real or imagined) disapproval of another (Williams 1993; cf. Bedford *et al.* n.d.). But, there is currently little, if any, shame attached to a carbon-heavy way of life for many, perhaps most, of those who comprise 'the global elite', 'the advantaged', etc., (nor is such a lifestyle recognized as harmful).

There is one further possibility to discuss: shame might come not from the negative judgment of our peers, but from posterity. McKinnon claims, 'Knowing that posterity will fail to respect us, will judge us as unjust, indeed, will be ashamed of being descended from us, gives powerful motivating reasons for doing intergenerational justice' (2011: 210). I just do not know if this is true. It seems to me that when we judge those who have gone before us, we might think ill of individuals who stood out in their time as particularly morally bad, or who held particularly influential positions, and we might judge as unjust previous generations' collective moral standards, but when we condemn a whole generation's moral failure, we soften the moral judgment against the individuals within it, accepting that it is difficult to act against, or indeed *think* against, the pervasive moral codes of one's time. If this is accurate then it is worrying for climate justice as an irreducibly collective task, for we know that if we fail to act and are blamed for our moral failure, we will not be blamed alone. The shame of posterity is thus an uncertain motivator.

4. Concluding remarks

Theorists of climate justice substantially agree that: (i) climate justice is an urgent moral problem; (ii) the greatest share of the burdens associated with climate justice should fall on 'the advantaged', 'the global elite', etc.; and (iii) failure to accept these burdens on the part of the advantaged will implicate them in relations of harm towards future generations. I have argued that the justificatory architecture underpinning both ATP and PPP arguments depend upon this notion of harm for its motivating force. I have also defended the view that climate justice is irreducibly a collective problem, and one that arises not so much from identifiable harmful actions, as from a widely accepted and valued way of life. Both of these factors present challenges to political philosophers who accept the basic principles of liberal individualism and neutrality with respect to conceptions of the good. Liberalism, however, is undoubtedly the dominant game in town, and so it is not surprising to find that theorists typically draw on resources available within liberal political philosophy in order to justify duties of climate justice.

If McKinnon is right that justifying climate justice is a practical activity, then she is also right to say that the motivating potential of justificatory arguments matter, and that the question of motivation should matter to political philosophers. Motivating climate justice does seem to be an enormous challenge, and one where philosophers might not be thought to have much to contribute. However, I have tried to show here that there is work to be done; namely clarifying the motivational claims on which justifying principles depend, and exploring the extent to which these cohere both with assumptions being made about agents and with the content of the duties prescribed for agents. My sense is that the argument from harm, on which both ATP and PPP ultimately depend, relies on an elastic notion of harm that is at odds with conventional understandings, and that this weakens the motivational potential of shame, and its legal cousin, coercion, which the argument from harm is intended to make accessible. One way forward from here, which I have only gestured at in the space available, but which I suggest better fits the scale and complexity of the challenge of climate justice, is to return to a task embraced by an earlier generation of environmental ethicists, and elaborate the notion of what it is to lead a good life as ecologically embedded beings.

Notes

1   This is from the thesis statement of RESOLVE, an interdisciplinary research project exploring the links between lifestyles, values, and environmental sustainability: http://resolve.sustainablelifestyles.ac.uk/about-resolve.

2   See, for example, White Jr. (1967), Hardin (1968), Naess (1973), and for an overview, Marshall (1995).

3   For example, Caney (2010b) and Bell (2011) draw on human rights; Cripps (2011a) draws on Mill's harm principle and McKinnon (2011) draws on John Rawls' Just Savings principle. Tim Hayward, who has defended an account of environmental human rights, asks, 'what reason is there to presume that liberalism provides a suitable framing for political theory relating to global justice and the environment?' (2007a: 276).

4   Indeed, by 2011 McKinnon notes that it is 'burgeoning'.

5   Some also hold that some people in developing countries should bear a smaller portion of the costs. Since the consensus is on 'the global elite', the 'advantaged' and so on noted at the beginning of the chapter, I will focus my attention here.

6   Steve Vanderheiden (2011), for example, argues for the separation of mitigation and adaptation costs, and for the allocation of these costs to be governed by distinct principles that he characterises as distributive justice (for mitigation) and corrective justice (for adaptation). The underlying norms of each seem to me to be reflected in the two principles I discuss here, but I accept that my necessarily brief characterization of the debate about who should shoulder which burdens, and why, is to some extent reductive.

7   Caney rejects an argument against attributing climate justice obligations to those able to pay but not directly responsible for the GHG emissions thus: 'The objection rests on the following assumption: it is wrong that some bear a burden for a problem that is not of their doing. This assumption seems to me highly implausible but the most important point to make in this context is that whatever happens some will be bearing a burden that it is not their fault' (2010a: 214).

8   The structure of McKinnon's argument is explicitly Rawlsian (drawing on his Just Savings principle), so does not share this affinity with Singer's principle of sacrifice. However, it does disclose an orientation sympathetic to ATP as a significant principle: 'Those who make the most malleable contributions to global GHG emissions are rich individuals (and countries and corporations): the "Sienna Millers" of the world. The motivation problem is most forceful with respect to this group because their wealth renders them most able to adapt (at least in the short-term) to the conditions that CC could create' (McKinnon 2011: 211).

9   On Caney's formulation of it, the advantaged agent ought to pay what she is able to without sacrificing reasonable interests. 'Reasonable interests' seem likely to be open to interpretation, so the demandingness objection would have more or less bite depending on how these were interpreted. But even on a generous reading of reasonable interests, it still seems plausible to think that B faces quite extensive obligations here.

10   See also Bell, who defends the view that anthropogenic climate change violates the human rights of future generations: 'each of us has a duty not to accept benefits that

result from human rights violations, therefore, each person has a duty now not to emit more than they would be allowed to emit under effective institutions' (2011: 120). While I can see that this is a credible proposal for a non-ideal theory of climate justice directed towards individuals, as an action-guiding principle it seems to be a bit of a spare wheel, since it tells us really very little about the content of an agent's duties.

11 That is, they were free to act as they did, they are rationally capable adults.

12 Of course, some GHGs persist in the atmosphere for a very long time, meaning that those responsible for generating a portion of GHGs are now dead. In fact, the proportion of GHGs to which this applies is small relative to the substantial contribution being made today, so we need not worry too much about this issue.

13 There are plenty of websites with carbon footprint calculators and the opportunity to carbon offset.

14 I leave aside here the role of markets in coordinating action.

15 It also, of course, depends upon the view that collectives can be culpable agents – see Cripps (2011b) for a defence of this view.

16 Recall Caney's argument; harm will fall somewhere, the advantaged have the power to determine where, they can either accept it for themselves, thereby protecting future persons, or they can carry on contributing to the problem, thereby harming future persons.

17 Cf. Hayward (2007a), which raises worries about thinking in terms of a 'right to pollute', and instead proposes thinking about climate justice within the framework of rights to ecological space.

18 There is a fair bit of equivocation within the literature on this point. For example, within a single article, McKinnon (2011) makes the following claims: 'There is one further, crucial, fact about GHG reductions which adds the final layer of intractability to the CC problem: the changes required to meet the 60% target within five years are root and branch, and swingeing' (197); then, with respect to, 'the Sienna Millers' of the world, 'these cuts could be effected immediately by relatively straightforward changes to lifestyle that are easily made and impose little cost, e.g. ceasing to travel by air' (211). The Sienna Millers of the world may represent a special case of the advantaged, but the point stands; the advantaged are held to be liable for costs because they will find it easy to bear them, and yet the costs are held to be pretty comprehensive.

19 To take just one part of this, a recent report recommends that, to tackle climate change, people in Western states should reduce the amount of meat that they consume. Levels of meat consumption in the West have risen steadily in the past 50 years and are rising in countries such as India and China as well. The rationale for reducing the amount of meat consumed is that in principle, agricultural land used for growing crops will feed more people than land used for raising livestock, and agricultural processes account for the majority of nitrous oxide emissions, a GHG. But this piecemeal, action-based approach misses some important points. Eating less meat will not tackle climate change if instead what people eat are fruits and vegetables grown out of season in energy-intensive greenhouses or flown in from other climates. Consuming a lot of meat, as well as fruit and vegetables from all over the world at any time of year, have become a normal part of Western lifestyles.

20 To give just one example of the complexity here: one of the biggest contributors to the carbon footprint of my university is the GHG emissions generated by international students travelling to the UK each year, yet the recruitment of international students is central to my university's vision of what it is to be a good university. I am not suggesting that we should stop recruiting international students; rather, I am trying to illustrate the ways in which our GHG emitting behaviours are intimately tied to our conceptions of the good.

21 Caney (2011) claims that we need not be rigidly prescriptive about how a decent standard of living is defined, but it is clear that there are some normative assumptions in play here, and that these must spill over into a notion of living well.
22 Hayward's discussion of the Clean Development Mechanism (CDM) is illustrative here: rather than generating a substantive reduction in polluting behaviours, he argues, the CDM 'yields piecemeal, small-scale, and sometimes dubious results, allowing the rich to cherry-pick cheap development projects abroad in order to achieve low-cost emissions credits that allow them to continue evading their emissions reduction responsibilities at home' (2007: 449).
23 It is difficult to see how this collective/social dimension of the problem does not also raise the vexed question of population size; it is self-evident that one way of managing the scale of GHG emissions would be to reduce the total population.
24 For an overview, see (again) Marshall (1995) or Dobson (2000).
25 The essays collected in Barry and Wissenburg (2001) and Wissenburg and Levy (2001) give a flavour of the beginnings of the liberal turn.
26 Bernard Williams' (1993) discussion of ancient Greek attitudes to slavery is illustrative here. It is not that the ancient Greeks failed to recognize that slavery was bad, they recognized it as a tragedy, but could not imagine a good way of life that did not depend upon it.
27 On the other hand, nor is it not completely unknown to contemporary agents. The recent UK parliamentary expenses scandal is instructive. What generated public outrage was not primarily that MPs who had claimed substantial sums of taxpayers' money had broken the rules; on the contrary, it was that they had found inventive ways to contravene the spirit of the rules whilst painstakingly observing them. In short, it was MPs' evidently vicious (in this case, greedy) *characters* that were the subject of public ire.
28 See, *inter alia*, Barry (1999), Connelly (2006), and Hursthouse (2007).
29 Interestingly, Rawls himself finds it fitting to explain shame in terms of virtues: '[S]omeone is liable to moral shame when he prizes as excellences of his person those virtues that his plan of life requires and is framed to encourage', quoted in McKinnon (2011: 209).

References

Attfield, R. 2009. 'Mediated Responsibilities, Global Warming and the Scope of Ethics'. *Journal of Social Philosophy*, 40(2), 225–236.
Ball, T. 2001. 'New Ethics for Old? Or, How (Not) to Think About Future Generations', in M. Humphrey (ed.), *Political Theory and the Environment: A Reassessment*. London: Frank Cass, 89–110.
Barry, J. 1999. *Rethinking Green Politics: Nature, Virtue and Progress*. London: Sage.
Barry, J. and Wissenburg, M. (eds). 2001. *Sustaining Liberal Democracy: Ecological Challenges and Opportunities*. Basingstoke: Palgrave Macmillan.
Bedford, T. et.al., n.d. 'Guilt: An Effective Motivator for Pro-Environmental Behavioural Change'. RESOLVE Working Paper 07-11.
Bell, D. 2011. 'Does Anthropogenic Climate Change Violate Human Rights?' *Critical Review of International Social and Political Philosophy*, 14(2), 99–124.
Caney, S. 2005. 'Cosmopolitan Justice, Responsibility, and Global Climate Change'. *Leiden Journal of International Law*, 18(4), 747–775.
Caney, S. 2010a. 'Climate Change and the Duties of the Advantaged'. *Critical Review of International Social and Political Philosophy*, 13(1), 203–228.
Caney, S. 2010b. 'Climate Change, Human Rights, and Moral Thresholds', in S.

Humphreys (ed.), *Human Rights and Climate Change*. Cambridge: Cambridge University Press, 69–90.

Caney, S. 2011. 'Justice and the Duties of the Advantaged: A Defence'. *Critical Review of International Social and Political Philosophy*, 14(4), 543–552.

Connelly, J. 2006. 'The Virtues of Environmental Citizenship', in A. Dobson and D. Bell (eds), *Environmental Citizenship*. Boston, MA: MIT Press, 49–74.

Cripps, E. 2011a. 'Climate Change, Collective Harm, and Legitimate Coercion'. *Critical Review of International Social and Political Philosophy*, 14(2), 171–193.

Cripps, E. 2011b. 'Collectivities without Intention'. *Journal of Social Philosophy*, 42(1), 1–20.

Dobson, A. 2000. *Green Political Thought*. London: Routledge.

Dobson, A. 2003. *Citizenship and the Environment*. Oxford: Oxford University Press.

Elliot, R. 1988. 'The Rights of Future People'. *Journal of Applied Philosophy*, 6(2), 159–169.

Gardiner, S. 2004. 'Ethics and Global Climate Change'. *Ethics*, 114, 555–600.

Gardiner, S. 2010. *A Perfect Moral Storm: The Ethical Tragedy of Climate Change*. Oxford: Oxford University Press.

Hardin, G. 1968. 'The Tragedy of the Commons'. *Science*, 162, 1243–1248.

Hayward, T. 2007a. 'Human Rights versus Emissions Rights: Climate Justice and the Equitable Distribution of Ecological Space'. *Ethics and International Affairs*, 21, 431–450.

Hayward, T. 2007b. 'International Political Theory and the Global Environment: Some Critical Questions for Liberal Cosmopolitans'. *Journal of Social Philosophy*, 40(2), 276–295.

Hursthouse, R. (2007) 'Environmental Virtue Ethics', in R. L. Walker and P. J. Ivanhoe (eds), *Working Virtue: Virtue Ethics and Contemporary Moral Problems*. Oxford: Oxford University Press, 155–172.

Intergovernmental Panel on Climate Change (IPCC). 2007. *Climate Change 2007: Synthesis Report*, Geneva: IPCC.

Jackson, T. *et al.* n.d. RESOLVE thesis statement. Available at: http://resolve.sustainablelifestyles.ac.uk/about-resolve (accessed 20 March 2012).

Jamieson, D. 2005. 'Adaptation, Mitigation and Justice', in W. Sinnott-Armstrong and R. B. Howarth (eds), *Perspectives on Climate Change*. Amsterdam: Elsiever, 217–248.

Jamieson, D. 2007. 'The Moral and Political Challenges of Climate Change', in L. Dilling and S. C. Moser (eds), *Creating a Climate for Change: Communicating Climate Change – Facilitating Social Change*. Cambridge: Cambridge University Press, 475–484.

Lichtenberg, J. 2010. 'Negative Duties, Positive Duties, and the "New Harms"'. *Ethics*, 120, 557–578.

Marshall, P. 1995. *Nature's Web: Rethinking our Place on Earth*. London: M.E. Sharpe.

McKinnon, C. 2011. 'Climate Change Justice: Getting Motivated in the Last Chance Saloon'. *Critical Review of International Social and Political Philosophy*, 14(2), 195–293.

Moore, M. 2008. 'Global Justice, Climate Change and Miller's Theory of Responsibility'. *Critical Review of International Social and Political Philosophy*, 11(4), 501–517.

Murphy, L. B. 1993. 'The Demands of Beneficence'. *Philosophy and Public Affairs*, 22(4), 267–292.

Naess, A. 1973. 'The Shallow and the Deep, Long-Range Ecology Movement: A Summary'. *Inquiry*, 16, 95–100.

Neumeyer, E. 2000. 'In Defence of Historical Accountability for Greenhouse Gas Emissions'. *Ecological Economics*, 33, 185–192.

Page, E. 2006. *Climate Change, Justice, and Future Generations*. Cheltenham: Edward Elgar.

Parfit, D. 1987. *Reasons and Persons*. Oxford: Oxford University Press.

Shue, H. 1999. 'Global Environment and International Inequality'. *International Affairs*, 75, 533–537.

Shue, H. 2011. 'Face Reality? After You! A Call for Leadership on Climate Change'. *Ethics and International Affairs*, 25 (1), 17–26.

Singer, P. 1972. 'Famine, Affluence and Morality'. *Philosophy and Public Affairs*, 1(1), 229–243.

Sinnott-Armstrong, W. 2005. 'It's Not My Fault: Global Warming and Individual Moral Obligations', in: W. Sinnott-Armstrong and R. B. Howarth (eds), *Perspectives on Climate Change*. Amsterdam: Elsiever, 285–307.

Vanderheiden, S. 2011. 'Globalizing Responsibility for Climate Change'. *Ethics and International Affairs*, 25(1), 65–84.

White Jr., L. 1967. 'The Historical Roots of Our Ecologic Crisis'. *Science*, 161, 1203–1207.

Williams, B. 1993. *Shame and Necessity*. Berkeley, CA: University of California Press.

Wissenburg, M. and Levy, Y. (eds). 2001. *Liberal Democracy and Environmentalism: The End of Environmentalism?* London: Routledge.

7 Sustainable action and moral corruption

Roland Mees

The concept of moral corruption has been pointed at as the root cause of our failure to make progress with acting towards a sustainable future. This chapter defines moral corruption as the agent's strategy not to form the intentions needed to overcome the motivational obstacles of sustainable action. Moral corruption is considered similar to Kant's radical evil; it causes our practical identities to be divided. The question then arises: how could we possibly strive for moral integrity, while simultaneously being infected with the 'disease' of moral corruption? It is argued that we have an indirect motive for sustainable action in wanting to prevent our practical identity from falling apart.

1. Introduction: the problem with motivation for sustainable action

A common experience these days is that conversations between proponents and opponents of environmentally friendly action end abruptly, when the sceptic touches upon the motivational aspect by asking: 'what's in it for me?' In common sense language, this means that in matters concerning sustainability, we seem in some way to be seriously hampered in making the step from *worth doing* to *doing*.

Within the spectrum of human action, those actions related to accepting certain restrictions with the aim to preserve the planet for people who will live in the distant future seem to be most vulnerable to overriding motives that pull us in a different direction than the one we cognitively agreed to (Ott 2004; Baumgartner 2005; Birnbacher 2009; Gardiner 2011). That is, whatever reasons we have to support environmentally friendly action, at the motivational level we have to deal with the potential psychological inconsistency between what practical reason commands, and the actions that we in fact carry out. This happens, for example, when we increase the rate of depletion of natural resources, despite the fact that we are perfectly aware that these resources are finite, and people in the distant future will also need to benefit from them.

The problem of motivation in ethics arises, since normative statements cannot, by themselves, force agents to act in conformance with them. 'All they do is to prescribe, or recommend, a certain course of action. In order to make someone act accordingly they have to rely on further factors' (Birnbacher 2009:

273). The motivational problem of sustainable action for us as individual human agents then, could be formulated as the problem of overcoming the potential psychological inconsistency between our *moral judgement* in favour of some environmentally friendly action, and the *action* that we in fact carry out following up on that judgement. Dieter Birnbacher (2009: 285) argues that next to normative statements indirect motives are needed to solve the problem with motivation for sustainable action, since they aim at objectives in the present or in the near future from which current people benefit.

In his analysis of the motivational problem to care for the distant future, Stephen Gardiner has pointed at the concept of moral corruption as the root cause of an agent's attitudes of complacency and procrastination when it comes to taking environmentally friendly action; even when such action is supported by the agent's moral judgement (Gardiner 2011: 45). In his book, Gardiner's goal is mainly to *explain* the global environmental tragedy (3). The book analyses the causes of the problems we face globally in the context of an ethics of the distant future, and presents the research in a way that is also accessible to a non-academic agent, who would want to implement a policy of sustainability under real world conditions. As to the main problem of moral corruption, however, the book remains relatively silent, and it does not say anything about potential solutions or ways in which it could be dealt with.

This chapter will start with an argument of why people in high-income OECD countries, that are supposed to contribute to the goals formulated for example, by the UNFCCC, must consider the motivational problem for sustainable action first. It will then analyse why the problem of caring for the distant future is so difficult from a motivational point of view. I will show some psychological obstacles that we, as agents in highly industrialised countries, have to overcome in order to strengthen our motivation for environmentally friendly action. I will then continue by giving a more detailed formulation for the concept of moral corruption than provided by Gardiner (2011: 307). Subsequently, I will discuss the concept of moral corruption in relation to the ethical concepts, weakness of will and radical evil.

I will then argue how we can overcome moral corruption by giving an account of the effect of moral corruption on our practical identity as socialised moral agents. As it turns out, moral corruption causes our practical identity to be divided, and this leads to a discussion of moral corruption in relation to the concept of integrity. I will argue that morally corrupt agents, who consistently disregard their obligations towards future generations, face difficulties in being called persons of integrity. As a way to avoid moral corruption and keeping up our striving for integrity, I propose to use our best endeavours for sustainable action. I conclude by revisiting the common sense sceptical question this chapter started with.

2. Why should we deal with the motivational problem first?

The problem of motivation for sustainable action can be illustrated by considering the UNFCCC framework (including its successor the Kyoto Protocol) as a commonly shared moral judgement being embodied in a contract between 192 states. It has now been in place for two decades. Various scientific reports have indicated that the realisation to date of the goals laid down in the UNFCCC is far from where it should be (IPCC 2007). Given the lack of major progress to realise the objectives of the framework since 1992, it could be argued that agents who are responsible for taking the necessary actions (for example those politicians who signed the framework), face some form of motivational problems in following up on the moral judgements entailed by the UNFCCC, and in any event, could be subject to strong ethical criticism (Gardiner 2011: 404).

The starting point of my argument in this chapter is not only with those politicians, but also with most people in highly industrialised countries who share *some* responsibility to act in accordance with the goals laid down in the UNFCCC. That is, the lack of progress in living up to the UNFCCC is not only a moral burden for those who are responsible in their role as politicians, but for many of us. My argument for this claim is as follows.

First, suppose that scientists are right in their judgement that current greenhouse gas emissions are too high to keep global warming within the level aimed for by the UNFCCC.[1] Based on the scientific projections, this means that any responsible policy would require that at some moment in the not too distant future, global emissions of greenhouses gases should peak and from there on start decreasing substantially for at least a couple of decades. This global course of action to reduce greenhouse gas emissions must continue until the desired levels are reached.

Second, if for example the parties of the UNFCCC agree that action is required, and the rough task of the burden is clear, then who is responsible for making it happen? Here, it could be objected that the institutions in the developed countries have never been set up with the idea that they should be able to handle problems of the magnitude and complexity of the global climate change problem that came about over many generations. Nevertheless, many of these institutions have been created by following a process of delegation of individual responsibilities and powers, since the problems of each and every individual could be solved more effectively when the institution can organise the implementation of their solution (Gardiner 2011: 432). In other words, in the liberal democracies that the high-income OECD countries happen to be, there is a principal-agent relationship between voters and politicians, respectively. This implies that in the case that politicians have been given the authority to propose and implement plans for reducing greenhouse gas emissions, and they fail to do so, then these politicians can be held accountable and be the subject of moral criticism.

On the other hand, the delegation of responsibility and powers from the individual voters to the institutions do not discharge the individual agents fully of their responsibilities in the case that the politicians fail to do their job. With or without responsible politicians, the problem of climate change still remains, meaning that if delegation to the agents does not work, then the responsibility to solve the climate change problem falls back on the principal, i.e. the individual citizens. Hence, in the event that delegation to politicians fails, the individual citizens are likewise subject to moral criticism. This means that citizens in high-income OECD countries cannot entirely waive their responsibility for failing to meet the goals of the UNFCCC.

It could then be argued, that doing something about the motivational problem to care for the distant future for individual agents is simply unfeasible. What might remedy the problem instead is to create new institutions or change existing institutions in high-income OECD countries so that they can help steer our behaviour towards more sustainable action. The recently published psychology of nudging could serve as an example in this regard. Citizens of a particular country could gently be stimulated ('nudged') to decrease their energy consumption by showing them – in an anonymised way – the annual energy bill of their neighbours. Generally, this will indeed stimulate the lowering of energy usage, though not as a result of moral reasoning, but as a result of psychological manipulation (Thaler and Sunstein 2008).

There is, however, a fundamental difficulty with the view that the creation of new institutions (such as nudging) should be preferred to solving the motivational problem for individual agents. The difficulty is that it mixes up what the primary problem is, as well as what the secondary problems are. Choosing the way of creating new institutions, or changing existing ones to solve the motivational problem of individual agents, presupposes that we are motivated to do so. In order to accomplish the action to create new institutions or change existing ones, one has to be convinced that executing this is valuable in itself in the first place. At least a politically relevant coalition of agents has to solve the motivational problem for itself first, in order to start creating new institutions or changing existing ones. Solving the motivational problem for individual agents, therefore, is the first problem to be solved, and the question of creating or changing the institutions that steer our actions towards more sustainable ones comes thereafter.

The above arguments justify that this chapter focuses, in the first place, on the motivational aspects. The paper puts in the centre, the motivational problem of those agents who ought to contribute to the reduction of the global emission of greenhouse gasses. In the following sections, a short phenomenology of the motivational challenges of sustainable action will be presented, followed by the analysis of a concept that could be seen as one of the major roadblocks on the way towards a sustainable world: moral corruption.

3. Motivational characteristics of sustainable action

In this section, I will study more closely the nature of the motivational problems that agents encounter when their actions concern the distant future. In order to facilitate this, I undertake a phenomenological analysis of the full spectrum of morally non-trivial human actions that require intensive moral deliberation by the agent, and have an impact both on the agent herself, as well as on their environment; the magnitude of the impact varying with the action. The action X under consideration could, for example, be: becoming a vegetarian regarding red meat by any agent; developing and marketing products with a substantially reduced ecological footprint by the product manager of a medium-sized family owned business; implementing a policy to put severe tax penalties on the use of fossil fuels in favour of renewable energy sources by the prime minister of an OECD country; but also, closing a loss-making factory in an area with high unemployment by the CEO of a multinational company.[2]

Below I will consider certain aspects ('dimensions') of action X that will help us to clarify why sustainable action is so difficult from a motivational point of view. By scoring all actions with respect to the dimensions mentioned below, we will be able to distinguish between sustainable actions and other actions, in the sense that the extraordinary nature of an agent's motivation for sustainable action compared with other morally relevant actions becomes apparent. The agent's action (X) will be classified along the following dimensions.

Effectiveness

The degree to which the agent is causally effective in successfully carrying out action X. It is meant to distinguish between actions that can be initiated and executed entirely by the agent herself; and actions where the agent can only exercise a marginal influence on whether the action succeeds. The extent to which the action can be carried out fully by the agent, is given by three values: high, medium and low.

Coordination

The complexity of coordination needed for the agent to execute X. Independent from the question of effectiveness, the level of coordination with other people or institutions required to perform the action can vary considerably. Coordination is a main factor that discriminates between the private and public roles of agents. Even when the level of effectiveness an actor can exercise is high, the level of coordination can vary from low to high, depending on the field in which the agent operates. The degrees of this dimension are again, given by the values high, medium and low.

Geographical scope

Geographical scope within which action X directly affects current people. This dimension specifies whether the action has a local impact, confined purely to the immediate surroundings of the agent; has a regional impact (i.e. province, country or group of countries); or even impacts many countries and people around the globe.

Effect on current people

The degree to which action X goes against the immediate self-interest of current people (other than the agent) affected by X. This dimension indicates the level of resistance the agent will likely encounter while executing X, whether there will be a high, medium or low level of resistance.

Effect on the living conditions of future people

The degree to which action X will have morally significant effects on the living conditions of people in the distant future. Equally important for a moral judgement about the agent carrying out X is the question that to what extent future people will be worse off compared to the situation of not performing X.

Possibility for free rider behaviour by the agent

Shifting the moral problem of not achieving the ultimate end of action X to future generations by not executing X with negligible negative consequences for the agent. Perhaps this is the most severe temptation for agents to not undertake environmentally friendly action: the low price they have to pay in terms of diminished self-interest if they do not undertake X in relation to the potentially large collective impact that inaction will have for people living in the distant future.

Although obviously, evaluating human actions along these dimensions does not at all pretend to say something empirically definitive, I would still like to make the following observations that, in my view, concur with the conclusions other authors have drawn based on conceptual analyses and references to empirical psychological studies (Ott 2004; Baumgartner 2005; Birnbacher 2009). Actions, which aim to care for people who will live in the distant future, can be characterised by:

- the environment, in which the agent operates, seems to be such that the agent can hardly be causally effective;
- the environment has a high degree of complexity, which requires strong social coordination capabilities of the agent;
- a geographical scope that is at least regional; effects on current people and future people that are at least medium to high;
- there is a high possibility for free riding, showing that agents who perform these actions will hardly be forced by their immediate surroundings to undertake the actions, but to rely mainly on their own will power and persuasiveness to be efficacious.

The above-mentioned characteristics suggest that agents, who want to undertake actions to care for the distant future, especially in their professional roles, face considerable practical difficulties compared with agents in other roles executing other actions. Agents who undertake sustainable action will need to overcome (at least) three types of psychological obstacles. First, they face the task as agents to change something in the world for which they prima facie will not be praised, since it goes against the immediate self-interests of current people. Second, the action to be executed is hard work, i.e. it requires the agent's utmost dedication and competence in order to follow through with it. Third, since the ultimate end to be achieved with the action will be to the benefit of people who will live in the distant future, the agent will need to overcome her own sceptical attitude, fuelled by the first two obstacles, inviting her to go back to the original moral judgement that formed the starting point for her sustainable action by questioning: 'is it worth it?' Moreover, as a result of our 'asymmetric causal power and time-dependent interests' (Gardiner 2011: 184), we as current people are susceptible to our motivation not being strong enough to overcome these types of psychological resistances when those actions are concerned, which aim to preserve the planet for people who will live long after us.

Our potential failure to overcome the practical and psychological difficulties of taking environmentally friendly actions gives rise to confining the investigation into the problem of motivation for sustainable action, as discussed so far, to considering the formulation of the concept of moral corruption. This will be my focus in the next section.

4. The concept of moral corruption

Given the observations made in the previous section regarding the motivational difficulties of taking action in favour of the interests of people living in the distant future, I propose to define moral corruption as: (1) pursuing a strategy; (2) with the objective to keeping up one's current, perfectly convenient status quo; (3) by deliberately and persistently not forming those intentions that are necessary to overcome the motivational challenges of taking action to care for people living in the distant future, both in the private and in the public sphere (e.g. in one's professional role as a teacher, police officer or banker).

Overall, one can say that morally corrupt agents do their utmost to not be confronted with questions about their commitment to ethics of the distant future. This means that morally corrupt agents do have moral prescriptions about taking environmentally friendly actions as part of their shared background assumptions, and they know that they possess these assumptions somewhere in what we call their conscience; but they have decided to leave this part of their life world aside, not letting it exercise any influence over the practical considerations they deem relevant for justifying their actions. In short, morally corrupt agents are deaf to principal moral questions regarding sustainability and climate change, and they are conscious of the risk they take that their deafness to these questions may result in the irreversible corruption of their moral character, thereby potentially losing a few moral virtues. That is, corruption is not only a moral concept, but also a causal or quasi-causal concept (Miller 2011: 10). Some of the terms used in this definition need further clarification.

First, moral corruption should be understood as pursuing a strategy, very much in the same way as one chooses a strategy in the context of decision theory. That is, one does not give up easily when attempting to achieve a certain goal that has a high utility to the agent (to be defined in the next paragraph). More specifically, if after having carried out action X, action Y is required to reach that particular goal, the agent will be strongly inclined to undertake Y; even when Y involves a morally blameworthy situation for the agent. It also means that one's endeavours are strategic in the Habermasian sense, that is, the agent has set herself unilaterally on a course of action in which she wants to achieve a specific goal, without having made this course of action subject to the inter-subjective critique of other people; for example those people affected by the strategy that has been set (Bohman and Rehg 2011: 14).

Second, the strategy of the morally corrupt agent is aimed at preserving their current convenient status quo in the high-income OECD countries. As Gardiner points out, it is an almost universal characteristic of decisions by agents about their ordinary consumption patterns that these are focused on the short and medium term at most, and that their spatial scope is limited to local circumstances (2011: 58–9). It means that people currently living in Western industrialised countries define their good lives in terms of certain social-economic, material conditions to which they want to hold fast. They seem of the opinion that whatever happens, their wealth should be impacted only minimally, if at all, very much as it was expressed by the former president of the USA, George H. W. Bush, during the Earth Summit in Rio de Janeiro 1992: 'The American way of life is not negotiable'.

Third, the principal characteristic of morally corrupt agents is that they do not form intentions to act in order to preserve the planet for future generations, which is in my account, why global accords negotiated by politicians remain in the eyes of the public, weak and without substance. Morally corrupt agents know very well 'that intentions involve characteristic kinds of motivational commitments. Intentions are conduct controlling, in the sense that if you intend to F at t, and nothing changes before t, then (other things equal) you will F' (Wilson and Shpall 2012: 32). The reason why they do not form intentions to overcome the motivational challenges of acting in the interest of future generations (Section 3) is that if one intends to do F, one is already in progress towards doing it. In that sense, deliberation is over: one has begun (Setiya 2011: 8). This is exactly what morally corrupt agents try to prevent.

The definition of moral corruption given above should be understood as a concept, analogous to how Christine Korsgaard elaborates on the four types of vices in Plato's *Republic* (Korsgaard 2009: 165). It does not make sense to go out on the street and look for primary examples of morally corrupt agents, or to look in one's organisation for agents that more or less fulfil the characteristics of the definition. Rather, we should acknowledge that our motives to take action to live up to our obligations to people living in the distant future might be morally corrupted in a way similar to how Plato describes people striving for a good, i.e. aristocratic constitution: they have to fight against the timocratic, oligarchic, democratic and tyrannical tendencies that try to overrule the aristocratic governance of their soul. Many people living in high-income OECD countries have to face moral corruption as a serious obstacle to take action to care for the distant future. Moral corruption is a 'shadow' of moral agents, with which they are confronted when they feel hampered in acting in the interest of people who will live in the distant future.

5. Moral corruption versus weakness of will and 'radical evil'

The following section will deepen the understanding of moral corruption by discussing it in relation to other well-known concepts in ethics: weakness of will and Kant's 'radical evil'.

The formulation of the motivational problem to care for the distant future at the start of the chapter as 'the problem of overcoming the potential psychological inconsistency between our *moral judgement* in favour of some environmentally friendly action, and the *action* that we in fact carry out following up on that judgement', might suggest that this problem falls within the 'classic' formulation of weakness of will as *akrasia*. This formulation says: 'weak-willed or akratic action is (free, intentional) action contrary to one's better judgment … Rather than the two – action and judgment – being in concert, there is a dissonance or lack of correspondence between the two that marks off the action as akratic' (Stroud 2010: 55). Given that, according to the classic definition, the agent's action at t must be synchronous with her unfavourable judgement at t about that same action, it should be clear that moral corruption is not an example of this form of *akrasia*. On the one hand, the morally corrupt agent has agreed to the judgement that carrying out an environmentally friendly action is the right thing to do. On the other hand, she has decided that it is not up to her to carry out that action. Therefore, she has never formed an intention to do the action in favour of the environment. The morally corrupt agent does not even arrive at t, where a discrepancy between her action and her judgement could be observed, since she has not formed an intention to act in an environmentally friendly way in the first place.

So far, we have dealt with the essentially synchronic definition of *akrasia*. However, Stroud gives still another definition of weakness of will, namely that 'it is a species of irresoluteness, or failure to follow through on your intentions. It is a failure to do what you have decided you will do – a failure to stick to your plans' (Stroud 2010: 60). Here, it seems that we get to a critical feature of a morally corrupt agency: although these agents might have agreed to the moral judgement that caring for the distant future is the right thing to do, they – deliberately and persistently – have never formed an intention to act according to that judgement. In that sense, they have never failed to carry out their intention to care for the distant future. They never decided to take action in favour of the distant future. This means that also according to this second definition as an essentially a diachronic phenomenon, moral corruption cannot be regarded as a form of weakness of will.

This is not to say that morally corrupt agents make no future-directed intentions at all. As I have construed them, these are as a rule, strongly willed agents who know perfectly well that having certain clear future-directed intentions are necessary for them to accomplish their strategies; if only in order to coordinate their activities with other agents. That is, on the one hand they form future-directed intentions with regard to the strategies they have chosen; and on the other hand, they do not make any plans or intentions with regard to actions to take care of the distant future. Morally corrupt agents are aware that when they abandon prior intentions, they may be criticised for that on rational grounds. This is one of the reasons why they do not form intentions to act in favour of the environment: they could be accused of weakness of will if they did not manage to execute their plans. Morally corrupt agents do not make a commitment to care for the distant future, by forming an intention or adopting a plan to do so because this binds them to realise that plan, which is not their objective. Being regarded by other agents as someone who has failed at self-management is something morally corrupt agents particularly want to prevent.

If moral corruption cannot be considered as an example of weakness of will, which other ethical concept could we bring into connection with the phenomenon of moral corruption? As morally corrupt agents have set themselves on pursuing a strategy to keeping up their convenient status quo, it seems that they have freely chosen maxims of their will that are not universalisable to all human beings. That is, they have decided on a principle to guide their actions that potentially could be at odds with the principle of morality, e.g. the categorical imperative.

In his account of the evil nature of the human being, Kant indicates that human agents both integrate the principle of self-love and the moral law into their maxims. According to Kant, the deciding feature of 'radical evil' is the agent's action to reverse the moral order of her motives by putting the principle of self-love above the universal law. In subordinating the moral law and making her motives and inclinations of self-love a prerequisite for following it, the agent voluntarily and consciously chooses to take her inclinations to be reasons for action (Kant 1974: 33–34). On my account, this comes closest to what morally corrupt agents do.

In addition, drawing on Plato's account of evil, Korsgaard notes:

> the bad or evil person is powerful, ruthless, unconstrained. The evil person is prepared to do *whatever is necessary* to get what he wants, and determined to let nothing stand in his way. He is clever enough to circumvent the law, and both willing and able to outwit, outsmart, or if necessary outshoot whoever and whatever comes between him and the satisfaction of his desire.
> Korsgaard 2009: 170 (emphasis Korsgaard)

The morally corrupt agent has decided that she will leverage her powerful position in society and use her (considerable) instrumental intelligence to achieve the goal of keeping up her convenient status quo. She does not really choose a maxim, which means that she does not make laws for herself. In that sense, morally corrupt agents have deliberately given up their autonomy and freedom in order to pursue their strategy (Korsgaard 2009: 173). This might, however, have consequences for the way these agents constitute themselves as the cause of their actions.

6. Moral corruption and our self-constitution as agents

In the previous sections, we have given a phenomenological analysis of the motivational challenges specific for taking action in the interest of people living in the far future, and we have formulated a concept of moral corruption, based on this analysis. Thereafter, we have compared the concept of moral corruption with two concepts that have a much longer history in ethics: weakness of will and radical evil. It turns out that moral corruption should not be viewed as an instance of weakness of will, but as an example of defective action that might have consequences for the way we conceive ourselves as moral agents.

As a result, we see ourselves faced with a few inconvenient questions: can current people claim to be moral agents, that is claim to be acting morally as agents with regard to a certain class of actions (for example those affecting current people or children or grandchildren), and at the same time act defectively with regard to another class of actions, namely those regarding people living in the distant future? Is there a view on human agency that combines acting responsibly towards current people and our immediate offspring, and irresponsibly towards people living in the distant future? Finally, how can we possibly strive for moral integrity, while being infected with the 'disease' of moral corruption?

As defined above, being morally corrupt means pursuing a strategy with the objective of keeping up one's convenient status quo, by deliberately and persistently not forming those intentions that are necessary to overcome the motivational challenges of taking action to care for the distant future, both in the private and in the public sphere. Given the motivational challenges, current agents in high-income OECD countries have to overcome, the twenty year history of the UNFCCC has proven that it will be highly unlikely that these agents will undertake a meaningful effort to carry out an action to care for people living in the distant future; even if – if people in the affluent countries do not change their behaviour – the level of urgency to do so increases every year in the sense that keeping global warming below 2°C becomes more and more difficult. That is, they primarily see the difficulties for themselves (and the strategy they are pursuing) of carrying out such an action, instead of mobilising the best capabilities they have in order to bring the ideal of a world in which people of the distant future will be able to live under similar conditions as people currently living in the affluent countries a step further. With Stephen Gardiner, we might be tempted to conclude that there is only room for expecting an ethical tragedy, i.e. a scenario in which humanity will not be able to save itself, and the only hope is that humanity will be saved by causes external to it.

There is, however, one last card I want to play that could allow us to cope with moral corruption. This is to reflect on how we ought to understand ourselves as moral agents in relation to the concept of moral corruption. As Korsgaard argues, to act is 'to determine yourself to the cause of a certain end. So to act *self-consciously* is to conceive *yourself* teleologically – as the cause, that is, the *first* cause – of a certain end' (Korsgaard 2009: 41 (emphasis Korsgaard)).

Suppose that a very experienced and talented agent A, being one and the same person, would be in the position to take up all the roles and carry out all of the actions mentioned in Section 3. Suppose also that A would act in a morally responsible way concerning her actions that affect current people, and in a morally corrupt way with respect to actions that concern primarily people living in the far future. This means, according to Korsgaard, that A will conceive herself as a first cause of the ends that affect current people, whereas for ends that affect people in the distant future, A will not conceive herself as any sort of cause. More specifically, as a result of A's free riding regarding the ends that affect people in the distant future, A will these ends, but does not will the means to those ends. In particular, morally corrupt agents do not say that they do not will the ends to preserve the earth for future generations, but they keep questioning the means and do not propose actions that better promote the ends than those actions on the table for deliberation and decision; since they have decided not to form any intentions that are required to overcome the motivational burdens of taking environmentally friendly action. As A has judged in favour of environmentally friendly action, but does not form those intentions necessary to carry out that action, A acts according to Kant's hypothetical imperative regarding actions that concern current people; whereas this imperative, in A's eyes, does not apply to actions that affect people living in the distant future.

Translating this into the self-constitution of agents means that A constitutes herself as the cause of the ends of current people, whereas she does not constitute herself as the cause of ends that affect people living in the distant future. At the same time, when A deliberates about her actions and which ones to choose, she regards her choices as hers, as the product of her own activity, because she regards the principle of choice as expressive, or representative, of herself – of her own causality (Korsgaard 2009: 75). In particular, A views her choices regarding the ends promoted for current people and those for future people as an expression of her practical identity. The actions promoting the ends for current people are constitutive of A's practical identity, whereas actions in favour of the ends of people living in the distant future do not constitute A's practical identity, since she will the ends, but does not will the means, and consequently, has chosen not to form intentions to carry out those actions. That is, A's practical identity is constituted by the actions that she carries out that aim for an end to the benefit of current people, and by her *action not to form intentions to act* with the objective to save the planet for future generations.

What effect then, does this division between sets of ends and corresponding actions have on A's practical identity? The effect on A's practical identity of actions promoting the ends of people in the future that resides primarily in the private sphere (e.g. becoming a vegetarian), in first instance, could be considered as somewhat remote, since only her private surroundings will hold A accountable; in this example, for eating lots of red meat.[3] However, actions that A undertakes in her role as a professional leader might have a far greater and immediate influence on A's practical identity.

As a result of preserving her convenient status quo in the highly industrialised countries, A has deliberately chosen not to make public the reasons for which she does not undertake actions that further the interests of future people. This means that in a way, A socially cooperates with other agents, as she will share those reasons for actions concerning the ends to be promoted for current people, whilst remaining silent on her reasons not to take action in the interest of future generations.

Since A cannot control whether there will be certain actions required of her and her organisation that further the interests of people living in the far future, her difference in treating the interests of current and future people leads to problems in the practical deliberation about common courses of action in A's social interaction with other agents. This is so, because it is not clear a priori whether other agents will understand A leaving out certain types of arguments from the discourse about these commonly shared courses of action. In the course of their deliberation, it might appear to other agents, who do not distinguish between ends in favour of current people and future people the way A does –that is, who do not follow a strategy of moral corruption like A – that A does not share with them certain types of reason, which could make it difficult for them to agree with A about what should be done in a situation in which certain actions are required.[4] Given this, it follows that A will find it difficult to engage in relations of reciprocity with other agents, since they 'must be prepared to share their ends and reasons; to hold them jointly; and to act together. Reciprocity is the sharing of reasons, and you will enter into it only with someone you expect to deal with reasons in a rational way' (Korsgaard 1996: 196). This is what A fails to do.

Coming back to the question about the effect of moral corruption on A's practical identity, we can now say that it causes a division of A's self into parts: one that is constituted by the actions carried out to promote the ends affecting current people, and another that is formed by the action not to form intentions to act in the interest of people who will live in the distant future. Morally corrupt action, as I have defined it, is an example of defective action in the sense that it fails 'to constitute their agents as the unified authors of their actions' (Korsgaard 2009: 32).

Moral corruption causes A's self to be divided, which raises the problem that A cannot unambiguously claim that her actions are issued from her constitution by giving herself a law (Korsgaard 2009: 160). Assuming that A performs a leadership role, the other agents with whom A socially interacts will be disorientated, not knowing at a certain moment in time with which part of A's divided self they are dealing. Since A has a leadership role, as a result of which there will be strong reciprocal relations between A and the other agents, this uncertainty for the other agents affects their motivation negatively to act in accordance with any mutually agreed course of action in a given situation. For A and the other agents, it seems impossible to establish a unity between them, that is, to form a single common will. A's divided self hampers her and the other agents from meeting in the noumenal world (Korsgaard 2009: 190). As it seems fundamental for us as human beings that we understand ourselves as self-conscious agents, as noumena *and* as participants in the social-communicative relations with other human beings, we might question A's ability to be an efficacious moral agent at all.

To what conclusion does this account bring us so far? The least we can say about the self of a morally corrupt agent is that it is divided. On the one hand this self is constituted by actions that pertain to the interests of current people and on the other hand it is formed by the agent's strategy of keeping her current, perfectly convenient status quo, which is being achieved by persistently ignoring the obligations we have to people living in the distant future. The next section will discuss the question of whether we can be held responsible for such a divided self.

7. Integrity and our 'best endeavours' as a way to cope with moral corruption

The conclusion of Section 6 leads us directly to the question of how our reflections about moral corruption, and the divided self that have resulted from it, could be related to a conception of integrity. In this paper I understand integrity to be a complex and thick virtue term, namely:

> a capacity to respond to change in one's values or circumstances, a kind of continual remaking of the self, as well as a capacity to balance competing commitments and values and to take responsibility for one's work and thought.
>
> Cox *et al.* 2003: 41

Integrity so understood means that there certainly is a connection between living with integrity and living a morally good life. 'Integrity is a complex aspect of character that serves to link or dissolve disparate goals, values, emotions, aspects of self and periods in one's life' (Cox *et al.* 2003: 56).

Can agents be morally corrupt as defined in this chapter, and simultaneously strive for integrity in the above sense? Recall that being morally corrupt means pursuing a strategy with the objective of keeping up one's convenient status quo, by deliberately and persistently not forming those intentions that are necessary to overcome the motivational challenges of taking action to care for the distant future, both in the private and in the public sphere. In other words, with respect to treating the interests of current people and future people, the least we can say about morally corrupt agents is that they operate with different moral standards. As we have seen in Section 6, as a consequence morally corrupt agents develop two sorts of self: one that cares for the interests of current people including those of the agent herself, and one that deliberately and persistently does not care for the interests of people who will live in the distant future.

Deliberately and persistently not forming those intentions that are necessary to overcome the motivational challenges of taking action to care for the distant future means that one of the selves of morally corrupt agents has the potential to act in good faith regarding current people, whereas their other self does not act in good faith with respect to people who will live in the far future. The morally corrupt agent does not seem to be able to form a moral point of view from where she can evaluate her actions regarding current people and future people based on an integral set of normative standards. For professional leaders, of whom we have legitimate expectations about their consistency (e.g. politicians, CEOs), this seems to be a defeater of integrity (Cox *et al.* 2003: 112).

Alasdair MacIntyre argues that moral agents are justifiably and uncontroversially held responsible for their actions that are intentional (MacIntyre 1999: 312). As morally corrupt agents have compartmentalised their intentions regarding current people and future people, it could be argued that these agents can be held responsible for their divided selves as well. Morally corrupt agents actively refuse to form intentions that could lead to actions in the interest of people who will live in the distant future. These agents have deliberately closed their minds to certain possibilities of action, which could be expected of them both in their private and professional roles. As MacIntyre argues:

> This divided self has to be characterised by what it lacks. It is not only without any standpoint from which it can pass critical judgement on the standards governing its various roles, but it also must lack those virtues of integrity and constancy that are prerequisites for exercising the powers of moral agency.
>
> MacIntyre 1999: 324

I conclude that our integrity is at risk when we consistently do not care for the distant future whilst living an active life as a present moral agent. Persistently not living up to our obligations to future people, does negatively affect the circumstances in which future people will live, it also casts doubts over us current people, when we still believe that we can be regarded as persons of integrity. Not striving for a sustainable world in the sense of being a morally corrupt agent, that is not being able or willing to find good reasons and forming the intentions needed to voluntarily carry out those actions needed to fulfil the obligations we have to people in the distant future, will hamper us in viewing ourselves as candidates for being persons of integrity.

What then, ought we to be doing as current moral agents in high-income OECD countries, which could release us from the suspicion of moral corruption, whilst keeping us candidates for being attributed the virtue of integrity? The answer I propose is: giving ourselves the law to use one's best endeavours to act in a sustainable way. It means that current agents should demand themselves to execute all those reasonable courses of action that further the interests of people living long after us. Simultaneously, the requirement that an agent uses her best endeavours means that the agent should give reasonable consideration of her own interests. That is, the agent must consider her own interests in order to be able to continue using her best endeavours for sustainable action. For example, it is not implied that the agent runs into financial ruin as a result of carrying out sustainable action.

The requirement of best endeavours imposes an obligation to act in good faith and to the extent of the agent's own total capabilities.[5] What current agents in the affluent countries, as a minimum, *can do and ought to do* as part of using their best endeavours is form those intentions needed to overcome the motivational obstacles that we have found to be among the reasons why sustainable action seems difficult to accomplish. The forming of the right intentions, that is those intentions that favour undertaking action in the light of sustainability, is something very many agents in high-income OECD countries *can do and ought to do.* Thereafter, obviously, it will also be a matter of contingency whether these intentions become reality. Having a plan to act in good faith in the interest of future generations, however, is a minimum we can ask from ourselves.

8. Returning to 'what is in it for me?'

We started this chapter by referring to a typical conversation between a proponent and an opponent of some environmentally friendly action, in which the sceptic utters her reason for not forming those intentions necessary for the action under discussion by asking 'what is in it for me?' We started by arguing that solving the problem of motivation for sustainable action is the first thing people in high-income OECD countries should do. We continued by giving a phenomenological account of the motivational challenges that one faces when one intends to undertake a sustainable project with a scope that goes beyond merely one's private sphere. Based on this description, we formulated a definition of what it is to be a morally corrupted agent. Moral corruption turned out to be a particular sort of defective action, one that forces our practical identity to become divided. An agent with this divided self cannot claim to be a person of integrity, since the agent herself can be held responsible for her own self being compartmentalised. Finally, I proposed that agents in affluent countries set themselves the law of using their best endeavours to further the interests of people who will live long after us.

In reply to the question 'what is in it for me?' we now can say: an indirect motive for undertaking sustainable action is that you will have the possibility to remain undivided, being deprived of moral schizophrenia, and even remain a candidate for becoming a person of integrity understood as a virtue. You can achieve this by fighting the tendency towards moral corruption that we all have, through making your best endeavours in the sense of 'leaving no stone unturned' to will those sustainable projects that preserve the planet for generations of human beings who will live in the distant future. Given the lack of progress in meeting the goals of the UNFCCC by people currently living in the high-income OECD countries, we not only *can do* something about our moral corruption, we also *ought to do* this to prevent our practical identity from falling apart.

Notes

1 The UNFCCC, Article 2, states: 'stabilization of greenhouse gas concentrations in the atmosphere at a level that would prevent dangerous anthropogenic interference with the climate system'. Although the Copenhagen conference (2009) did not agree on the target to keep the global temperature rise below 2°C, recently thinktanks such as the International Energy Agency have started to base their projections on this scenario.

2 Note that it is beyond the scope of this chapter to present a detailed analysis here. For an elaborate analysis of the motivational aspects of environmentally friendly actions in relation to other human actions, I refer to my forthcoming PhD thesis.

3 There are good reasons, however, to argue that our consumption patterns are under moral scrutiny as well. By our behaviour as private consumers in the economy, we directly influence the 'what', 'how' and 'when' of the production methods of corporations that produce the goods and services we have just bought. There is a causal chain between our reasons for buying certain goods and services and the actions that agents in corporations carry out to further the ends of current people or those of people living in the distant future. Hence, our practical identities are constituted by our consumer patterns as private individuals as well. Due to the space limitations of this chapter, however, I will not develop this argument further.

4 In common sense language, other agents may refer to A as having a 'hidden agenda'.

5 I draw here on the literature concerning the meaning of 'best endeavours' or 'best efforts' in UK and US case law, e.g. Miller (2006).

References

Baumgartner, C. 2005. *Umweltethik – Umwelthandeln: Ein Beitrag zur Lösung des Motivationsproblems*. Paderborn: Mentis.

Birnbacher, D. 2009. 'What Motivates Us to Care for the (Distant) Future?' in A. Gosseries and L. Meyer (eds), *Intergenerational Justice*. Oxford: Oxford University Press, 273–301.

Bohman, J. and Rehg, W. 2011. 'Jürgen Habermas' in Edward N. Zalta (ed.),*The Stanford Encyclopedia of Philosophy*. Available at: http://plato.stanford.edu/archives/fall2011/entries/habermas/.

Cox, D., La Caze, M. and Levine, M. 2003. *Integrity and the Fragile Self*. Farnham: Ashgate.

Gardiner, S. 2011. *A Perfect Moral Storm: The Ethical Tragedy of Climate Change*. New York: Oxford University Press.

IPCC. 2007. *Fourth Assessment Report, Summary for Policy Makers*. Cambridge: Cambridge University Press.

Kant, I. 1974. *Die Religion innerhalb der Grenzen der bloßen Vernunft*. Stuttgart: Reclam.

Korsgaard, C. 1996. *Creating the Kingdom of Ends*. Cambridge: Cambridge University Press.

Korsgaard, C. 2009. *Self-Constitution. Agency, Identity and Integrity*. New York: Oxford University Press.

MacIntyre, A. 1999. 'Social Structures and their Threats to Moral Agency'. *Philosophy* 74, 311–329.

Miller, S. 2011. 'Corruption' in Edward N. Zalta (ed.),*The Stanford Encyclopedia of Philosophy*. Available at: http://plato.stanford.edu/archives/spr2011/entries/corruption/

Miller, Z. 2006. 'Best Efforts? Differing Judicial Interpretations of a Familiar Term'. *Arizona Law Review* 48, 615–638.

Ott, K. 2004. 'Essential Components of Future Ethics' in R. Döring and M. Rühs (eds), *Ökonomische Rationalität und praktische Vernunft*. Würzburg: Königshausen & Neumann, 83–108.

Setiya, K. 2011. 'Intention'. in Edward N. Zalta (ed.), *The Stanford Encyclopedia of Philosophy*. Available at: http://plato.stanford.edu/archives/spr2011/entries/intention/

Stroud, S. 2010. 'Is Procrastination Weakness of Will?' in C. Andreou and M. D. White (eds), *The Thief of Time, Philosophical Essays on Procrastination*. New York: Oxford University Press, 51–67.

Thaler, R. and Sunstein, C. 2008. *Nudge: Improving Decisions about Health, Wealth, and Happiness*. New Haven, CT: Yale University Press.

Wilson, G. and Shpall, S. 2012. 'Action', in Edward N. Zalta (ed.), *The Stanford Encyclopedia of Philosophy*. Available at: http://plato.stanford.edu/archives/sum2012/entries/action/.

8   Ideology and practice of the 'Green Economy'

World views shaping science and politics

Joachim H. Spangenberg

Even for persons with shared values, their world view or ontology choices make a significant difference when it comes to developing or endorsing policies. For instance, while an environmental economics ontology trusting in solutions from yet unknown technologies, from commodification of nature and from market forces is not a suitable basis for solving sustainability problems, an ontology of nested systems, with the environment the metasystem as in ecological econom-ics, fits as the basis for developing substantial sustainable development strategies. Changing the world view is a necessary condition for successful sustainability policies, and transparency regarding the basic world views is crucial.

1. Introduction

Moral ideals – for all the limitations they face in shaping living conditions – are considered one of the main determinants of human individual and political behaviour. However, it is not only ideal principles that determine which motiva-tion to act results from them, but also the world view, the ontology held by decision makers (for the purposes of this chapter, world view, pre-analytical vision, metaphysics and ontology do not need to be distinguished) which is deter-mining the practical conclusions from moral principles and ethical attitudes.

This can be illustrated by the vexed relationship of ecology and economics, in particular the turn of concerned ecologists to economics (as 'the language of power') in the search for more attention for their worrying insights, and the attempts of concerned economists to broaden their discipline's pre-analytical vision to include the thus far neglected environment. This apparent convergence, however, tends to hide the deeply different world views that are characterised by mutually exclusive topologies. As a result, the relationship remains an uneasy one; solutions suggested by economists do not necessarily find support amongst ecolo-gists (or for that, the population at large, as far as it has not undergone an economics education, like the majority of the political, business and cultural elites) and vice versa. However, while without understanding the basically diverg-ing ontologies it is not possible to understand the reasons for the differing conclusions, and to make an informed choice as condition of any democratic process, the world views behind the positions are hardly ever made explicit.

Science for sustainability, in the sense of disciplinary contributions to sustainability problems, has to accommodate such divergences. Any meaningful inter- and trans-disciplinary science of sustainability, however, must insist on transparency regarding the underlying ontologies and on the struggle for joint – or at least non-contradictory – world views, as otherwise a synthesis of results as a starting point for problem-solving strategies and advice is impossible (Spangenberg 2011). This holds true for environmental problems such as climate change or biodiversity loss (the case we analyse here in some more details) as much as for global social problems.

2. Ecologists and economists: the biodiversity case

In the beginning, there was a shared concern: wetlands, rainforests, deserts and iconic species were recognised to be at risk, locally and globally. Due to climate change and management attitudes, agro-biodiversity and food security are threatened, locally adapted but less productive animal races and plant varieties are getting lost. Addressing these challenges to biodiversity requires both scientific knowledge and changes in politics, business and consumption practice. Some ecologists (admittedly, a minority) recognised that to contribute to this, they had to collaborate with those more familiar with political and social (and less with ecological) systems. Similarly, some economists (admittedly, a small minority) saw that such problems could not be addressed within the prevailing neoclassical world view. This ontology sees the economy as an exchange of goods against money, and of money against labour – society, production, resources and the environment are exogenous to this world view, they play no role, do not even exist. Environmental and ecological economists realised the need to modify their perception of the world to include the environment – environmental economists by extending the scope of their models to include the environment, ecological economists by redefining the economy as a part of the larger systems society and nature.

3. A change of the ecologists' world view: convergence

The group of social scientists with whom ecologists seem at first glance to have the most in common is economists:

- a shared preoccupation with the role of competition for scarce resources, which gave the impression of a common intellectual heritage;
- a largely positivistic and quantitative orientation, which made them open to seemingly similar statistical techniques;
- the vogue for mathematical modelling, albeit with different kinds of models.

For ecologists, such an engagement with social sciences is a major shift of strategy (not necessarily of their ontology), involving them not only in novel subject matter but also in unfamiliar research methods required by the increasing complexity of the system under analysis, modes of understanding and measurement/indication standards and traditions (Figure 8.1).

As a consequence, ecologists developed an instrumental and a non-instrumental attitude towards economics (with intermediaries). The *instrumental approach* does not adopt the economic world view but translates ecological claims into the dominant discourse of money: 'We value what we can put a price on' (UNEP 2011). This results in endorsing three steps thought to save biodiversity:

1. Allocating a monetary value to biodiversity, ecosystems and ecosystem services (ESS) makes their real, currently neglected value visible to decision makers and the public at large.
2. Internalising the cost incurred by biodiversity loss, ESS degradation or ecosystem restoration into the market mechanism makes it possible to achieve optimal results in the most efficient manner.
3. This message has to be conveyed to policy makers in money terms, as that is what really counts in these circles.

The *non-instrumental attitude* buys into the economic system of value determination, accepting that the value of ecosystems is determined by their price. Doing so, they – often unconsciously – change the object of analysis and implicitly endorse a change of methods, leaving the natural science domain.

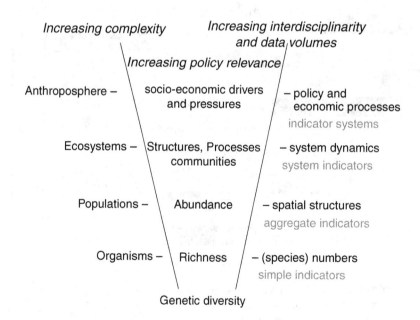

Figure 8.1 Increasing system complexity requires increasing interdisciplinarity – a challenge for ecologists as much as for economists

Discipline	–> Biology	–> Ecology	–> Economics
Object of analysis	–> system traits	–> functions	–> ecosystem services
Kind of method	–> *descriptive*	–> *analytical*	–> *social: subjective, collective*
			–> *economic: preference based*

This attitude fits well with the world view of environmental economists as it implies applying the 'laws' of economics to natural systems, instead of vice versa as ecological economists would have it. Thus, for tactical reasons or whole-heartedly (the latter based on a change of their ontology), these ecologists endorse an economic world view – made possible by the fact that environmental economists have modified the neoclassical world view, offering the apparent opportunity for convergence. Most often economy and society are treated as 'external', and their impacts as 'external influences' the ecosystem has to deal with. The instrumental approach to economics sustains this world view, while the non-instrumental attitude tends to endorse the dominant environmental economics ontology (see Figure 8.2).

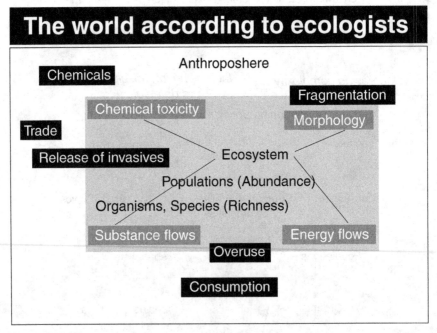

Figure 8.2 The ecologists' world view: most often economy and society are treated as 'external', and their impacts as 'external influences' the ecosystem has to deal with. The instrumental approach to economics sustains this world view, while the non-instrumental attitude tends to endorse the dominant environmental economics ontology

4. Distinct world views in economics

While different schools of thought co-exist in all disciplines, their differences are much more pronounced in the social than in the natural sciences. While – at least for external observers – different approaches in natural science are often complementary, in economics the different paradigms tend to be mutually exclusive, resulting in a discourse not aiming at a synthesis of different theoretical approaches, but at the exclusion of minority positions without falsification (the widespread lack of an empirical basis may be one of the reasons). The different ontologies tell mutually exclusive stories about how the world really is and how it should be perceived.

Comparing the ecological economics and the neoclassical environmental economics ontologies, two basic discrepancies can be identified causing all or most of the differences between the two bodies of theory and the resulting policy recommendations: the topology and the integration of thermodynamics into the world view. While the latter issue has long been an item of debate (since Georgescu-Roegen 1971), the former has not been dealt with extensively; it is the focus of this analysis.

Environmental economics is a derivate of neoclassical economics; like neoclassic economics it is based on an 'atomic' view of humans and society (agents are independent individuals, not interacting except through the market). Value is determined by demand and supply in (mostly perfect) markets, there is no inherent value of goods or services (Rink and Wächter 2002). Instead, value is considered as an externally attributed utility, a subjectively defined quality that does not permit interpersonal comparisons; without any supra-individual standard individual utility can be re-defined case by case so that every human action can be interpreted ex post as an attempt to maximise it. Ex ante assessments are not possible as the definition refers to the results and is thus only available ex post. As utility is not measurable, often the price is used as a proxy for utility. The purpose of neoclassical environmental economics is to describe the optimal allocation of goods in exchange processes, thus increasing the overall exchange value that is considered as a proxy for welfare.

Environmental economics is about to become the mainstream variant of neoclassical economics. It emerged when it became obvious that environmental influences are relevant cost factors for the economic process, be it that the cost of resources were increasing (the 2011 rare earths price shock was an important trigger), or that the disposal of waste and other effluents became expensive (in European manufacturing about half of all expenditures are for materials management, and only a quarter for labour (Bleischwitz *et al.* 2009)). This led to the necessity to extend the body of theory to 'internalise' the formerly 'external' environment. In doing so, environmental economics builds upon the neoclassical market equilibrium approach and the optimum expected from undisturbed market forces in welfare economics. The extension provided is recognising the value of nature as a production factor: as the environment made itself felt in the economic process, it was conceptually integrated *as a part of the economic system.*

Nature and its components are consequently considered economic goods, commodities, as this is the only category of goods the theory seriously deals with. Thus nature and its services need to be priced to be used efficiently. Producing the maximum welfare possible from scarce resources requires allowing the market mechanism to function.

It is in this sense, that environmental damage is the most severe market fail-ure ever (UNEP 2011). According to the environmental economics explanation, this failure has been caused by the fact that nature, with its sources and sinks a part of the economic system, had no price, and was overexploited due to this undervaluation. The environmental economists' topology can be represented as shown in Figure 8.3.

Another implication of viewing nature and its components as commodities is that the components of nature and its services are seen as essentially independ-ent entities, which can be traded individually, each fetching its own market price that will then guarantee a welfare maximising result. To achieve this, the compo-nents of nature – often common pool goods or public goods – need to be transformed into objects that can be bought and sold, with privatising them the preferred means towards this end. If they become scarce, their price will rise and cost-effective protection measures will be taken. Cost effectiveness is given if the costs of protection are not higher than the value of the good or service rescued,

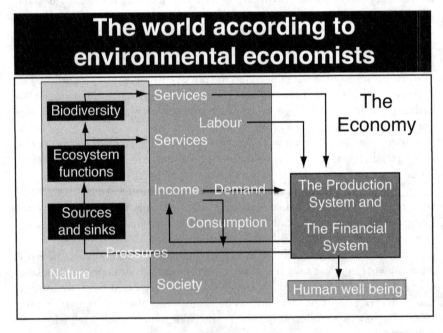

Figure 8.3 The environmental economists' topology: the economy is the metasystem

leading to a welfare maximum of the outcome (Coase 1960). If privatisation is not possible (such as for the air to breathe), cost internalisation can be achieved by levying fees or taxes on the consumption of these resources reflecting their (externalised) value and bringing it back into the market mechanism (green taxation, eco-taxes; see Pigou 1932).

Ecological economists are a later brand of environmentally concerned economists; the sub-discipline was interdisciplinary from the outset. Although some forerunners can be identified (e.g. K. E. Boulding in the USA or K. W. Kapp in Germany), ecological economics emerged as an independent school of thought only in the early 1970s, influenced by the prevailing zeitgeist. It perceives the economy as part of the larger system of society, and society as a part of the overall ecosystem. In this view, it is necessary to clearly distinguish an object and its price: the market, based on price mechanisms, may provide the economic optimum (under certain, not too realistic assumptions, beyond damage costs etc. to be included in market prices), but not necessarily a social or ecological optimum. These are determined according to criteria of the larger systems, i.e. outside the economy and its mechanisms. H. Daly (2000) illustrates the difference by emphasising that some environmental economists do not expect major damages from climate change as the sector most affected, agriculture, only makes up for less than 3 per cent of the GDP in most affluent countries, so the economic loss would be limited – but what, Daly asks, would these people eat once the 'negligible' 3 per cent have collapsed? This case exemplifies that ignoring the physical economy of material and energy flows leads to gross misperceptions of challenges such as biodiversity loss and climate change (see Figure 8.4).

The ecological world view considers ecosystems as complex entities that cannot be subdivided into discrete, independent objects to be traded, and thus as having no market price. However, what can be and is traded are specific products, goods and services, such as all harvested goods. Over-exploitation of harvesting opportunities may however decrease the environmental value of a system, i.e. its capability to provide (at least partly) economically unvalued, but ecologically important functions and services. Thus, in this world view, not extending the market regime to biological objects, functions and services is considered the most appropriate tool, and instead limits to the market mechanism are highlighted. Decisions have to be taken according to a set of societal values, with cost consideration one legitimate but not necessarily decisive concern as 'economic value is not an adequate measure of how important a service may be to human survival' (Aronson et al. 2009: 10).

While sharing the call for political decisions based on societal values, some ecological economists disagree even with this limited role of economic values, for conceptual reasons. Sagoff (2008) describes biospheric and climate systems as 'lumpy', explaining that 'lumpy goods' are goods that cannot be provided incrementally, divided into pieces and sold in units. The choice is either to save, protect, 'buy' the whole system, or let it go bust. There is no way to trade marginal amounts – and thus no price: politics and not markets are needed to provide solutions (Sagoff 2008: 232).

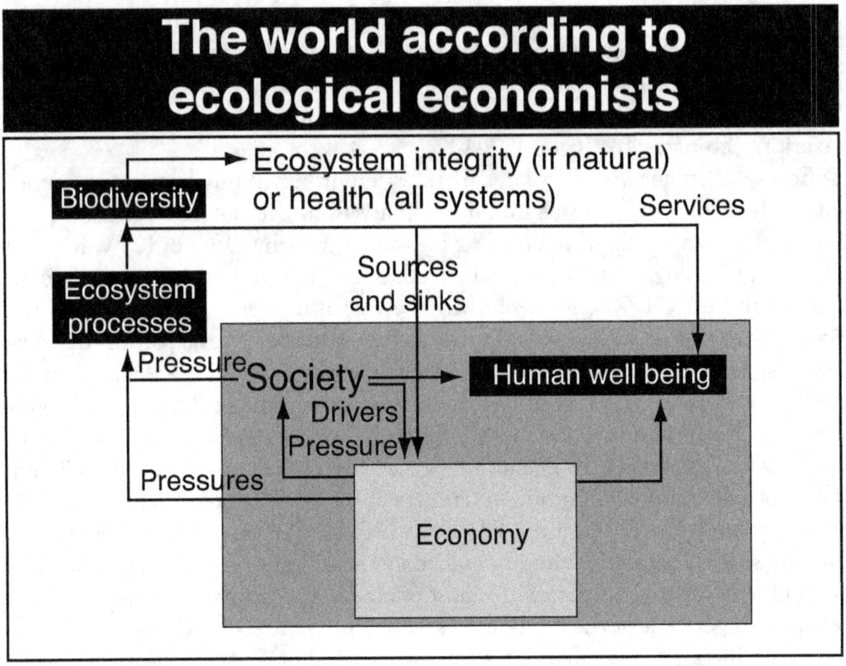

The world according to ecological economists

Figure 8.4 The ecological economists' topology: nested systems, the environment as metasystem

The ecological attitude also alters the role of economic instruments: they no longer measure the value of nature to include it into the market (commodification), but they are incentives introduced to bring about behavioural change. Their effectiveness, assessed by monitoring behavioural change, is more essential than their efficiency, and thus their level is independent of any value calculation. This avoids economically optimal solutions that may include the loss of 'useless', and thus not 'valuable' ecosystems or species.

Environmental and ecological economists are thus easiest distinguished by the fact that the former perceive nature as part of the economy, to be managed according to economic rules, while the latter consider the economy to be part of nature and subject to its laws, not least the entropy law, and to be managed according to the limitations set by these laws.

5. Disappointment and divergence

In the course of time, some of the problems of working on the basis of an unfamiliar ontology became obvious. They range from more technical aspects (common terms such as resilience may have different normative and analytical connotations between human and ecological systems; even common methods such as regression analysis can be applied and interpreted differently) to strategic disappointments and value conflicts.

Strategically, many ecologists adopted the language of economics instrumentally, hoping for increased resonance with decision makers. However, it has become obvious that politics does not react to all kinds of economic figures; in particular, hypothetical value measurements such as those based on contingent valuation (willingness to pay analyses) have hardly any political influence. Politics reacts sensitively to economic figures only if real money flows are affected. They can be, for example:

- damage costs, e.g. cost of harvest losses caused by the loss of pollination, and thus the cost of inaction;
- repair costs, e.g. the cost of labour and pesticides against weeds and pests no longer kept in check by biocontrol;
- avoidance cost, e.g. the investment needed to avoid avalanches and the damages they cause;
- replacement costs, e.g. the cost of hand pollination replacing pollinators;
- option values, i.e. the value of options no longer available due to damages and the expenditures they cause.

However, while these kinds of cost figures effectively influence policy makers, they are not at all new – the hope behind embarking on economic arguments was to monetise, in addition to them, the ecological and inherent values of ecosystems and biodiversity to turn them into pro-conservation arguments. This hope has mostly failed in political reality, undermining one of the strategic motives for 'going economics'.

Finally, bioscientists, whether they phrase their request in economic terms or not, tend to be morally motivated when arguing for the conservation of biodiversity. The value system they hold is distinct from the economic one (at least for those endorsing economics only instrumentally); realising this discrepancy (see Table 8.1) makes the instrumental use of economics a questionable undertaking. In a nutshell (and admittedly simplifying a complex issue), *ecological value* is a characteristic of a system component, describing the importance for its environment. It is an externally defined, location and context dependent value FOR something. Social and economic value are externally defined, with *social value* the value OF something for a specific group, and *economic value* a location independent exchange value determined by the market, the value OF something in general.

A *value described in monetary terms is a price or a price offer* (before a market equilibrium is reached, offers are made comprising the later price plus the consumer or producer surplus) and implies, as for all market goods, substitutability against other goods of the same price; non market goods have a (use) value that cannot be expressed in monetary terms. Unique goods like species have an inherent, non-instrumental value. They have no price but a dignity (Immanuel Kant).

Table 8.1 Values and value creation processes in environmental economic and in ecological perception

Economic value	Ecological value
Integrall linked to the number of beneficiaries and the socio-economic context (TEEB for Pol. Makers: 8)	A natural property of ecosystems, with other ecosystem elements the relavant context
Subjective value	Inherent, objective value
Maximises returns	Maximises resilience

Economic drivers	Ecological drivers
Scarcity	Energy and resource availability
Not: energy and resource availability	Not necessarily: rareness

Evolution driven by	Evolution and species formation by
innovation, competition, globalisation	mutation, selection, isolation

Economic measurement	Ecological measurement
Analysing	Valuing
Incremental change, at the margin, no real time	Multiple parameters, time series

Economic conceptualisation of ESF	Ecological conceptualisation of ESF
Functions = service potentials	Functions = biological traits
Linear development assumed	non-linear behaviour (the margin can be a threshold), cyclic behaviour possible

6. Down to earth: the green economy

The diverging world views described lead to different policy receipts, even in the case of shared intentions such as climate protection or safeguarding biodiversity. Worse, what is recommended under one world view may be identified as devastating under the other. The 'Green Economy' (UNEP 2011) can be used as a case in point to illustrate these effects.

The 'Green New Deal', 'Green Growth' (the OECD mantra) or 'Green Economy' (UNEP 2011; in EU Commission parlance the 'inclusive green economy') threaten to shift the focus away from sustainable development. But where do they shift it? This is not exactly clear; extended discussions including the Rio+20 UNCSD summit have not produced a broadly agreed definition of what a 'Green Economy' really is or should be. The promises are striking (conserving nature, overcoming poverty, providing equity and creating jobs), but the means, measures and philosophy behind look all too familiar, *environmental modernisation* reloaded, and freshened up with a significant dose of neo-liberal political thinking. In consequence, in particular the ways how the social objectives are to be achieved remain either unspecified or lack credibility (changing power structures is not an issue). In the versions promoted by UNEP, OECD and the EU Commission, despite their differences, it clearly is an environmental economics concept. This becomes obvious not only by the choice of concepts and models, but already by the terminology applied (as in most discourses, the way of describing reality reveals the way of perceiving it, i.e. the ontology).

To UNEP, the sustainability crisis is the biggest market failure ever. Describing it this way reveals a specific kind of thinking: a market failure occurs when the market fails to deliver what in principle it could have delivered, and once the bug is fixed the market will solve the problem. However, unsustainable development is not a market failure to be fixed but a market system failure: expecting results from the market it cannot deliver (not even a hypothetical ideal market could), like long-term thinking, environmental consciousness and social responsibility. Whoever considers the failure of sustainable development to be a market failure must call for better markets, not for replacing market decisions by political prioritising.

Another aspect of the environmental economics paradigm is revealed by the EU when describing the world in terms of capital stocks, natural, manufactured and financial (which do not really fit together – manufactured capital is stuff to produce other stuff, a means, while financial capital is money to produce money, an end in itself) as the basis of the green economy, and human and social capital outside it. The capital terminology indicates the economic world view: humans and the environment are resources or production factors to be exploited, and their value lies in their contribution to the economic process, i.e. to profit generation. It is a key terminology in environmental economics, as shown essentially neoclassical economics endogenising the environment as a resource. The key difference to the environmentalist (and ecological economics) view that, vice versa, the economy is just one part of the environment, and dependent on it for its functioning and survival, has been described above.

As capital stocks are usually measured in monetary units, prices not qualities are the basis of their analysis. In this situation each capital stock is a substitute for any other, meaning that accumulating wealth (manufactured and financial capital) compensates for the destruction of nature, health and human relations. This possibility of compensation is the basic assumption in what has been called 'weak sustainability' (but too weak to be sustainable).[1] Substitutability is the basis for 'market solutions', and the market is relied upon to stimulate the technical solutions to political problems environmental modernisation/weak sustainability relies upon. As a result, the business orientation towards maximum profit without obligations to preserve public goods remains unrestricted, trusting that the 'invisible hand' of the market, as the neo-classical dogma contends, will turn private greed into public benefits. Facts on social polarisation do not shake or brake this ideological confidence.

Another characteristic of neoclassical economics prevailing in environmental economics is the strong belief in technology (much more so than amongst engineers): for whatever problem is emerging, market forces will successfully stimulate the development of problem-solving technologies. Of course, any substantial sustainable development will require replacing much of the prevailing set of technologies with environmentally and socially benign alternatives, embedded in sustainable consumption patterns. But will such technologies be available (leaving aside for the moment the fact that technology is not a panacea to sustainability problems)? In order to reduce resource consumption to a sustainable level, investment in innovation is necessary (with the emphasis on developing sustainable – or less unsustainable – technologies: that is more needed than the transfer of not sufficiently efficient current technologies), with volumes of investment significantly higher than the current level in the affluent countries. For instance, in the USA today the investment into the real economy is close to a 30-year low, while profit margins are higher than at any time in the past 65 years, and expected to increase even further (Buttonwood 2012), making the current casino capitalism also economically unsustainable. For the transition to a low carbon, dematerialised production system, investment must be mobilised on a large scale, by re-domesticating capital. This requires reforms of the international financial institutions, the multilateral trading system, the big banks – but these issues are dismissed as being beyond the remit of the 'Green Economy' discourse. However, with a financial system running amok, sustainable development cannot be achieved, and not even a 'Green Economy'. Stronger regulation of corporate accountability and financial markets is needed. Requiring private companies to 'consider sustainability issues' and include them in reporting is part of this, but grossly insufficient. Instead, building sustainability concerns into the heart of the international financial institutions and the world trade system is sorely necessary, but this will require enormous political efforts. Unfortunately, the political will to invest in them is not (yet) visible anywhere, and the 'Green Economy' debate nurtures the illusion that sustainability challenges could be overcome without such efforts.

Without question, many of the components of a 'Green Economy' are important and have been long since demanded by environmentally concerned citizens from all walks of life – for instance the improvement of energy and resource efficiency by means of ecological tax reforms and the abolition of environmentally harmful and socially unnecessary subsidies, more recycling, a transition to renewable energies in industrial as well as in so-called developing countries, and more. But decoupling of resource use and economic growth, the transition to green technologies, and ecological modernisation have been propagated for more than 30 years. So questions remain whether the 'Green Economy' as advocated by leading institutional actors will really make a difference.

7. Three flaws: objectives, tools, and the not-so-hidden agenda

The objective of the green economy strategy is essentially to revitalise the conditions of doing business. Faced with peak oil and global resource limits (sources and sinks), which make a reduction of consumption a realistic perspective, it is the attempt to turn the challenge into a business opportunity. This resonates well with the business sector, where sustainability, understood as resource efficiency, has become the buzzword of so-called 'Corporate Social Responsibility' or CSR strategies.

> [Although CSR] has a hard earned reputation for flakiness [today] managers are increasingly aware that they must squeeze the most out of finite resources. Sustainability thus fits nicely with lean production and tight supply-chain management. Indeed, it provides new ideas for reducing cost ... Gone are the days when it was mainly about managing corporate reputations – or 'greenwashing' ... Today's iteration of CSR is ... encouraging businesses to become more frugal in their use of resources and more imaginative in the way they think about competitive advantage.
>
> Spangenberg 2012a

Pricing nature as a production factor turns 'frugality' into a competitive advantage welcomed by major corporations. As pointed out above, it is understood to heal a market failure, and with this 'correction' the market is expected to deliver an 'optimal' result (again).

Thus, the pricing of environmental 'externalities' (damages which are considered external to the market economy, and not recognised as its necessary outcome as already shown by Kapp (1950); social 'externalities' are mostly ignored) is expected to solve the environmental problems; green technology is perceived as the basis of the next growth cycle. So what IT technology has delivered (and what genetic engineering and nanotechnology failed to realise) is now expected from green technology: to provide the technological basis for another period of unfettered economic growth. This is why ministries of the economy and business corporations convert from hostility towards environmental demands to endorsing them – but only as long as they do not imply less consumption (and thus profit), but more technology.

However, this expectation is flawed in more than one sense: a decoupling of resource consumption that would permit a >95 per cent reduction of CO_2 emissions as needed in industrialised countries is hardly imaginable, so even the technologically greenest growth will imply that necessary reduction targets are missed (a 3 per cent growth rate over 50 years overcompensates a factor 10 efficiency improvement). Economic growth intensifies the problems; for instance, the 20 per cent gain in carbon intensity of the global GDP since 1992 has been by far overcompensated by economic growth. Secondly, the technologies developed or under development are dependent on scarce resources (the role of rare earths has become a prominent example in the last years), so that the strategy is dependent on the unlimited access to resources mainly located in the South. Enforcing free trade, free inflows of investment and free outflows of profits (supported by military superiority and where necessary military interventions) are the methods of choice to guarantee access to those resources. International trade agreements granting corporations the right to claim compensation if democratically decided policy changes affect their profit expectations, as now under negotiation between the EU, USA and Canada, are a prominent means to this end.

This has been labelled a neo-colonial attitude, which is only partially right. After the experiences in Iraq and Afghanistan, the appetite for semi-colonial occupations has been largely lost, and instead economic take-overs (such as the OECD's MAI, which failed due to citizens' protests, but also the new EU raw materials strategy) are preferred (Spangenberg 2010), supported by the threat of short-term, maritime based interventions (the 'offshore strategy'). US, EU and NATO military strategies are explicitly aimed at securing free access to crucial resources. Joseph Nye, formerly chairman of the US National Security Council, summarised this attitude in one sentence: 'Markets and economic power rest on political frameworks, and American military power provides that framework' (Gerson 2012).

The market and the political frameworks are thus at the core of the environmental economics-based environmental modernisation strategy, presented as a new green economy idea. Here again, the green economy strategy does not appear very new, but a repetition and extension of former approaches: there is no resource sovereignty, no limits to resource consumption, no minimum resource supply for all humans, as the basic assumption is that 'the market rules okay'. As long as environmental (and social) damages are considered to be 'externalities', and the economic optimum expected from market mechanisms to simultaneously be the social and environmental optimum, and markets to be the most efficient kind of regulatory mechanism, it appears plausible to minimise environmental damage by turning environmental goods and services into market goods. Thus a further commodification of nature and a regulation by market instruments is considered the most promising way forward, making nature an exchangeable good regardless of local human needs and natural carrying capacities, let alone the dignity of nature itself. The commons need to be privatised to turn them into market goods, goes the argument, this being a superior way of protecting them, ignoring the fact that they are goods in the possession of communities, or belong to humankind as a whole, and this non-economic value is destroyed by turning them into commodities.

Privatising public goods and commodification of the commons are not an instrument for safeguarding a green future but hand out the common heritage of mankind to private profit interest. Public wealth is spoilt to increase private riches, use value turned into exchange value, publicly owned abundant goods in scarce market commodities. The 'tragedy of the commons' (Hardin 1968) is still frequently cited (according to which public or common pool goods are necessarily overexploited and run down) although being counterfactual (Ostrom *et al.*

1999) and representing a racist and right-wing extremist point of view (Clark 2010). Instead of turning even more public goods into private property, sustainable development requires re-establishing the primacy of politics over the market and of public over private interest, and a decommodification of human labour, rather than a commodification of nature. This criticism is not new – in the nineteenth century the inverse correlation of public wealth and private riches was known as the Lauderdale paradox (Foster and Clark 2009), but still private goods are protected in almost every constitution, but common goods in almost none. In consequence, greening the business world, although overdue for at least 35 years, is a necessary step, but a far cry from leading to a sustainable economy, let alone a sustainable society.

However, rejecting all economic instruments out of hand would mean throwing out the baby with the bath water: some of these instruments, like an ecological tax reform and the abolition of environmentally and socially harmful subsidies, are urgently needed. They are economic tools to achieve politically defined targets. As opposed to that, artificial markets for public goods, where – as we currently experience – the market sets the targets, offer no effective protection but rather create new risks for humankind, nature and the environment, as seen in the EU emission trading scheme and the REDD mechanism.

Besides the ideological attitude, there is an economic reason why the commodification of nature and its services is promoted: creating a new kind of tradable goods constitutes new fields for business activities, and provides enormous opportunities for growth and profit. As high profits and low investment into the real economy create a huge surplus of money looking for profitable investment opportunities, and as these are mostly found in speculation, it is no surprise that after the IT and the housing bubble have burst, speculators are now focussing on minerals, oil and food, causing skyrocketing prices with devastating impacts on the global poor and their daily life. While resource prices in real terms have been falling throughout the twentieth century, that trend has changed since the turn of the millennium. The price rises in the twenty-first century, for all resources, from minerals to metals, energy carriers and food, have already overcompensated the whole decrease accumulated in the last century.

Resource efficiency strategies (as the recent EU one) and changing consumption patterns are overdue attempts to manage not the supply side, but the demand side of the economy. Although a necessary element of any really green economy, they are so far rather considered a complement than an alternative to the expansionist strategy: they tend to be too weak and mobilise too little support in business and politics to be able to replace supply securing expansionist strategies. Overall, expansionist strategies securing supply are dominating demand management, the attempt to do with what we have, i.e. the sustainability option (Spangenberg 2010).

The primary macro-level objective of the green economy initiative is enabling future economic growth by decoupling growth from environmental limitations. Decoupling as such is not bad – compare it to current policy, e.g. in Canada where oil production from tar sands is set to rise from 2m barrels a day (b/d) to

3.3m b/d by 2020, each barrel causing three to four times the greenhouse gas emissions the same amount of conventional oil does – a nightmare for the climate and a reason for Canada to withdraw from the Kyoto protocol. And what is the reason? It is 'because natural gas exports, long the mainstay of the energy industry, are threatened by shale gas in the United States' (another unsustainable means of energy production emitting greenhouse gas, banned for instance in France, Bulgaria and in parts of Germany) and 'replacing gas exports with tar-sand oils is vital for economic growth' (Spangenberg 2012b). Demonising environmentalists, threats to charities and dismantling environmental legislation and democratic rights in this case go hand in hand with growth mania.

However, decoupling economic development and resource consumption is necessary but by no means sufficient. As reducing resource expenditure is reducing operating cost, efficiency is another driver of growth and in the end can lead to increasing consumption (a phenomenon known to economists since the nineteenth century as 'Jevons' paradox'). Furthermore, for a capitalist market economy a stationary state is not an option: the advanced goods-producing economy requires the permanent generation of new demand (dressed and partly perceived as needs); otherwise saturation and a marginal profit of zero are threatening. Thus ever new products are pushed into the market, advertising suggests their indispensability for human well-being, or their character as essentials for social status; the critique of these phenomena is not new and goes back to Veblen (1899).

The second, less explicit objective is avoiding distribution debates – without growth, more justice cannot be generated by distributing surplus, but only by taking from those who have and giving to those who do not, taking from the 1 per cent and giving to – let's say – the lower 50 per cent. It is against this backdrop that the social attitudes of the wealthy groups in the affluent countries is eroding – their recognition of poverty in and between countries is fading away, their willingness to donate money or even share their riches is reaching historical lows. They consider their wealth as something they deserve, even feel that they do not get their fair share and feel called upon to give to 'undeserving', 'worthless' lower income groups (Zick *et al.* 2010). Redistribution instruments like the pre-Reagan US income tax level of 94 per cent (an element of the New Deal shining up in none of the 'Green New Deal' proposals) are no longer imaginable, the bourgeois society is eroding. Less equality contributes to less social cohesion, and – empirically – to a more violent society with more compensatory or addictive consumption (Wilkinson and Pickett 2009).

Another downside of the neo-classical environmental economics world view is its image of society as composed of independent individuals – accommodating collective processes is not within its reach. This 'methodological individualism' did not prevail in classical economics: Adam Smith acknowledged the right of every citizen to have access to goods sufficient to lead a dignified life in her respective society. In fact, Adam Smith went well beyond the standard characterisations of living conditions and considered such functionings as not being 'ashamed to appear in public', and analysed how the commodity requirements for this achievement – clothing, shoes, etc. – varied with social customs and cultural norms (Smith 1776). 'In analysing these relationships, Adam Smith not only distanced his own approach from commodity fetishism and wealth maximisation, he also showed the social nature of these relationships between commodities (and opulence), on the one hand, and capabilities (and achievements of living conditions), on the other (Sen 1986).

However, this societal context plays no role any more in modern neoclassical economics (they are 'delegated' to other disciplines), and thus justice as an inter-personal value relation, and democracy (as government for and of the people) as an interpersonal process both play no role, neither in economic models nor in policy prescriptions. For sustainable development, however, democracy, stake-holder empowerment and human rights are the key pillars of the most neglected dimension, the institutional one (Spangenberg 2007). Unlike Agenda 21, which emphasises the need for empowerment of women, youth, trade unions and civil society organisations like environmental and development NGOs, the main-stream sustainable development discourse has neglected this dimension. As opposed to that, the economic dimension was not neglected, but severely misin-terpreted: maximising profits is a far cry from creating a resilient economic system which can be sustained in the long run (Spangenberg 2005).

8. The really green economy alternative: applying the ecological economics world view

If the environmental economics world view, and the 'Green Economy' derived from it cannot plausibly deliver on substantial sustainable development, what about the ecological economics approach with its distinct world view? For obvi-ous reasons, it will advocate other tools and targets. Starting with the very beginning of the modern Sustainable Development debate, the 1987 Brundtland Commission report 'Our Common Future', criteria can be derived to assess the sustainability of policy proposals based on the ecological economics world view. The World Commission for Environment and Development defined Sustainable Development as:

> Sustainable development is development that meets the needs of the pres-ent without compromising the ability of future generations to meet their own needs. It contains within it two key concepts:
> 1. The concept of 'needs', in particular the essential needs of the world's poor, to which overriding priority should be given, and
> 2. The idea of limitations imposed by the state of technology and social organisation on the environment's ability to meet present and future needs.
>
> WCED 1987: 43

The Brundtland report's praise for economic growth has to be understood in this frame: economic growth was justified and considered necessary as far as it is instrumental to reach both objectives, satisfying needs and respecting limits. Instead, all too often, only the first part of the definition is quoted and its lack of precision bemoaned, to come up with 'complementary' explanations based on a neo-classical and neo-liberal world view, promoting economic growth as a priority issue for sustainable development.

In consequence, any policy for a substantial 'Green Economy' must address both these criteria, the concept of needs and the idea of limitation, if it is to contribute to sustainable development. Ecological modernisation programs either not addressing human needs and poverty eradication, and/or discussing resource efficiency without referring to limits in absolute terms cannot claim to be implementing a 'Green economy in the context of sustainable development' as propagated at the UNCSD 2012 conference. Unlimited growth, however green, is not sustainable (it is not even development).

Furthermore, besides the environmental, social and economic dimensions, UNCED 1992, for all its weaknesses, highlighted questions of influence and power which were completely off the agenda at UNCSD 20 years on. This is not due to a lack of knowledge or insight – it would be unfair to say that nothing has been learned from 20 years of failures. The UN World Economic and Social Survey 2011 (United Nations 2011) has taken a closer look at technology potentials (including renewable energies and organic agriculture, but – with limited plausibility – combining them with genetic engineering and nuclear power). The report concludes that: (a) technology is not enough and must be accompanied by behavioural and consumption change; and (b) that strong governments, able and willing to act, setting up a politically defined framework forcing business sector investment and innovation in a direction towards sustainable development are indispensable. UNCTAD draws similar conclusions: technological, population-expansion and governance constraints, as well key systemic issues cast a long shadow on the Green Growth hopes, and continued growth intensifies the challenges, in particular for the necessary global greenhouse gas emission reductions. A reductionist, limited and gradual change approach such as the 'Green Economy' will not be sufficient; it may rather offer false hope and excuses (Hoffmann 2011). The International Trade Union Confederation ITUC, while supporting a substantial 'Green Economy' strategy based on investments of at least 2 per cent of GDP per year into greening, and expecting hundreds of millions of decent new jobs from it, insists that 'governments must set targets for green jobs and provide the legislative and regulatory conditions so workers can have secure jobs, living wages and creating a healthy society and environment' (Burrow 2012). All these global organisations are aware that deregulation, privatisation and market solutions will not bring about what is needed and promised. Without taking the structural factors of societies (their institutional and economic system) into account, and without changing them for the better, any sustainable development strategy is bound to fail. Thus, all four dimensions have to be taken into account when trying to develop effective strategies; UNCSD neglected half of them, and in the emerging Sustainable Development Goals (SDGs) environmental objectives had a hard time to be taken on board, while institutional objectives are missing rather completely.

Sustainable development is meant to give (back) a purpose to the economy, serving human needs. These needs, however, are not identical with the greed of capital owners and shareholders. The needs of the global poor in particular are needs not underpinned by purchasing power, and thus do not resonate in the market. As meeting them is the first key criterion for sustainable development, and the market cannot serve their needs, it is the wrong distributive mechanism – free market shareholder value capitalism cannot be sustainable.

Instead, sustainable development can be described as a development with resource consumption between the upper and lower limits of our environmental space (FoEE 1995). The upper limits have been quantified recently by science, identifying the 'safe operating space for humankind' (Rockström *et al.* 2009), which can be translated into upper limits for resource consumption (Spangenberg 2014). Such limits can of course be extended by social and technological development (the former including redistribution mechanisms), but cannot be replaced to give way to unlimited growth; but this is exactly what Green Growth (and essentially also the UNEP Green Economy (UNEP 2011)) are calling for. Limits to growth, or resource capping, are not part of these policy concepts. Thus, they are not sustainable (Lorek and Spangenberg 2014).

Regarding the lower limit or floor of the environmental space, indicating the minimum resource availability required for a dignified life (known in Latin America as the *Linea de Dignidad*), it cannot be quantified like the ceiling (already Adam Smith knew this), but quality criteria and provision processes can be identified. The 'social protection floor' promoted by the International Labour Organization, a concept combining human rights (including labour and social rights) with a concept of minimum social security, human dignity and good work, has been endorsed by the 2012 UNCSD conference, and subsequently by the UN General Assembly. It provides an excellent basis for further elaboration and concretisation of the 'floor' sustainability criterion (Spangenberg 2014). Addressing human needs in a market economy implies guaranteeing sufficient purchasing power to all citizens. In an economy based on paid labour, sufficient wages (no working poor) and full employment contribute to this end, as do the welfare state transfers for those who do not have a job in the formal economy (the informal economy also produces significant contributions in the fight against poverty). Measures like a basic income entitlement, right to employment etc. have been discussed for decades, while primary income distribution adjustments are an upcoming issue. Similarly, for the 'limitations' criterion, efficiency standards have long been discussed, but not so consumption caps. All these issues must be part of any policy programme for sustainable development living up to its name.

As the current fiscal and currency crisis demonstrates, a primary objective for public policy must be to regain the ability to act (i.e. not only to react) to address any relevant issue, including structural change. Re-establishing the primacy of policy is a necessary condition for transition management. This includes thinking out of the box. Two fields are crucial in this respect: extending the public domain – by stopping privatisation, financialisation and corporate capture, and by reclaiming public goods from private exploitation. For instance providing free access to all environmentally relevant patents emerging from publicly financed research, and by buying up and publishing such patents currently in private ownership, would make green knowledge and technology a public good (again). The second field for new policies is changing the economic logic by modifying the policy framework, in order to put the dynamics of the economy at the service of minimising resource consumption and environmental sustainability (social sustainability must be secured by other measures).

9. Conclusions

The transition to a sustainable society requires a fundamental cultural change, which in turn will only be possible if the prevailing neo-classical world view is replaced by one recognising that the laws of nature, and the limits they imply, apply to economic processes as much as to the environment. This leads to the insight that setting social as well as environmental limits is a necessity. It indeed means limiting the freedom of choice of some individuals, but a different world view would make obvious that such limitations are the precondition for the free flourishing of all members of society. It would help overcome the economic liberalism interpretation of human freedom as freedom to consume, and replace it with a democracy-based definition, freedom as the freedom for sustainable livelihood and lifestyle choices, and a freedom from political and economic oppression.

While the term 'Green Economy' suggests a beneficial effort to address the twin environmental and economic crises afflicting the world today, the strategies presented by the OECD, UNEP and World Bank are in fact being constructed by the same financial and global institutions that have underwritten climate change, income polarisation in and between countries, and brought us to the brink of global economic collapse. Deregulation, free markets, free trade and the preference for economic instruments and voluntary agreements in politics have turned out to be a safe recipe for disaster. Following Paracelsus' (1536) famous insight that 'the dose makes the poison', what might have been a cure for some ills has been applied in a dose making it a poison. In such a situation it is urgent to reduce the overdose, not increase the prescription and thus the toxic effect, as the 'Green Economy' as suggested by UNEP and OECD, does. Private multinational corporations, international financial institutions and influential individuals are pushing governments (nationally and as actors within the UN system) towards policies that will increase the commodification of nature and the earth's resources, at the expense of people and the environment. They find firm supporters in all parts of the classe politique – the neo-classical world view is their shared ideology, defining the environment and its resources as part of the economy to be exploited as the basis for sustained (not sustainable!) economic growth. These policies would negatively impact current efforts – across the spectrum of natural resource and global economy issues – to promote the rights of communities over their own resources and to stop land grabs, big dams, water markets, extractives, false climate solutions and other corporate grabs.

Instead, we need a 'right-sizing' of the economy, which in the affluent countries means slimming the economy (not the state, which is already suffering from anorexia in many countries), and in the emerging economies the recognition of ceilings they are reaching soon or have already transgressed. Sustainability requires accepting:

1. The primacy of meeting human needs, regardless of their purchasing power, instead of maximising shareholder value. This includes (social) justice, and in Europe a participatory welfare state. Enhanced citizen participation requires a social protection floor, and honouring unpaid work, mostly done by women.
2. The acceptance of limits in absolute figures as efficiency is not enough, and incremental change will not suffice. What is needed is basic (social, institutional and technological) innovation, and product rather than process innovation (including ex-novation, getting rid of outdated products). This includes, for instance, a transition to a nuclear and carbon free energy system, dematerialisation, ending land use extension (and of course land grabbing), limiting transport volumes, and sustainable agriculture on 100 per cent of the land.
3. Sustainable consumption patterns. These require not predominantly consumers' initiatives but choice editing, i.e. policies redirecting consumer choices, bans on unsustainable products, extended warranty times, effective top-runner approaches and the like.
4. Better respect for non-economic values in political decision making. This is a cultural as much as a political necessity. The prevailing criteria, dominant interests and power structures are clearly unsustainable (business interests explain only a fraction of this). Growth is no development – citizens' quality of life must become the overarching objective of economic policy again (within environmental limits).
5. International relations based on peaceful cooperation amongst equals, with leadership by example, not by prescription. This includes better cooperation, keeping promises regarding transfers (technology and ODA), and a reform of the world trade and finance systems. As 20 per cent of the global military expenditures would be sufficient to finance the implementation of the Millennium Development Goals, and as war (including civil war) is the ultimate unsustainability, disarmament, peaceful conflict solution and a ban on nuclear testing, weapons export and invasions would be a key contribution to sustainable development. Phasing out nuclear weapons is a medium-term sustainability objective.

However, what is considered 'right-sizing' the economy under an ecological economics world view, is perceived as a 'disaster in the making' seen through the lenses of a neo-classical ontology. Without changing the view, the turnaround to a sustainable society, choosing the appropriate world view as a basis for strategy development is a necessary condition for deriving substantial sustainable development strategies. An environmental economics ontology that trusts in solutions from unknown technologies, from commodification of nature and from market forces is not a suitable basis for problem-solving strategies. A different world view, like the ecological economics ontology, is a necessary condition for successful sustainability policies. Stakeholders in the sustainable development discourse should begin asking such deeper running questions, and request transparency regarding their basic world views from the decision makers in business, politics, media and civil society.

Note

1   As opposed to 'weak sustainability', 'strong sustainability' rejects the idea of substitution *between* capital stocks and insists on their complementarity. However, proponents of this idea have to permit substitutability of the elements within each capital stock – the capital stock concept would completely lose its meaning and function if the stock elements were considered as incommensurable.

References

Aronson, J., Gidda, S. B., Bassi, S., Berghöfer, A., Bishop, J., *et al.* 2009. *TEEB for Policy Makers – Summary: Responding to the Value of Nature.* Geneva: TEEB: The Economics of Ecosystems and Biodiversity.

Bleischwitz, R., Steger, S., Onischka, M., and Bahn-Walkowiak, B. 2009. 'Potenziale der Materialeffizienz erschließen'. *Ökologisches Wirtschaften* 24(2): 34–38.

Burrow, S. 2012. '48 million jobs in the green economy of 12 countries in the Americas, Asia, Africa and Europe – New report forecasts huge job growth'. ITUC press release of 19 April. Available at: www.it uc-csi.org.

Buttonwood. 2012. 'Marginal improvement'. *The Economist*, 31 March, 71.

Clark, B. 2010. 'The tragedy of common sense. Part one: The power of myth'. *Capitalism, Nature, Socialism* 21(3): 35–54.

Coase, R. 1960. 'The problem of social cost'. *Journal of Law and Economics* 1960(1): 1–44.

Daly, H. E. 2000. 'When smart people make dumb mistakes'. *Ecological Economics* 34(1): 1–3.

European Commission. 2011. 'Communication from the Commission to the European Parliament, the Council, the European Economic and Social Committee and the Committee of the Regions: Roadmap to a resource efficient Europe'. Document no. COM 571 final, 20.9.2011, Brussels: European Commission:.

FoEE (Friends of the Earth Europe) and Spangenberg, J. H. (eds) 1995. *Towards Sustainable Europe.* Nottingham: Russel Press.

Foster, J. B., Clark, B. 2009. 'The paradox of wealth: capitalism and ecological destruction'. *Monthly Review* 61(6). Available at: http://monthlyreview.org/2009/11/01/the-paradox-of-wealth-capitalism-and-ecological-destruction.

Georgescu-Roegen, N., 1971. *The Entropy Law and the Economic Process.* Cambridge, MA: Harvard University Press.

Gerson, J. 2012. 'NATO in crisis and the agendas for Chicago'. *Global Responsibility* 63, 5–7.

Hardin, G. 1968. 'The tragedy of the commons'. *Science* 162, 1243–1248.

Hoffmann, U. 2011. 'Some reflections on climate change, green growth illusions and development space'. UNCTAD Discussion Paper 205, Document No. UNCTAD/OSG/DP/2011/5.

Kapp, K. W. 1950. *The Social Costs of Private Enterprise*. Cambridge, MA: Harvard University Press.

Lorek, S. and Spangenberg, J. H. 2014. 'Sustainable consumption within a sustainable economy – beyond green growth and green economies'. *J Cleaner Production* 63: 33–44.

OECD. 2011. *Towards Green Growth*. Paris: OECD.

Ostrom, E., Burger, J., Field C.B., Norgaards, R. B., Policansky, D. 1999. 'Revisiting the commons: Local lessons, global challenges'. *Science* 284(5412): 278–282.

Paracelsus. 1536. *Die große Wundarzney*. Ulm: Hans Varnier

Pigou, A. C. 1932. *The Economics of Welfare*, 4th edn. London: Macmillan.

Rink, D. and Wächter, M. 2002. 'Naturverständnisse in der Nachhaltigkeitsforschung. Sozial-ökologische Forschung', in I. Balzer, M. Wächter (eds), *Ergebnisse der Sondierungsprojekte aus dem BMBF-Förderschwerpunkt*. Munich: ökom-Verlag, 339–360.

Rockström, J. et al. 2009. 'A safe operating space for humanity'. *Nature* 461, 472–475.

Sagoff, M. 2008. 'On the economic value of ecosystem services'. *Environmental Values* 17(2): 239–257.

Sen, A. 1986. 'The standard of living: Tanner Lectures on human values'. Available at: www.tannerlectures.utah.edu/lectures/documents/sen86.pdf (accessed 25 March, 2011).

Smith, A. 1776 [1910]. *An Inquiry into the Nature and Causes of the Wealth of Nations*. London: Home University Library.

Spangenberg, J. H. 2014. 'Institutions for sustainable consumption – sustainability: science, policy'. *Practice* 10(1): 62–77. Available at: http://sspp.proquest.com/

Spangenberg, J. H. 2007. 'The institutional dimension of sustainable development', in Tomáš Hak, Bedřich Moldan and Arthur Lyon Dahl (eds), *Sustainability Indicators. A Scientific Assessment*. SCOPE Books Series No. 67, Washington, DC: Island Press, 107–124.

Spangenberg, J. H. 2010. 'World civilisations at crossroads: Towards an expansionist or a sustainable future – Lessons from history'. *Futures* 42(6): 565–573.

Spangenberg, J. H. 2011. 'Sustainability science: a review, an analysis and some empirical lessons'. *Environmental Conservation* 38(3): 275–287.

Spangenberg, J. H. 2005. 'Economic sustainability of the economy: concepts and indicators'. *Sustainable Development* 8(1–2): 47–64.

Spangenberg, J. H. 2012a. 'Good business, nice beaches: corporate social responsibility is evolving, and becoming a little less flaky'. *The Economist*, 19 May, 66.

Spangenberg, J. H. 2012b. 'Energy in Canada: the great pipeline battle'. *The Economist*, 26 May, 40.

UNEP. 2011. *Towards a Green Economy. Pathways to Sustainable Development and Poverty Eradication*. Available at: www.unep.org/greeneconomy (accessed 28 October, 2011).

United Nations. 2011. *World Economic and Social Survey 2011: The Great Green Technological Transformation*. New York: United Nations.

Veblen, T. B. 1899. *The Theory of the Leisure Class. An Economic Study of Institutions*. London: Macmillan.

WCED (World Commission for Environment and Development) (Brundtland Commission) 1987. *Our Common Future*. Oxford: Oxford University Press.

Wilkinson, R. and Pickett, K. 2009. *The Spirit Level: Why Greater Equality Makes Societies Stronger*. London: Bloomsbury Press.

150   Joachim H. Spangenberg

Zick, A., Küpper, B. and Heitmeyer, W. 2010. 'Prejudices and group-focused enmity ? A
socio-functional perspective', in A. Pelinka, K. Bischof and K. Stögner (eds),
Handbook of Prejudice. Amherst, NY: Cambria Press, 273–302.

Part 3

Pathways to sustainability

9   Some moral pragmatics of climate change

Dieter Birnbacher

There is a more striking discrepancy between the motivation to accept principles of future ethics and the motivation to act in accordance with them than in other areas of ethics. This is diagnosed as mainly due to three general factors: time preference, uncertainty and limited altruism, as well as to three 'system variables' specific to the present industrialized world: individual freedom, consumerism, and egalitarianism. The remedy singled out as being most compatible with ethical demands of autonomy and democratic principles is self-binding, internal and external, preferably based on 'nudges' instead of massive social or political pressure.

1. Introduction: future ethics and the idea of moral pragmatics

The branch of ethics that deals with questions reaching far into the future, in short, *future ethics*, is primarily concerned with ends rather than means. It is interested, in the first place, in the moral quality of the ends to which future-directed actions pertain and much less with the means by which these are, or might be, attained. It is primarily 'outcome-oriented'. The most controversial questions in future ethics are, however, not questions of ends but questions of means, i.e. questions of what might be called *moral pragmatics*. While philosophical ethics is primarily concerned with giving an account of the *structure, content*, and *foundations* of morality as a system of legitimate ends, moral pragmatics is primarily concerned with questions concerning the means of implementing moral principles under real-world conditions. This implies, among others, that it has to take account of the strictures in resources, individual and social, cognitive and motivational, required to transform moral principles and ideals into concrete behaviour. As these resources are limited, moral pragmatics works from the start in the framework of what has been called, by John Rawls and others, a 'non-ideal theory'. Realistically, it takes moral principles to act as useful orientations that guide our way into a better future but has no illusions about the fact that morality as such is largely impotent to influence how we behave unless backed up by non-moral motivations such as egoism and adaptation to what is socially expected.

There is little controversy about what the most pressing moral challenges concerning the global future are, but there is a great deal of uncertainty about the potential efficacy of strategies to meet them and, indeed, about whether there are strategies at all with a reasonable prospects of success. The most important of these challenges is, no doubt, to feed a more than nine-billion population of humans projected for the year 2050 on limited resources of arable land, limited water resources and limited energy supplies. The more general challenge is to achieve sustainability in man's dealings with nature in a world with continuing population growth and rising expectations of material well-being. Other challenges concern long-term security: to secure peace on the background of continuing enmity and distrust between nations and groups; and to limit the long-term risks of the use of fossil fuels and nuclear energy while at the same time satisfying the 'hunger for energy' that can be expected to increase with more and more countries of what is now the developing world becoming industrialized.

With all these challenges there is far less controversy about their moral urgency than about the strategic options open for confronting them. Even on the level of theoretical modelling, it is far from clear whether these challenges can be met. Even greater are the difficulties in making any of these models work in practice. In many cases, however, what is unclear is not only the feasibility and efficacy of strategies but also their moral defensibility. For any strategy that can be expected to be successful, given its aims, it still is an open question whether it is defensible from a moral point of view. Examples of morally problematic strategies that have been adopted over time are population and deterrence policies: is a rigorous one-child policy such as that practised in China defensible, all things considered, in spite of its being incompatible with the idea of reproductive freedom set down in the UN Declaration of Human Rights? Is it morally defensible to build up a second-strike nuclear threat in the service of peacekeeping? Other strategies that are at present under discussion raise similar moral questions: how much moral pressure is justifiable in trying to change the vested interested and lifestyles in the highly industrialized world so far as these are incompatible with a reduction of greenhouse gas emissions? What changes in the existing social and legal institutions and procedures are justified to make provisions for future risks that are highly probable but do not yet make themselves felt directly to people living at the present? Would it be legitimate, as other authors suggests, to give up the principle of democratic government altogether because of its inefficiency in implementing long-term policies that meet with massive resistance both from interest-groups and from the electorate (cf. Shearman and Smith 2007)?

Any strategy that presents itself as a possible solution to one of these issues has not only to be tested for its probability of success and the costs and opportunity costs it imposes on people but also for its moral quality. Furthermore, it can be expected that in many cases there is no uniform standard to judge this quality. Judgements on how far the moral urgency if the ends justify morally problematic means is, and will be, no less controversial than controversies about the efficacy and efficiency of the means. In this respect, moral pragmatics is not too far from 'normal' political controversy concerning strategies. In fact, it is, one might say, the continuation of political controversy on a more theoretical level of discourse.

The likeliness of controversies partly results from the fact that the principles on which the moral quality of long-term strategies are assessed are not of the nature of strict constraints providing yes-or-no answers. As a rule, they allow for negotiations between the moral quality of ends and the moral quality of the means by which these may be achieved. A balance of some kind has to be struck between the moral urgency of the ends and the moral imperfection of the means on the background of, among others, an assessment of their probable efficacy. Though there are some means that are evidently acceptable and others that are evidently unacceptable, most strategies will lie somewhere in between. To give an example: in assessing potential incentives to change present lifestyles in the highly industrialized countries in the direction of more sustainable consumption patterns, there is a long way to go from more or less innocuous 'nudges' (Thaler and Sunstein 2008) to massive moral and social pressure. The difficulty is to say where the threshold lies between means that are justified and those that are not. Even if the goodness of the ends to which the potential changes of lifestyle serve goes undisputed, there may be doubt, or dissent, about where the borderline lies between the adequate and the excessive.

Moral pragmatics understood as the systematic study of mean-ends-relations in this sense requires contributions from more than one discipline: philosophy, psychology, sociology, political theory and the theory of education (cf. Gardiner 2011: 442). As far as sustainability and climate change are concerned, all of these disciplines have something relevant to say. Some of the factors relevant to sustainability and long-term orientation have been an object of study for quite a long time. *Time preference*, the preference for what is present over what is future, has for long been a subject of study in Motivation and Developmental Psychology, especially as an indicator of character formation from childhood to adulthood; Moral Psychology has been interested in finding out what conditions are favourable and unfavourable to *altruism*, both in motivation and in performance; Social Psychology tells us a lot about the extent to which individual action depends on *social expectations* and the motivation to act in accordance with what is seen as the 'done thing'; Empirical Decision Theory has a lot to say about the conscious and unconscious *heuristics* people use in making decisions under risk and uncertainty and about the complex determinants of how present and future risks are perceived in non-ideal epistemic situations; and Political Science can offer important insights into how much leeway there is for *collective agents*, especially governments and international organisztions, in adapting their policies to what seems ethically called for within the field of forces between public discussion, lobbying and legal pre-commitments. There is a lot that can be learned from these different fields of study. Nevertheless, it is a formidable task to integrate what they have to say into a coherent over-all picture. The following contribution cannot hope to present this picture. It will be content to provide some fragments from the point of view of a moral philosopher.

2. Concern about the future – theory versus practice

One of the central challenges the moral pragmatics of future ethics has to face is the gap between, on the one hand, the degree to which concern about the future is present in the consciousness of present individual and collective agents and the degree to which these agents are convinced of the necessity to contribute to meeting them by adaptive changes in behaviour, and, on the other hand, the degree to which these agents in fact act in accordance with these convictions.

If there was anything in the diagnosis given by Tocqueville in the nineteenth century about North America that 'people want to think only about the following day' (Tocqueville 1961: 156), it is no longer true, neither of North America nor of Europe. Long-term preservation of the natural conditions on which human life depends and maintenance of a satisfactory quality of life seem to be widely recognized values. The same seems to hold for what Hans Jonas has called the 'first commandment' of future ethics, the imperative not to endanger the future existence of mankind (Jonas 1979: 36). In a study of attitudes to anthropogenic climate change Russell *et al.* found that imposing climate changes on future generations by present energy use is predominantly judged to be morally unjust to these generations. They also found a clear correlation between the feeling of injustice and the expressed readiness to act in ways appropriate to reduce the risk of long-term climate change (Russell *et al.* 2003: 167). Similar results were found in a study of attitudes to the environment conducted by the American ecologists Minteer and Manning. The primary aim of this study, which was based on a representative sample of the population of Vermont, USA, was to find out about what matters to people in policies of environmental protection (Minteer and Manning 1999). One of the results was that there is a considerable pluralism of environmental values even within the relatively closed New England population. Not surprisingly, values with a religious background are more important to some than to others. The most interesting result was, however, that the three values most often nominated and on which there is the highest degree of agreement were also the three values with the highest values in relative importance, namely 'future generations' (with the representative statement 'Nature will be important to future generations'), 'quality of life' (with the representative statement 'Nature adds to the quality of our lives (for example, outdoor recreation, natural beauty)') and 'ecological survival' (with the representative statement 'Human survival depends on nature and natural processes'). This points to the conclusion that a justification of environmental protection can be expected to be the more successful the more it invokes anthropocentric but unselfish values of a collectively 'prudential' sort: the values of stewardship and of keeping nature intact for future generations.

There is no reason to doubt that the future-directed values expressed by large portions of present populations are authentic. Nevertheless they seem to have relatively little impact on behaviour, both individually and collectively. Everyday experience shows that future-oriented norms, laudable as they are, largely fail to make an impression on the motives of individual and political agents. Most initiatives to save fossil fuels and thereby lower carbon emissions are thwarted, partly by what is called the *rebound effect*. Though each new car makes more miles with the same amount of fuel, as a rule, it consumes more fuel because drivers use it more often, thus consuming the same amount of fuel in the same time interval. Paradoxically, in the developed world, there never have been so many gas-guzzling cars around than at present, no doubt most of them with drivers subscribing to future-oriented values. Similarly, energy for room heating per square meter has decreased in Germany between 1990 and 2004 by 9 per cent, but at the same time the area used for living per person has increased by 13 per cent, so that the gain in efficiency has been more than compensated for (Koch and Zech 2011: 392).

An analogous paradoxical situation prevails in politics. The same governments that strongly subsidise alternative energy sources actively pursue, or at least tolerate, projects of carbon-fired power stations on an unprecedented scale with a correspondingly high discharge of greenhouse gases. On the same line, the national balance of emissions is kept low by increasingly importing goods from Asian countries such as China that are known to care less about climate politics than about their economic development.

Why do future-oriented values and motives fail to influence action more than they do? One answer is that the values people have and the norms they think to be ethically justified are mutually inconsistent, or that inconsistent strategies follow from them, with the agent either knowing about the inconsistency or not. Given the multitude and heterogeneity of influences that impact on our moral thinking during our formative years it does not come as a surprise that our values are monolithic. In the political sphere, compromise formulae such as 'sustainable development' are even deliberately chosen to serve as integrative catchwords to assemble as many parties as possible under one common, though ultimately non-committal umbrella, though it is doubtful whether their elements really cohere. In the case of 'sustainable development' it is an open question whether it is really more than a piece of wishful thinking, however useful that may be as a diplomatic device.

A second answer is that, on the background of the biological origins of morality, universalistic ethics is overly demanding. It is illusory to expect that abstract universal norms can by themselves make anyone behave in accordance with it. In successively extending the range of 'moral patients' that have to be taken into consideration in judging the morality of action, universalistic ethics deeply challenge the anthropological drive towards keeping morality within the limits of emotional bonds. Indeed, there can be no more conspicuous contrast than that between what universalistic ethical systems such as Kantianism and utilitarianism expect of moral motivation and the evolutionary origins of morality in the low-distance-morality of the family, the clan and the tribe. While this origin is deliberately disavowed in the *principles* of these moralities, it stubbornly reappears in the limits of *motivation* documented by moral psychology. Moral emotions such as love of humanity, a sense of justice and international solidarity are readily affirmed in the abstract but rarely lived in the concrete.

It is a common-place of everyday psychology that acceptance of values and principles is not by itself sufficient to prompt action in accordance with them. It is a long way from accepting a principle or maxim to acting in accordance with it. Four steps seem to be involved: acceptance, adoption, application, and action (cf. Birnbacher 2009; 276). It is a necessary condition of acting in accordance with a maxim that the agent *accepts* the maxim, in the sense of judging it to be right and justified. This, however, is not enough to make an impact on his motivation to act accordingly. As a further step, the agent must *adopt* the maxim as a principle by which to guide his behaviour, to incorporate it, as it were, into his own identity. Moral psychologists tend to insist on the distinction between acceptance and adoption because empirical evidence suggests that the capacity to make moral judgements is largely independent of the readiness to act in accordance with them (cf. Montada 1993: 268). Tests that measure the capacity of making moral judgements (like the dilemma tests of the Kohlberg school of moral psychology) have little prognostic validity about moral behaviour. Making moral judgements is mainly a cognitive affair and does not involve any strong commitment to act appropriately. In contrast, adopting a maxim is more than assenting to it on a purely intellectual level. It has an emotional impact. It means that acting against it is accompanied by feelings of shame, at least of unease. A further step that must intervene between acceptance and action is *application*. An agent must relate the maxim he has adopted to the realities that confront him in experience. He must apply it to situations of the appropriate kind, i.e. identify situations to which his maxim is relevant, which can require considerable intellectual effort. This will be so especially in the case of consequentialist maxims because of the necessity to calculate consequences. Application is a separate step also for other than intellectual reasons. In cases where there are strong motives to deviate from an accepted rule, the empirically well-established theory of cognitive dissonance (Festinger 1957) predicts that even the capacity to identify the situations in which it should be applied will be weakened. It is probable that a situation that objectively is a case for which the rule is relevant is re-interpreted as a situation to which, for some reason or other, it does not apply. We do not only fail to observe the principles we have adopted but even fail to see that we do so by unconsciously, or half-consciously, misrepresenting the situation to ourselves. The same motives that make us act in ways incompatible with our principles blind us about the nature, and, given the case, the consequences of our actions.

3. Motivational obstacles to future ethics: time preference, uncertainty and limited altruism

Future ethics poses more stringent problems of motivation than other branches of practical philosophy. There is a more striking discrepancy between the motivation to accept principles of future ethics and the motivation to act in accordance with them than in other areas of ethics. This is mainly due to a combination of three factors: time preference, uncertainty and limited altruism.

Time preference is a complex phenomenon that is best explained as the preference for present over future consumption of a good. The Austrian economist Eugen von Böhm-Bawerk distinguished three motives because of which present consumption is preferred to future consumption: (1) pure (positive) time preference, the preference of the present merely because of being present; (2) the expectation of a decreasing marginal utility because of increasing possibilities of consumption in the future; and (3) the chance to realise technological progress through present consumption with the expectation of thereby increasing future possibilities of consumption (Böhm-Bawerk 1889: 262). Of these motives, pure time preference is the most problematic from the point of view of rationality. It does not seem reasonable to place value on the pure point of time at which a certain benefit is reaped. It does not come as a surprise that for the rationalist Spinoza, for example, pure time preference was one of the most evident (though at the same time, one of the most common) cases of irrationality that should be counteracted by reason. From a rational point of view it cannot matter whether a thing is present or future, and if future, how far in the future (Spinoza 1910, 184). Likewise, for Sidgwick, the assumption that temporal position of an action is relevant to its moral evaluation was incompatible with the claim to universality inherent in moral principles and maxims (Sidgwick 1907: 381). In fact, a great number of psychological experiments on delayed gratification with children and young adults have shown that pure time preference is negatively correlated with a number of conditions that can be associated with rationality and maturity. The probability of the choice of delayed over immediate gratification increases with prudence and the readiness to think about the future ('future perspective'). It increases with age, intelligence, ego-strength, achievement motives and social responsibility. It decreases with neurotic pathology and delinquency (cf. Mischel and Metzner 1962).

Pure time-preference seems a contributing factor to what has been termed 'obliviousness of the future'. Future dangers rarely find our spontaneous attention without constant efforts to keep them on the agenda. It seems part of the explanation of the relative ease with which the Montreal convention was established, the convention that banned gases that contributed to the dramatic increase in skin cancer around the globe by destroying the protective ozone layer. Apart from the fact that only small adaptations on the part of producers were necessary to reduce emissions, the fact that the consequences became visible massively in the immediate present greatly helped in finding an agreement. In the case of greenhouse gases this is much more uncertain, not only because much more comprehensive changes in energy use are at stake but also because the victims of global warming have not yet made their appearance and the impact of present styles of production will mainly be felt in the generations to come. All this explains why future ethics does not, in general, provoke the 'visceral response' (Weber 2006: 103) prompting appropriate action. It appeals to the cold intellect rather than to the heart.

The second factor is the inevitable *uncertainty* of the forecasts on which future-directed action has to be based. Uncertainty about the future has more than one dimension (cf. Jamieson 2012: 191). First, there is the residual uncertainty about the scientific validity of the theories and scenarios on which the prognosis of future risks is based. Though, in the case of climate change, there seems to be little room for doubt about the physical side of the matter, there is room for doubt about the impact of rising temperatures on local economies, living conditions and, ultimately, quality of life. Since motivation to effectively lower greenhouse gas emission depends, to a large extent, on the explicit or implicit calculation of consequences for oneself or for one's immediate descendants, uncertainty is most important as far as it concerns how Europeans will be affected by global warming. What is the probability that living conditions in some parts of the developing world will be worsened by climatic change to an extent that massive migration occurs to the North, putting a heavy strain on its infrastructure and its assimilation capacity?

Second, there is the uncertainty about future technical fixes. It seems improbable that the technologies discussed at present will be succesful. Carbon capture and storage, even if feasible, will not suffice to lower total emissions of greenhouse gases on a climatically relevant scale, and present blueprints for geo-engineering carry with them too many incalculable risks. It cannot be excluded, however, that technical solutions of an as yet unknown kind will present themselves that lower the impact of continuing greenhouse gas emissions on vulnerable economies.

Third, and most importantly, there is uncertainty about whether present efforts to lower emissions will make more than a minimal contribution to the reduction of impacts. One reason is that we have much less empirical control about the consequences of present saving. Lacking appropriate feedback, we have no effective 'control beliefs' about present saving, i.e. beliefs that appropriate action will be effective in attaining the desired goals. However, control beliefs are an important precondition for action motivation. Without relevant 'control beliefs', the motivation to enter upon a course of action can be expected to be unstable. Another reason is that we have no certainty about whether future people will share our values and continue the strategies initiated now. In order to attain their goal, long-term strategies have to be undertaken by a series of successively co-operating generations. However, no single individual and no single collective can be sure that its descendants will honour their efforts by carrying on the process into the distant future. There can be, in the nature of the case, no certainty that countervailing interests of later generations will not annul the beneficial effects of the efforts of the first generation. We cannot expect that later generations will co-operate simply because our generation has taken the lead. After all, we know from the series of post-Kyoto conferences how difficult it is to make even present agents co-operate with the nations leading the lowering of greenhouse gas emissions. It is true, it is a real possibility that one-sided saving may serve as a model for others, especially if those taking the lead are able to demonstrate that saving fossil fuels is compatible with (further) economic growth. But it seems more probable that, on the condition that the supply in fossil fuels remains constant, the fuels saved by the countries resorting to alternative energy sources will be bought at (possibly) lower prices and consumed by the rest of the world, so that, in the total, no reduction occurs.

The third factor standing in the way of putting high-flung future-directed maxims into operation is *limited altruism*. The fact that moral emotions and motives of universal scope such as love of humanity, a sense of justice and international solidarity are readily affirmed in the abstract but rarely lived in the concrete has something to do with the fact that the prospective beneficiaries of these actions are primarily people spatially and temporally distant from the relevant agents. The great majority of people who have been asked whether they think they are themselves directly affected by global warming and climate change answer in the negative (Giddens 2009: 113). Thus, any change in lifestyle that might be required by a coherent policy of reducing greenhouse gas emissions has to rely on altruistic motivations. The fact that the beneficiaries of present action are not only distant but, in addition, for the most part unidentified, anonymous and abstract, does not make things better. It is well known that people are in general significantly more willing to expend resources to save identified victims than for merely statistical victims, and future victims are in general statistical victims.[1] It is true, altruism includes 'self-referential altruism' (Mackie 1977: 158), the love of one's immediate descendants, of one's group and of one's country. However, though emotional attachments to the 'near and dear' may be an important factor in increasing the 'imaginability' of future generations (Wade-Benzoni 1999: 1401), this kind of altruism will hardly be sufficient to support future-directed action in the case of climate change. Though some of the risks of climate change will affect, at least indirectly, the inhabitants of the northern parts of Europe, the main beneficiaries of reducing greenhouse gas emissions will not be our own descendants but the descendants of today's populations of the South. It is an open question whether Northern Europe has very much to fear from climate change. It is not at all clear that, apart from large-scale migration from the South and minor ecological changes, there is anything in climate change that makes it threatening to the populations contributing most, by their lifestyles, to its further course. The risks falls mainly on those populations that are already very much at risk, both by poverty as well as by ecological damages like desertification and scarcity of water supplies.

4. Short term objectives and 'system variables'

Probably the greatest threat to present motivations to implement a coherent climate policy in accordance with people's professed long-term concerns is the attention paid by citizens and politicians to short-term objectives that counteract the effects of long-term climate strategies but promise more immediate benefits. In general, these objectives are in line with what Renate Hübner has identified as the five most dominant orientations of consumers in modern industrial society: mobility, flexibility, convenience, safety and hygiene (Hübner 2000: 126). To take only the first of these orientations: will it be possible to maintain, or even increase, the present level of mobility and at the same time reduce fossil fuel use to the extent required by the ambitious aims, say, of the European Union? The answer is uncertain given that, for reasons of security, the contribution of nuclear energy is likely to be cut down at the same time. The surveys of the last ten years leave no doubt that even those who are seriously concerned about climate change have other, competing concerns that might not be compatible with a coherent politics of climate protection. A study of a representative sample of the population of Baden-Württemberg in 2001 showed that 50 per cent of the people interviewed associated the climate problem with a 'high' or even 'very high' catastrophe potential and 54 per cent saw great or very great societal dangers in it. However, this did not correlate with a willingness to find the causes for this problem in their own behaviour. Only 11 per cent associated the responsibility for climate change with their own ways of acting (Zwick 2001: 302). Roughly the same proportion of people who attributed a high catastrophe potential to climate change think that individual car traffic provides important individual and social benefits. Correspondingly, sociologists of consumption are extremely sceptical as to the chances to change consumption patterns in the direction of sustainability. Consumption seem to be as little affected by ecological as by economic concerns. At least, according to some social scientists, the dominant behavioural orientation in the household concerns much less economic or environmental rationality but the quality of the goods and services provided. Energy saving is, according to these authors, 'not compatible (with this orientation) and might even put in question the qualitative core of what constitutes the meaning and purpose of the household as a social and productive system' (Götz *et al.* 2011: 278) A survey in the late 1990s in the USA showed that, as one might expect, knowledge about climate change and its causes, perception of the riskiness of climate change as well as general environmental beliefs, defined as non-issue specific cognitive orientation about environmental issues are determinants of intentions to adapt individual behaviour voluntarily as well as to support corresponding policies. At the same time, the survey shows – at least for the USA – that there is strong reluctance to adapt behaviour in sensitive areas such as car-driving. A majority of Americans are opposed to driving less (and using trains and buses more often) and especially to additional taxes on petrol (O'Connor *et al.* 1999: 464). In a similar study of the attitudes of 623 residents of central Pennsylvania, O'Connor *et al.* found that 'many … are not willing … to support policies that threaten their jobs or the health of the economy' (O'Connor *et al.* 2002: 15).

This is not to say that clinging to 'bad habits' in the face of what one's own rationality and morality demand is peculiar to the industrialized world. That behaviour is more regulated by habit, custom and social expectations than by rational insight is a, anthropological commonplace supported by a plethora of evidence. In the context of adaptation to climate change, Grothmann and Patt recently emphasized the importance of what they call 'avoidant maladaptation' to explain the inadequate and seemingly irrational responses of people to perceived risks (Grothmann and Pratt 2005). They rightly point to the limited explanative power of explanations focussing on financial, technical and institutional limitations of the capacity to adapt to new risk situation. What is equally crucial is, in their view, the subjective factor which they locate in the individual's perceived adaptive capacity. It seems doubtful, however, whether the ultimate explanation of 'avoidant maladaptation' is to be sought in the realm of the purely cognitive. A more adequate explanation seems to be by affective factors. Perceived personal capacity to adapt depends crucially on motivation to adapt. This is also made plausible by one of the field studies from Zimbabwe the authors quote as evidence (Grothmann and Pratt 2005: 208). It shows that an adequate response to climate forecasts on the part of subsistence farmers is greatly facilitated by role-playing games and an explicit confrontation of subjects with the alternatives between which they have to choose. Both learning methods involve the emotions significantly more than a pure transmission of information.[2]

'Avoidant maladaptation' in the industrialized world is best explained by the 'system variables' characterizing modern industrialized countries and gradually becoming universal values, including parts of the world under dictatorial regimes: *individual freedom*, *consumerism*, and *egalitarianism*. These values have become so much taken for granted that it needs considerable efforts to confront them with the prospect that they may not be sustainable in a world with finite resources. To quote Eduard Müller, a social ecologist working in Central America: 'Modern society has been structured under paradigms that typically ignore unsustainable human activities, making change seem like an impossible or absurd task' (Müller 2011: 346).

Initiating fundamental changes in consumption patterns is extremely difficult in societies in which consumption of material goods is seen as an indicator of well-being and status and in which there is a latent pressure for economic growth in order to prevent feedback loops with negative effects on the economic system. Further pressure for economic growth comes from egalitarianism. Growth seems necessary to satisfy the expectations in the improvement of social transfers for those below the average and to prevent social disruption and estrangement by evening out the most glaring discrepancies in income and status.

Though short-term objectives of economic growth and social peacekeeping can be in harmony with long-term objectives such as climate protection, reality shows that more often than not they are not. In general, they challenge the adherence of governments to their long-term commitments and greatly reduce the chances of introducing more than minimal structural changes. At present, the German government, for example, presents the picture of an almost acrobatic performance in trying to reconcile its ambitious climate protection programme with its continuing support of the German car industry with its focus on the production of so-called 'premium' cars on which more than a sixth of the national economy depends. The paradoxical consequence can be seen all over the world: a nation that claims to be a forerunner in climate politics produces and successfully exports motor vehicles that exhaust tons of greenhouse gases simply for fun, as luxury toys for adults.

5. Self-binding as a check on myopia

One way to maintain long-term policies in the face of short-term challenges is to make ever renewed efforts to keep them at the top of the agenda. Another, and probably more comfortable way, is *self-binding*. Self-binding functions either by raising the threshold to deviate from the road of virtue defined by one's own principles, or by deliberately limiting one's freedom to deviate from these principles. In either case, an attempt is made to control in advance the extent to which future motivations that deviate from one's principles result in undesired behaviour, either by making deviations more difficult or less attractive, or by restricting future options.

Self-binding can take various forms. *Internal* self-binding consists of self-binding relying on mechanisms internal to the agent. In the case of the individual, internal self-binding can assume the form of adopting maxims by which internal sanctions are activated to avoid opportunistic deviations from one's principles, so that deviations are 'punished', for example by feelings of guilt or shame that are mobilized whenever the person does not live up to the obligations of his moral identity. Once these internal sanctions have been established, even the most extreme egoist has a reason to take these sanctions into account. In the case of collectives, internal self-binding can consist of establishing institutions within a society by which collective decisions are controlled and potentially revised. *External* self-binding consists of delegating these sanctions to an external agency, either by making it raise the threshold for deviations or by restricting the options open to oneself. Delegating the power to make one follow a rule according to the Ulysses-and-the-Sirens pattern (Elster 1979) can be thought of as a kind of self-paternalism, which, however, is without the moral problems characteristic of other forms of paternalism since the subject and object of paternalistic intervention are one and the same.

It may be doubted that self-binding can serve as a device in furthering observance of future-ethical commitments for the reason that self-binding is appropriate in cases of addiction or deeply ingrained bad habits one does not want as they dominate one's behaviour, but not for failures to act in accordance with one's most lofty and most demanding moral principles. According to this objection, the strategy of self-binding is simply misplaced when employed in the context of conflicts between principles of maxims of differing degrees of scope and abstractness instead of conflicts between principles and a strong and imperative craving to act against them. Time-preference, 'self-referential altruism' or egoism are not the kinds of urges that need restraining by devices such as self-binding. After all, the model of self-binding is the literal 'binding' Ulysses demanded from his crew when approaching the sirens. Obviously, the temptations, egoism and time-preference are too far removed from the irresistibility of the song of the sirens to justify similarly drastic methods.

I do not think that this objection carries much weight. Conceptually, self-binding is not as closely bound to situations of addiction as the objections assume. On the contrary, self-binding seems an extremely meaningful device not only in situations of addiction or irresistible craving but also in less exceptional situations in which weaknesses of a more everyday variety prevent us from following our principles. There is broad spectrum of such weaknesses, with love of comfort and ease, laziness, the wish to be left alone on the side of sloth and greed, envy and ambition on the side of passion.

The context of long-term strategies is only one of many in which self-binding seems to be relevant. Given the psychological facts about time preference and limited altruism, self-binding is, in principle, a potent device in effectively caring for the future, both on the individual and the social level. On the social level, internal self-binding might serve as a potent instrument of protecting collective long-term concerns from being weakened by myopic temptations, both by formal and informal means. The most important formal means are legal and constitutional safeguards that may act as a check on the temptations of politicians to serve themselves or their electorates at the expense of the future. In this respect, constitutional safeguards are clearly more reliable than legal safeguards. They are not only less easy to change than simple laws, they can also be expected to pre-commit future generations of politicians and other decision-makers, thus contributing to continuity in the pursuit of transgenerational objectives (cf. Elster 1979: 95). Though there can be, in the nature of the case, no guarantee that they will remain in force during future generations, they provide as much certainty as one can possibly hope for that the projects of today are carried on in the future. One of the procedural safeguards designed to control short-term orientation in political decision-making is the institution of indirect democracy, which requires that the members of the legislative organs are bound exclusively by their own conscience and/or party discipline and not by an imperative mandate. By assigning the control of the executive not to the constituencies themselves but to their elected representatives, potential pressure from the basis to prioritise short-term objectives over long-term objectives of preservation and development is effectively reduced. Again, this assignment of control will work in favour of long-term orientations only to the extent that the decisions taken by political representatives are in fact less myopic than those hypothetically taken by their constituencies. Whether this is so, is open to doubt.

Another procedural safeguard is the institution of an independent constitutional court with the power to control government policies by constitutional principles. Most constitutions contain material principles limiting the extent to which governments may indulge in 'obliviousness of the future'. In the German *Grundgesetz*, there are two articles to that effect, article 115, which limits the national debt to the sum total of national investments (which is going to be considerably extended in 2016 with the full implementation of the constitutional debt limit), and the recently introduced article 20a, which contains an explicit commitment to care adequately for the needs of future generations, especially by preserving resources and by protecting the natural environment.

There are other hopeful developments in establishing self-binding mechanisms by which collective agents keep their own myopia under control. In a number of political areas, such as economics, science, technology, environment, medicine and social security, there is a growing number of independent bodies whose counsel is heard, and often respected, in practical politics. Examples of such independent bodies are, on the one hand, research institutions, think tanks, and foundations designed to exist over longer periods of time and wholly or partly financed by the state, and, on the other hand, committees and commissions expected to work on more limited tasks. The intention in setting up these bodies is, partly, to make them act as a kind of collective 'future ethical conscience', a role that politics is often unable to play because of pressures of lobbying, party politics and election campaigns. Of course, there is no guarantee that the advice of these committees and commissions (even where it is unanimous) is respected. The advice coming from these bodies binds those to whom it is addressed as little as advice from a friend binds an individual. The alternative of endowing these bodies with executive or legislative powers, however, would hardly be compatible with basic democratic principles. The sovereignty of the people, or of its representatives, should not be usurped by experts.

Internal self-binding mechanisms gain momentum by the degree to which they are supplemented by external self-binding devices. On the level of the individual, self-binding by an external agency is the more attractive the more firmly an individual wants to act on its long-term principles and the higher its risk of impulsiveness. An extreme case is the situation of gambling addicts, some of whom have gone so far as to demand legal possibilities to make gambling casinos restrict access to them on an international scale.

Since time preference is a universal phenomenon, delegating responsibility for long-term provisions to an external agency like the state is often rational even for those who are less prone to succumb to their impulses. For one, control costs are shifted to an external institution. Self-restraint is wholly or partly replaced by restrictions coming from outside. Second, the individual can be more certain that his individual investment has an effect on the future in all cases where a cumulative effort is needed to make a difference. Third, it is more probable that the burdens of realising long-term objectives are fairly distributed and that free riding on the idealism of others is ruled out. Fourth, there are advantages of a moral division of labour made possible by institutional solutions. Instead of each individual making its own provisions for the future, those with an intrinsic interest in the class of objects to be protected can be assigned the task of keeping them in good order, with environmentalists caring for the conservation of nature and the continuation of biodiversity, and economists caring for the conservation of capital and the continuation of economic growth. Empirical surveys show that a large proportion of citizens is interested in the conservation of nature but that very few are willing to actively contribute to it by voluntary contributions.[3] In all such cases it is rational to lay these widely shared aims into the hands of those who are intrinsically motivated.

On the level of the collective, several external self-binding mechanisms with a clear relevance to future ethics are already in operation, some of them taking the form of international law and international contracts, others taking the form of transnational organisations and authorities. A model of an internationally effective agency able not only to give advice to national governments but also to implement their future directed policies independently of national politics is the European Central Bank. It functions independently of national governments and is bound exclusively by the criteria of the European Union Treaty. However, given the fact that governments are the key agents of most future hazards such as the destruction of large parts of tropical rainforest, the reduction of biodiversity, and the degradation of soils by intensive agriculture, there is still much to be done. There are quite a number of proposals about how this may be effected. One option that should be taken into consideration is the global court for future issues proposed, together with other options, by Weiss (1989: 121). A court of this kind, even if it lacks the authority to check the 'obliviousness of the future' of national governments by issuing sanctions, would at least be able to protest against policies that endanger the interests of future people and to encourage the search for sustainable alternatives.

6. How much moral pressure is compatible with individual liberty?

Given that mechanisms of internal and external self-binding work out success-fully, the central question, from the point of view of moral pragmatics, is how much pressure governments should be allowed to exercise on their citizens in order to gain support for their long-term strategies. What kinds of moral pressure are compatible with individual liberty? At what point does moral suasion and the implementation of 'nudges' of the kind recommended by libertarian paternalism change into illiberal paternalism or worse, moral dictatorship?

One accepted medium of spreading long-term orientations through all layers of society, though with some temporal delay, is *education*. By educating the young generation in the spirit of sustainability and by creating an atmosphere in which cautious use of resources, nature conservation, and the long-term stability of social security are strengthened against countervailing short-term interests, society might build up resistance to its own tendencies to overuse resources and to infringe on the integrity of its natural patrimony. Recently, Daniel Jamieson has drawn up a list of 'green virtues' that provides potential co-ordinates of an education for sustainability: *humility* (against nature), *temperance* (in consumption), *mindfulness* (in relation to the more distant consequences and side-effects of our actions) and *co-operativeness* (in coming to terms with the ecological problems before us) (Jamieson 2007: 181). The function of an education in the spirit of sustainability is not only called for by climatic change, reduction in biodiversity and other environmental problems lying ahead. It might also have the important function of opening up new horizons of meaning that in turn support future-directed action. In the developed world, a spiritual vacuum has made itself felt that can be traced back both to the continuing historical process of secular-isation and to saturation with purely economic private and collective (including corporate) objectives. There is a high degree of preparedness to contribute to causes or projects that reach further than one's own person, one's own personal context, and one's own lifetime. Ernest Partridge has called such motives motives of 'self-transcendence' (1980: 204). Future orientation and responsibility to the future offer themselves as the natural candidates for the longing for existential meaning in a secularized world. Acting for the future fits such motives neatly because a commitment to the future makes the individual feel his own value. It makes him feel embedded in a wider context of meaning that reaches from the past into the future. By acting for the future, the individual is able to see himself as a link in a chain of generations held together by an intergenerational feeling of community that joins obligations in the direction of the future to feelings of gratitude in the direction of the past. However modest his contribution, he thereby situates himself in a context transcending the individual both in personal and temporal respects.

This motive might gain particular momentum by being combined with the communitarian motive and supported by the feeling that one's own contribution is part of the objectives of a larger community. Concern about the future well-being of a group to which one has a close emotional relationship can be expected to be more reliable than the interest in the well-being of abstractions like humanity or future generations. Caring for the future of one's reference group can even be part of one's own moral identity. Whoever defines himself as German, Christian, or as a scientist, can hardly be indifferent to the future of the group to which his identity refers, though, with a plurality of identities and loyalties, there may be conflicts between the future-directed motivations associated with each. One's own contribution to the future is seen as a contribution to a common cause which one expects to be carried further by an indefinite number of subsequent generations of members of the same community. That 'community-bonding' (Care 1982: 207) can be a powerful support of future-directed motivation is also confirmed by experimental psychology (Van Vugt 2009). Of course, at least part of the robustness of this motivation depends on the fact that it cannot be disappointed by experience. In this respect, motivations to act for the future resemble religious commitments of a more literally transcendent kind. Both are, for the present agent, non-falsifiable. Partly in consequence thereof, they are liable to be abused. Whether there will in fact be the temporally overarching community with shared objectives and values and shared feelings of solidarity is highly uncertain. It is an open question whether our descendants will recognize, or honour by acting in accordance with them, the present generation's principles of intergenerational responsibility and visions of intergenerational justice. The more remote in time a later generation is situated and the more its principles are shaped by a long series of intermediary generations coming between ours and theirs, the less certain we can be that they will in fact be part of the same moral community. As historical examples of powerful ideologies like Marxism have shown, the risk of illusion does not inevitably detract from the strength of this motivation.

Another strategy to influence behavioural patterns in the direction of long-term objectives like climate protection and sustainability is *default*, the redefining of what counts as socially accepted and what stands in need of justification. Such processes of redefinition are going on all the time. The best example is the process of re-definition that has occurred in the 1980s with environmental pollution and the rise of the green movement. While pollution was accepted for a long time as a more or less inevitable by-product of economic progress, sensibilities changed radically with the awakening of the ecological conscience and redistributed burdens of justification. At present, there is no political party that has not integrated typically 'green' values into its programme that were originally proclaimed by small minorities at the fringe of society and hardly taken seriously if not even openly ridiculed by opinion leaders. Default strategies are, no doubt, a powerful instrument in the hands of politicians, company representatives and opinion leaders, especially if words are followed by actions and the virtues preached to others are lived, and seen to be lived, by those in power. To come back to the question of mobility, one of the main sources of irreversible environmental damage at present: that fact that politicians preaching sustainability to their own citizens congratulate the bosses of car companies for their high-emission models is surely one of the most scandalous inconsistencies in present politics. While the provision of drugs to addicts is heavily criminalized, providing the drug of high-speed driving, though hardly less dangerous, to car addicts is not only officially approved but even applauded.

From the perspective of moral pragmatics, the attraction of default strategies is that they set new standards of what counts as normal and accepted without restricting the freedom to act otherwise. One important condition for implementing such standards is appropriate information. Consumers, for example, should be able to judge how much their market transactions contribute to global warming. That means that goods should have labels not only with their prices on them but also with the rough amount of emissions that have gone into it (or by a climatic quality classification similar to the familiar quality classification). At least one big company, the British supermarket Tesco, seems seriously to consider such a strategy. It has promised to put 'carbon labels' on all its 80 000 product lines, so that consumers know what volume of greenhouse gases has gone into their production (Giddens 2009: 121). This initiative is to be welcomed. Of course, carbon going into production is only part of the carbon emitted during its whole lifecycle. Its lifecycle also includes average use and decommissioning. Without information about the complete emission load of goods, environmental and climate virtues run idle.

Attractive as these ideas are, it must be admitted that there is a whiff of ecological puritanism in them that might deviate into a public ecological moralism incompatible with liberty, at least if supported, and perhaps controlled, by a majority. A 'tyranny of the majority', to quote Tocqueville again, might develop that makes dissidents feel like outcasts. Something similar has recently happened with smokers for example, by legislation following a public vote against pubs with smoking licenses, a measure that massively infringes on the liberty of a considerable minority of citizens. After all, smokers are for the most part addicts who succeed at giving up smoking only at very high costs to themselves. It is difficult not to be ambivalent on this point. On the one hand one cannot easily dismiss the thesis put forward by some ecologically minded authors that the risk of libertarian paternalism degenerating into a downright dictatorial paternalism is negligible given the risks run by the unrestricted continuance of the wasteful lifestyles of industrialised societies (Heidbrink and Riedel 2011: 155). On the other hand, it is equally difficult not to sympathize with those who, in the libertarian spirit of John Stuart Mill, warn us of the social pressure resulting from an overdose of public ecological moralizing, especially if this comes not only from organizations and parties but from government and other state agencies (Petersen and Schiller 2011: 160). Not to have to feel ashamed for one's actions as far these are within the law and not obviously immoral is undoubtedly one of the great assets of a free society.

There are better strategies than moral pressure that states may consider in the service of climate protection, strategies that are both more in conformity with the market mechanism and probably more successful; namely either to tax goods according to the extent to which they directly and indirectly affect the climate through greenhouse gas emissions over their lifecycle or to install a system of cap-and-trade by auctioned emission permits on the line of the revised European Union Emissions Trading Scheme. Both alternative strategies have pros and cons that must be left to expert discussion (see, for example, Stern 2010). Both strategies, however, are not only more in line with libertarian paternalism than mere suasion plus information but also are more compatible with the pluralism of behaviour patterns characteristic of modern societies. One of the characteristics of modern society is that behavioural norms vary widely between social contexts. Moral and ideological criteria have a role to play in decisions concerning politics, for example in elections and political campaigns. They have little impact on the sphere of consumption in which most people think and act as *homines oeconomici*, i.e. by maximizing their personal utility irrespective of moral and ecological concerns. Even as ecological moralists we should accept the fact that the values actually followed in everyday life are strongly influenced by context and role and that only a few people are prepared to orient themselves by moral or ecological considerations in their daily visits to the supermarket. Nevertheless, a carbon tax would have good prospects to change consumption patterns because prices would, in many cases, change drastically in order to reflect the external costs of goods and services. Meat, for example, could no longer be as inexpensive as it is at the moment, given the costs in carbon emissions its production involves.

Notes

1   Experimental research has shown that this 'identifiable victim effect' depends on how the question is framed: whether the statistical victim is situated in a larger (e.g. percentage of the whole population) or narrower reference group (e.g. percentage of a more specifically characterised group) (cf. Jenni and Loewenstein 1997: 253). The narrower the reference group, the more it seems to cause empathic reactions. In contrast to other potential variables such as vividness of description, this variable works unconsciously and survives reflection.

2   Similar results are reported in Weber 2006: 110.

3   This may be different for the most well-to-do layer of society, hypothesized by Radermacher to be willing to make significant voluntary contributions, financial and political, to climate protection. The motive to which this author proposes to appeal is gains in reputation (2013: 92).

References

Birnbacher, D. 2009. 'What motivates us to care for the (distant) future?' in A. Gosseries and L. H. Meyer (eds), *Intergenerational Justice*. Oxford, 273–300.

Böhm-Bawerk, E. v. 1889. *Positive Theorie des Kapitals*. Innsbruck.

Care, N. S. 1982. 'Future generations, public policy, and the motivation problem'. *Environmental Ethics* 4, 195–213.

Elster, J. 1979. *Ulysses and the Sirens. Studies in Rationality and Irrationality.* Cambridge/Paris.

Festinger, L. 1957. *A Theory of Cognitive Dissonance*. Stanford, CA.

Gardiner, S. M. 2011. *A Perfect Moral Storm: The Ethical Tragedy of Climate Change.* Oxford.

Giddens, A. 2009. *The Politics of Climate Change*. Cambridge.

Götz, K., Glatzer, W. and Gölz, S. 2011. 'Haushaltsproduktion und Stromverbrauch – Möglichkeiten der Stromersparnis im privaten Haushalt', in R. Defila, A. Di Giulio and R. Kaufmann-Hayoz (eds), *Wissen und Wege zum nachhaltigen Konsum*. Munich, 265–282.

Grothmann, T. and Patt, A. 2005. 'Adaptive capacity and human cognition: the process of individual adaptation to climate change'. *Global Environmental Change* 15, 199–213.

Heidbrink, L. and Riedel, J. 2011. 'Nachhaltiger Konsum durch politische Selbstbindung'. *GAIA* 20/3, 152–156.

Hübner, R. 2000. 'Die Magie der Dinge. Materielle Güter, Identität und metaphysische Lücke', in O. Parodi, G. Banse and A. Schaffer (eds), *Wechselspiele. Kultur und Nachhaltigkeit. Annäherungen an ein Spannungsfeld*. Berlin, 119–150.

Jamieson, D. 2007. 'When Utilitarians should be Virtue Theorists'. *Utilitas* 19, 160–183.

Jamieson, D. 2012. 'Ethics, public policy, and global warming', in A. Thompson and J. Bendik-Keymer (eds), *Ethical Adaptation to Climate Change: Human Virtues of the Future*. Cambridge, MA, 187–202.

Jenni, K. E. and Loewenstein, G. 1997. 'Explaining the "Identifiable Victim Effect"'. *Journal of Risk and Uncertainty* 14, 235–257.

Jonas, H. 1979. *Das Prinzip Verantwortung. Versuch einer Ethik für die technologische Zivilisation*. Frankfurt am Main.

Koch, A. and Zech, D. 2011. 'Wirkungsanalyse im Rahmen des Wärmekonsums – Nutzerverhalten und thermische Energienutzung', in R. Defila, A. Di Giulio and R. Kaufmann-Hayoz (eds), *Wissen und Wege zum nachhaltigen Konsum*. Munich, 383–396.

Mackie, J. L. 1977. *Ethics: Inventing Right and Wrong*. Harmondsworth.

Minteer, B. A. and Manning, R. E. 1999. 'Pragmatism in environmental ethics: democracy, pluralism, and the management of nature'. *Environmental Ethics* 21, 191–207.

Mischel, W. and Metzner, R. 1962. 'Preference for delayed reward as a function of age, intelligence, and length of delay interval'. *Journal of Abnormal and Social Psychology* 64, 425–431.

Montada, L. 1993. 'Moralische Gefühle', in W. Edelstein, G. Nunner-Winkler and G. Noam (eds), *Moral und Person*. Frankfurt am Main, 259–277.

Müller, E. and Lindeman, K. C. 2011. 'Climate change in several Central and South American ecosystems' in G. Banse, G. L. Nelson and O. Parodi (eds), *Sustainable Development: the Cultural Perspective*. Berlin, 339–348.

O'Connor, R. E., Bord, R. J. and Fisher, A. 1999. 'Risk perceptions, general environmental beliefs, and willingness to address climate change'. *Risk Analysis* 19, 461–471.

O'Connor, R. E., Bord, R. J., Yarnal, B. and Wiefek, N. 2002. 'Who wants to reduce green-house gas emissions?' *Social Science Quarterly* 83(1), 1–17.

Partridge, E. 1980. 'Why care about the future?' in E. Partridge (ed.), *Responsibilities to Future Generations*. Buffalo, NY, 203–220.

Petersen, T. and Schiller, J. 2011. 'Politische Verantwortung für Nachhaltigkeit und Konsumentensouveränität'. *GAIA* 20, 157–161.

Radermacher, F. J. 2013. 'Klimapolitik nach Doha – Hindernisse in Lösungen verwandeln'. *GAIA* 22, 87–92.

Russell, Y., Kal, E. and Montada, L. 2003. 'Generationengerechtigkeit im allgemeinen Bewußtsein? – Eine umweltpsychologische Untersuchung',in Stiftung für die Rechte zukünftiger Generationen (ed.), *Handbuch Generationengerechtigkeit*. Munich, 153–171.

Shearman, D. and Smith, J. W. 2007. *The Climate Change Challenge and the Failure of Democracy*. Westport, CT.

Sidgwick, H. 1907.*The Methods of Ethics*, 7th edn. London.

Spinoza, B. de 1910. *Ethics and De Intellectu Emendatione*. London.

Stern, N. 2010. *A Blueprint for a Safer Planet*. London.

Thaler, R. H. and Sunstein, C. R. 2008. *Nudge: Improving Decisions about Health, Wealth and Happiness*. New Haven, CT.

Tocqueville, A. de 1961. *De la démocratie en Amérique*. Oevres completes, tome 1. Paris

Van Vugt, M. 2009. 'Averting the tragedy of the commons: using social psychological science to protect the environment'. *Current Directions in Psychological Science* 18, 169–173.

Wade-Benzoni, K. A. 1999. 'Thinking about the future'. *American Behavioral Scientist* 42, 1393–1405.

Weber, E. U. 2006. 'Experience-based and description-based perceptions of long-term risk: why global warming does not scare us (yet)'. *Climatic Change* 77, 103–120.

Weiss, E. B. 1989. *In Fairness to Future Generations: International Law, Common Patrimony, and Intergenerational Equity*. Tokyo/Dobbsferry NY.

Zwick, M. M. 2001. 'Der globale Klimawandel in der Wahrnehmung der Öffentlichkeit'. *GAIA* 10, 299–303.

10 Libertarian paternalism, sustainable self-binding and bounded freedom

Ludger Heidbrink

Environmental research shows that people have a strong environmental awareness, but in everyday life show only a relatively low willingness to sustainable action. Libertarian paternalism has developed an attractive program on how to make actors achieve what is in their own long-term interest by influencing their decisions through "nudges." On the basis of an overview of the critical discussion provoked by Sunstein and Thaler's book, it is argued that nudges are a legitimate and effective means of self-binding if they are designed openly and transparently, support the self-responsibility of actors and allow for learning processes.

1. Introduction

Generally, sustainable action does not only require a consciousness of relevant reasons of action, but also the readiness and ability to implement those reasons. Even if actors know what they should do, this insight is not necessarily being followed by them acting according to it. People very often not only have problems to acquire certain insights. They also tend to not adequately realize the insights they already have.[1]

Environmental research, for example, shows that people do have a strong environmental awareness, but show only a relatively low willingness to sustainable action in everyday life (Umweltbundesamt 2009; Borgstedt *et al.* 2010). In other words, many people actually want to act sustainably, but have a limited ability of putting their willingness into practice. In the literature, this phenomenon is often described as mind or attitude behavior gap and is ascribed to a motivational gap between insight and action.[2] From the perspective of psychological behavioral research and behavioral economics, however, problems reside primarily in the cognitive deficits of actors that lead to systematically biased and wrong action decisions (Ariely 2008; Kahneman and Tversky 2000; Beck 2009). While in one case the actors actually know what they are supposed to do, but still are not able to implement it, in the other case they are not able to gain correct insights of action. In both cases – according to the common diagnosis – actors "fail" because they do not have the "right" reasons and motives for their actions.

Libertarian paternalism, as it became known in the last few years through the book *Nudge* by Cass Sunstein and Richard Thaler (2008), tries to answer the question of why societal actors are only in a limited way able to do what they actually want to do and how they can be supported to achieve their goals of action in a better way. At first glance, libertarian paternalism has developed an attractive program on how to make actors achieve what is in their own long-term interest in spite of behavioral deficits. Libertarian paternalism is not about intervening in the freedom of individuals and restricting their autonomy, but about influencing their decisions with modest means so that individual welfare is promoted. Under the assumption that social actors have an interest in sustainable practices, but are held back by decision weaknesses and misperceptions, libertarian paternalism seems to have instruments at its disposal not only to promote individual welfare, but also to support the achievement of societal sustainability goals.

On closer examination, however, libertarian paternalism is characterized by a number of methodological and practical problems that make it questionable whether it is possible to achieve sustainable action with its help.

One problem is that libertarian paternalism takes individual preferences as its basis, has a dualistic understanding of the acting self, and adheres to the neo-classical ideal of rationality. This results in counter-productive consequences on the promotion of sustainable behavior patterns. However, the idea of libertarian paternalism to support the actors in realizing their own interests through the design of the decision environment contains a viable approach to supporting sustainable actions. In this chapter, I want to show that this way consists of the *sustainable self-binding* of actors that helps them achieve the common welfare goals they want to achieve through voluntarily limiting their freedom. The thesis of this chapter is that *bounded freedom* has welfare-enhancing and sustainability-promoting effects, if the boundary of freedom is in accordance with the principles of individual autonomy and democratic legitimacy. To show this, I will first discuss libertarian paternalism, then cover the problem of institutional self-binding, and finally go into the necessity of bounded freedom.

2. The idea of libertarian paternalism

The idea of paternalism has a long tradition, dating back to the political philosophy of the modern era. Essentially, it consists in the fact that interferences with individual spheres of freedom are allowed if they are accompanied by an increase in private and public welfare. "Paternalism is the interference of a state or an individual with another person, against their will, and defended or motivated by a claim that the person interfered with will be better off or protected from harm" (Dworkin 2010: 1). Paternalistic measures are justified if they increase the welfare of people without hurting the interests of others. This justification is only valid if the interests of the people whose welfare is supposed to be promoted are not injured in their autonomy. The means through which the actors experience welfare may not be applied against the will of the people concerned. "Any sensible view has to distinguish between good done to agents at their request or with their consent, and good thrust upon them against their will" (ibid. 5).

Based on these criteria, various forms of paternalism can be distinguished, which range between "hard" and "soft", "broad" and "narrow", "weak" and "strong" (ibid.). The main difference between the strong and weak forms of paternalism is that strong paternalism assumes stable preferences of the actors, which are steered in the direction of certain welfare objectives by statutes and rules, while weak paternalism assumes unclear or inconsistent preferences, which are guided in the direction of the actor's own interests by information and incentives. While strong paternalism has a tendency to be based on a negative conception of freedom, which is ensured mainly through regulatory measures and state intervention, weak paternalism is based on a positive understanding of freedom, which is primarily supported by subsidiary means of design and civic forms of self-organization.

Along with related phenomena such as "soft paternalism" (cf. Feinberg 1986: 12) and "asymmetric paternalism" (Camerer *et al.* 2003), libertarian paternalism belongs to the line of development of a "new paternalism" (Whitman 2006) that has emerged in response to a number of fundamental socio-economic changes and methodological revisions since the 1970s. These include the increase of global environmental and economic crises, which can no longer be dealt with effectively by the means of an intervening nation-state, but also growing health and psychological problems in affluent societies, which require changes in social policies (Whitman 2006). On the methodological level the criticism of the neoclassical paradigm of the informed expected utility by concepts of limited rationality and, above all, experimental and behavioral psychological research have contributed to the questioning of the ideal of the *homo oeconomicus* and its amendment by models of context- and situation-dependent decision making (Jones *et al.* 2010: 484).

Looked at that way, libertarian paternalism is directly related to the change of state governance services and social organization processes that in recent decades changed into ways of political context control and regulated self-regulation.[3] Furthermore, libertarian paternalism is a response to the factual limits of neoclassical welfare economics and empirically observable behavior anomalies that have led to a paradigm shift away from complete rationality and the ideal expected utility models.

This is the background against which libertarian paternalism has started out with the promise to be able to offer a "real Third Way" for future societal problems such as "savings, social security, credit markets, environmental policy, health care" (Thaler and Sunstein 2008: 253). A way that combines political control with individual freedom and allows "[to] nudge people in directions that will make their lives go better while also insisting that the ultimate choice is for individuals, not for the state" (254).

First, I would like to address the basic assumptions, means, and objectives with which libertarian paternalism is defending its program of the promotion of individual and societal welfare and then present the main criticisms of this approach, from which implications can be derived for the promotion of sustainable behaviors.

3. Basic assumptions of libertarian paternalism

One of the basic assumptions of libertarian paternalism is that people do not have "clear, stable, and well-ordered preferences" because they are influenced in their decisions by contextual factors whose effects they are not explicitly aware of: "What they choose is strongly influenced by details of the context in which they make their choice, for example default rules, framing effects (that is, the wording of possible options), and starting points" (Sunstein and Thaler 2003: 1161). Due to these biases, actors make choices that put them in a relatively worse position than if they had decided independently of the situational circumstances, because these circumstances cause a restriction of the ideal decision conditions. Thaler and Sunstein "emphasize the possibility that in some cases individuals make inferior choices, choices that they would change if they had complete information, unlimited cognitive abilities, and no lack of willpower" (Thaler and Sunstein 2003: 175). Due to the fact that actors act against their own interests based on incomplete decision conditions and therefore put themselves in a worse position unintentionally, it is not only politically legitimate but morally commanded "by private and public institutions, to steer people's choices in directions that will improve the choosers' own welfare. In our understanding, a policy therefore counts as 'paternalistic' if it attempts to influence the choices of affected parties in a way that will make choosers better off" (Sunstein and Thaler 2003: 1162).

The key requirements for "libertarian benevolence" (Sunstein and Thaler 2003: 1162) as propagated by Sunstein and Thaler are the actors' free choice and the absence of coercion. Actors should be influenced in a way that they are able to make decisions that are in their own interest and are not perceived by them as coercive measures. To this end, the effects must be designed in a way that a rejection by actors is possible if they are restricted in their interests or if the pursued welfare effects cannot be achieved: "Our only qualification is that when third-party effects are not present, the general presumption should be in favor of freedom of choice, and that presumption should be rebutted only when individual choice is demonstrably inconsistent with individual welfare" (Sunstein and Thaler 2003: 1201).

Under the assumption of missing coercion, and considering the freedom dictate and the promotion of welfare effects, the design of the choice architecture (cf. Thaler and Sunstein 2008: 89) is, from the perspective of libertarian paternalism, a justifiable method for improving individual decision-making processes that are subject to cognitive and motivational distortions. "Hence it is possible to preserve freedom of choice, and to allow opt-outs, but also to favor self-conscious efforts to promote welfare by helping people to solve problems of bounded rationality and bounded self-control" (Sunstein and Thaler 2003: 1184). Paternalistic measures are therefore allowed if the actors are given the opportunity of *opting out* without thereby imposing undue costs or burdens on them.[4]

But paternalistic measures are also, as a further argument states, inevitable in everyday practice. The inevitability of paternalism is based on factual and normative reasons. In fact people have always acted in socio-culturally shaped environments, are bound by rules and regulations, have subjected themselves to contracts and agreements, and are influenced by standards and routines that more or less directly guide their everyday actions.[5] In normative terms, paternalistic measures are necessary to address behavioral anomalies, reduce information and knowledge deficits, to overcome weakness of will and lack of self-control and thereby to achieve the desired betterment of actors.[6]

Sunstein's and Thaler's libertarian paternalism is thus characterized by the following basic assumptions (Sunstein and Thaler 2003: 1184): The planned measures are based on a *minimal paternalism*, which influences decisions of actors moderately through the design of action situations while the actors can choose otherwise at any time. Planners do not force actors to make certain decisions, but to make *active choices* that are taken explicitly in order to be able to take them back if they are not promoting welfare. By *procedural and substantive constraints* actors are encouraged by planners to pursue objectives in their own interest, which make them better off – even if still deciding under conditions of bounded rationality and self-control.

4. The means of libertarian paternalism

Libertarian paternalism combines the liberal freedom statute with a paternalistic consequentialism, subjecting the intervening actions to a cost-benefit analysis in terms of individual welfare effects. Thus, an extended rational choice approach takes the place of an autonomy dictate that sees an intrinsic value in the self-determination of individuals independent of actual influencing factors and expected utility results. The extended rational choice approach supports actors in taking the decisions they actually want to take by overcoming existing defects and anomalies.

This extended rational choice approach is based on an anthropological dualism that originates in behavioral psychological research. Following the behavioral research of Daniel Kahneman, who distinguishes between a fast-acting intuitive "system 1" and a slow-acting reflexive "system 2" that mutually influence each other in human decision making (Kahneman 2011: 19), Sunstein and Thaler assume an "automatic system" that is based on unconscious and direct reactions and a "reflexive system" that leads to controlled and conscious actions (Thaler and Sunstein 2008: 21). While the automatic system is a characteristic of *humans* who choose spontaneously, but flawed, the reflexive system is a property of *econs* who are trained to take well-considered, but time consuming decisions. The goal is to combine the advantages of the reflexive system with the advantages of the automatic system by supporting the actors in making decisions more directly and easily that are in their own interest (Sunstein 2013: 42).

Against the background of this two-selves model Sunstein and Thaler build on a cost-benefit analysis that is not based on the actors' "willingness to pay" which is influenced by contextual decision factors, but is attributed to an "open-ended (and inevitably somewhat subjective) assessment of the welfare consequences" (Sunstein and Thaler 2003: 1190) arising from the design of choice architecture. This cost-benefit analysis is part of a toolbox that – to put it paradoxically – should allow planners to generate welfare benefits without knowing the exact welfare costs for the actors. Since actors are not able to balance benefits and costs of welfare measures rationally due to their dualistic nature, it is the job of the planner to provide those means of decision, which are assumed to be helpful for actors in their own improvement.

To this end, three "rules of thumb" (Sunstein and Thaler 2003: 1193) are formulated: first, the libertarian paternalist should "select the approach that the majority would choose if explicit choices were required and revealed;" second, the libertarian paternalist should select "the approach that would force people to make their choices explicit;" and third the libertarian paternalist should select "the approach that minimizes the number of options" (178). Using these three rules of thumb, the appropriate means can be determined. They range from the establishment of "default rules" that preset the automatic default settings (as in the case of occupational pension or savings plans), "anchors" that ease the decision making as informative "starting points" (e.g. product labels or risk ratios), to "framing" that influences the decision-making process through the type of knowledge transfer and design of action situations (e.g. through the presentation of statistics on investments or the sequence of food in the cafeteria).[7]

Taken as a whole, libertarian paternalism aims at working against weakness of will and lack of self-control by an appropriate design of the choice architecture, at contributing to the formation of stable preferences under conditions of cognitive uncertainty, and at providing motivational support for behavioral change by overcoming inertia forces and status-quo effects, without restricting the actors' freedom of choice.

5. The aims of libertarian paternalism

The main goal of libertarian paternalism is to generate individual welfare benefits under conditions of bounded rationality and self-control by influencing action contexts (Sunstein 2006: 256). Libertarian paternalism shares the idea with asymmetric paternalism that paternalistic measures are justified (and politically have a majority appeal) if they produce benefits for the actors without at the same time causing excessive costs for actors acting without such restrictions.[8] Market oriented and liberal methods of welfare policy are not to be replaced by planning policy interventions, but complemented by subsidiary governance measures – by "regulation for conservatives"[9]– that reduce the risk of self-destructive behavior without leading to unjustified redistribution and burdens for third parties.

Libertarian paternalism thus joins the tradition of classical liberal paternalism, which has supported the welfare-promoting self-organization of collective societal processes by designing regulative frameworks and incentives for independent action (Wohlgemuth 2001: 155). In contrast to the classical liberal paternalism of, for example, Friedrich August von Hayek, libertarian paternalism, however, remains at a significantly greater distance to the "normative individualism" of liberalism, which is characterized by "respecting currently 'given' preferences, values and opinions even if they express themselves (according to abstract-general democratic processes) in harmful collective decisions" (ibid.: 174).

Libertarian paternalism is skeptical of normatively based practices of self-binding, since it regards the self as incapable of any long-term control of preferences and corresponding methods of self-control due to its dualistic nature and the influence of contextual factors. Instead, policy instruments that are based on the strategy of context design are used, which are supposed to lead to a "debiasing" (Sunstein 2006: 257) of influencing factors that enable actors to correct their wrongdoing by themselves without having to draw on normative reasons for action. Decision criteria are generated in processes of external control organized with the support of planners so that the actors will be automatically led to act in the way they would act reflexively.[10]

6. Objections

Libertarian paternalism has attracted numerous critical objections. With regard to the topic of this chapter, these objections focus on three points.

(1) Critique of libertarian paternalism's understanding of preference and rationality

Sunstein and Thaler have been reproached for having an understanding of individual preferences that is based exactly on the ideal of rationality that is questioned by behavioral economics research. The attempt to help actors to perform the actions that are in their own interest by designing a decision environment is based – despite contrary statements – on the neo-classical model of a rational, informed, and self-disciplined *homo oeconomicus* and an extended expected utility approach.[11] The libertarian-paternalistic idea of choice architecture is based on the assumption that actors are in principle able to develop consistent preferences if they are provided with the necessary information and decision criteria through an appropriate (counter-)framing (Sugden 2008: 228). This assumption is contrary to the basic diagnosis that parties involved are subjected to rationality defects and behavioral abnormalities in their action decisions due to contextual influences that prevent the realization of stable and revealed preferences (cf. Rizzo and Whitman 2009: 922).

Another objection is aimed at the term "preference" itself, which libertarian paternalism primarily bases on informed expectations instead of normative reasons. The focus on preferences overlooks the fact that real decision-making processes are not only based on individual interests and expected utility, but are a conglomerate of personal motives, beliefs, principles, and norms that cannot be derived from purposive-rational attitudes. In order to evaluate choices of actors appropriately, it is not enough to ascribe them to individual preferences, which are, furthermore, determined from an external observer position. Rather, an analysis of the normative and evaluative settings is required from the internal perspective of the actors and in conformity with their individual capacity for autonomous decision making and self-determination (White 2013: 34, 61).

(2) Knowledge and planning critique

The criticism of an abridged preference term and a perfectionist rationality ideal is directly followed by the criticism of the knowledge and planning understanding of libertarian paternalism. Subsidiary nudging does not only assume that planners are in advance of the actors, concerning information and knowledge about the actor's individual preferences, regardless of contextual destabilizing factors. The behavior control over the design of choice architectures also requires that the designers are able to estimate the long-term consequences and expected utility of their interventions better than those who benefit from them (cf. Rizzo 2005).

Regarding the basic idea of libertarian paternalism, both assumptions appear not only methodologically inconsistent but also objectively counterproductive. Thus, using their two-selves model, Sunstein and Thaler assume that the reflexive system stands above the intuitive system, or in other words: "that inside every Human there is an Econ" (Sugden 2009: 370). Libertarian paternalists claim that actors are not only in principle able to develop coherent preferences (if the conditions are right), but are also willing to act according to them. From the perspective of libertarian paternalism it is – despite the two-selves model – out of the question, that actors reflexively decide against their interests and wishes and intentionally choose, for example, an unhealthy way of life, excessive consumption, or an expensive use of resources.

Libertarian-paternalistic planners are therefore forced to interchange their expertise with lay knowledge and to organize welfare-enhancing measures as benevolent dictators, convinced of their cost-benefit advantages, although they are not only subject to the same risks of miscalculation like all Human-Econ-Actors,[12] but – and here is another problem – in this way produce unintended and counterproductive consequences on their own (cf. Saint-Paul 2011). These consequences can consist of the absence of individual learning processes and collective processes of spontaneous order formation due to the setting of defaults and behavior control by framing.[13] The external self-control by nudging measures – whether by taxes (particularly by *sin taxes*, see O'Donoghue and Rabin 2003), incentives for healthier behavior (order of food in the cafeteria, see Lades 2012) or the reduction of options through automation and standardization (organ donation, pension, or the terms of green power) – prevents the individual development of control skills and abilities of active self-binding to regulations (cf. Rizzo and Whitman 2009: 957).

In addition, nudging measures require stable control parameters that make it possible to influence future actors' decisions through the present design of the choice architecture in a beneficial and cost-neutral way. Libertarian paternalism assumes that the current self is willing to subordinate its interests and needs to the future self, without having any knowledge of how the contextual decision influences, social norms, and factual resources will change over time. It remains unclear if the future self would agree with the decisions of the current self and whether it can take advantage of the expected benefits. The libertarian paternalists underestimate the temporal change of decision factors and the feedback effects of nudging measures on actors. Therefore the effectiveness of the applied control means remains contingent and arbitrary (cf. Schnellenbach 2012). The internalized externalization of costs (from the current to the future self) can not only cause ineffective and unjustified consequences, but can also reduce the chances of developing individual methods of self-binding (e.g. through contracts, rewards or self-controls).[14]

(3) Power and legitimacy critique

Since libertarian paternalists assume that individual behavior anomalies are the rule, from their point of view, measures that go beyond the liberal means of economic incentive and political mainstream education are justified. Libertarian paternalism accepts the restriction of individual freedom in order to promote individual welfare. The justification for this approach is derived from the view that liberalism is based on an ideal of rational self-control, which has been empirically refuted, and therefore it is in the actors' interest to be supported by the design of a choice architecture in an external way.

Both justification arguments meet with significant concerns. First, one can point out that Sunstein and Thaler assume a distorted image of classical liberalism. It implies that classical liberalism is based on the ideal of the *homo oeconomicus* and the rational benefit maximizer. But it is not. It originates in the notion of the weak-willed and emotionally driven individual that is dependent on being bound to subsidiary regulations.[15] Therefore not only is libertarian paternalism's criticism of liberalism pointless, but there is also the suspicion that the overemphasis of unstable preferences is used as a justification of paternalistic policy strategies. Instead of promoting the ability of citizens to internalize political regulations, they are directed by external control mechanisms.[16]

Politically legitimate behavior rules are thereby replaced by strategic coercion mechanisms, which only seemingly leave citizens a choice between subjective action alternatives, while in reality forcing them to do what is necessary from the viewpoint of governmental welfare production (cf. Veetil 2011). State control measures become more paternalistic, paradoxically, the more they aim at supporting individual decision-making ability by moderate context design and intuitive framing. Especially, nudges meant to stimulate the automatic decision system of actors require – according to the critics – policy-making processes characterized by a lack of transparency and subtle forms of manipulation (Hausman and Welch 2010: 130). The method is illegitimate, according to the critics, because the choice of the means of design and the vote on the desirability of the objectives are not based on the autonomy and participation of the affected citizens, but are performed by benevolent, but heteronomous planning instances

(White 2013: 81, 127). Therefore libertarian paternalism is lacking an explicit reference frame with which one can distinguish between legitimate constraints and illegitimate coercion. In order to determine the legitimacy of the planning strategies, not only the personal consent of the actors is required, but also a democratic vote on the welfare objectives. Since both – the participation in the choice architecture and the deliberative participation in the regulation of public welfare aims – are absent, libertarian paternalism is only able to promote sustainable forms of action by sacrificing the principles of autonomy and political self-determination (Flügel-Martinsen 2010: 243).

7. Sustainable self-binding

Some of the objections mentioned above have been discussed by the protagonists of libertarian paternalism themselves.[17] Against the criticism that planning design measures lead to contra-productive political regulations and create a *slippery slope* of governmental control, Sunstein and Thaler defend themselves with the argument that political interventions are inevitable even in liberal societies, that they often lead to more effective results and are legitimate as far as the opportunity of opting-out is maintained. Against the objection that planning experts are subject to biases and behavioral weaknesses on their own, Sunstein and Thaler point out that expertocratic forms of governance are legitimate and effective if they are performed transparently and supervised by the affected actors. Against the criticism that the control force of political nudging is too weak and that in many cases strict regulations would have a greater welfare effect, Sunstein and Thaler invoke that individuals have a right to make mistakes and have to be allowed to decide actively for or against realized design architectures.

Anyway, three of the mentioned main objections cannot be swept out of the way easily: those of the lacking validity, efficiency, and legitimacy of libertarian paternalistic measures. *Lacking validity* refers to the question whether libertarian paternalism's image of humanity is compatible with its own basic assumptions. *Lacking efficiency* concerns the question of whether the used means actually achieve their planned effect of promoting welfare. *Lacking legitimacy* consists of the problem that welfare promotion and therefore the support of sustainable action are based on political coercion and unjustified limitations of individual freedom.

All three points show that the main deficit of libertarian paternalism consists of supporting the willingness of actors to implement sustainable reasons of action in a way that ensures that the main goals of action are achieved without thereby contravening the autonomy of actors. I have tried to show that libertarian paternalism follows a strategy of subsidiary self-binding. For this purpose actors are helped to focus their actions on goals they would realize through their own will, if they were not detained by bounded rationality and behavioral anomalies, with the decision architecture. The decisive question is, how a *sustainable self-binding* of actors can be realized according to their own will and at the same time support sustainable action.

Strategies of self-binding have the great advantage of being able to turn necessary coercion into voluntary limitations. In order to achieve certain goals more
easily, self-binding measures that help actors – similar to Ulysses – to limit their
freedom of action of their own accord, thus combining the principle of individual autonomy with the heteronomy of the conditions of actions in an effective
way. Procedures of self-binding are especially reasonable if actors are confronted
with the necessity of limitations of action and want to realize these limitations
themselves. Most procedures of self-binding aim at avoiding external interference with personal freedom of decision by encouraging the actors to subject
themselves to the necessary limitations.[18]

In this respect, methods of self-binding always refer to external factors of
action and external influences of action. The one who binds himself can never
do so entirely by himself. Self-binding is dependent on what one binds to and
what one is bound by. Procedures and techniques of self-binding – as the example of Ulysses shows, who had his companions tie him up – are taking place in
the name of self-determination, but require heteronomous regulations and mechanisms. If self-binding serves self-determination, self-binding goes beyond
self-determination, because the individual only achieves his aims of action by
giving away part of his freedom of action to someone or something else and
subjecting himself to the *limitation* of his personal freedom voluntarily.

Procedures of self-binding have a range of advantages. Self-binding in the
form of voluntary types of self-obligation reduce external – political and governmental – regulations and therefore the risk of sanctioning interventions (cf.
Beckmann and Pies 2009). Self-binding can contribute to the minimization of
transaction costs by actors committing themselves to self-contracts, deadlines or
joining support groups to achieve personal aims of action that would be more
difficult to control by external contracts or supervision.[19] Methods of self-binding are a suitable way of attaining one's objectives under circumstances of
incomplete rationality and imminent *akrasia*, by drawing on conventions,
routines, and habitual behavioral ways and rules of thumb (cf. Elster 1990: 36),
forcing oneself to stick to otherwise insecure agreements through promises
(Schelling 2006: 9) or adapting oneself to the change of the environment of
action through the self-constraint of demands.[20] Last, but not least, procedures of
self-binding have the advantage of intrinsic motivation, because actors are the
more willing to constrain their freedom of action if this constraint has an inter-
nalistic perspective and if the person achieves the things he "really wished for".[21]

Against this background, it is understandable that strategies of self-binding
have gained attraction in economical and political liberalization processes and
the pursuit of sustainability goals in the last few years. The more important it is
to keep in mind, besides their advantages, the problems and limitations of self-
binding procedures (cf. Di Fabio 1999). First of all, there is the problem of
initiating a stable and constant process of binding to rules, practices, or behaviors, which is implemented by actors but not necessarily initiated by them. Most
processes of self-binding depend on external initiatives that are not a part of the
self-binding procedure but precede them. If actors were able to bind themselves

by their own will-power, they would not need any techniques and strategies of self-binding. Self-binding procedures require an entity that starts and secures the process.[22] This raises the question of the efficiency and legitimacy of this entity. Actors have to be able to rely on the design of self-binding processes to be effective and to take place in their own name. The delegation of effective binding procedures has to be accompanied by the authorization of a legitimate binding entity in order to avoid the risk of a strong and illegitimate external binding.

Besides the risk of *overcontrolling* one's actions there is, on the other hand, the risk of *undercontrolling* them by rules and principles that are too weak. Voluntary procedures of self-binding often suffer from the fact that actors implement them only temporarily and under certain circumstances. When procedures of self-binding are characterized by a high extent of voluntariness, non-binding rules, and lacking control, actors tend to ease the binding to behavior standards and temporarily let go of them. Non-binding guidelines are often stuck to for purely strategic reasons and are revoked as soon as the binding does not pay off anymore. Therefore, not only the problems of a lacking credibility and so-called "greenwashing" emerge, as it is especially observed in the following of voluntary self-binding on competitive markets (Heidbrink and Seele 2008). Self-obligations can also be used as replacement actions and surrogates, by actors binding to standards and goals that are easier to achieve than those they actually wanted to implement or by setting the achieved goals against those they did not achieve.[23]

In short, procedures of self-binding are often subject to exactly those influences and biases against which they are directed.[24] Self-binding is not immune to the kind of self-deception it is designed to overcome. It is not guaranteed that methods of sustainable self-binding achieve their goal of rational self-control instead of being dominated by self-interest and impulsiveness.

How far strategies of self-binding can contribute to a permanent and stable orientation of individual action by common welfare aims depends mainly on the *type of self-binding* chosen. As described, self-binding is more than self-determination. It aims at the determination of the self under circumstances of incomplete rationality and *akrasia*. Self-binding is based on the limitation of one's own freedom of action in order to achieve self-chosen aims in a better way. Thereby individual tactics of self-binding distinguish themselves from forms of political self-obligation that come about through the contractual subjection of citizens under the rule of the state, which itself – just like in the Hobbes' sovereignty theory – is excluded from the subjection contract. In contrast to voluntary individual self-binding, Hobbes has solved the problem of the self-obligation of the citizens to peaceful forms of coexistence with an exclusive contract construction by which citizens give the power of self to the state for the sake of self-control (Hobbes 2003: 136; Kersting 2009: 142).

In order to avoid the fact that the individual self-binding is replaced by the governmental control of the self, the authorization problem has to be solved differently than in Hobbes' paternalism model. To make sure that the autonomous self-binding is not transformed into heteronomous forms of self-control, actors have to be not only the *authors* but also the *authorities* of the self-binding procedures. For sustainable practices of self-binding that are based on what the actors actually want to do, they have to be actively involved in the development of the self-binding procedures and at the same time form the legit-imizing authority before which these procedures are justified (Heidbrink and Reidel 2011).

Strategies of sustainable self-binding therefore require that actors do not only have the ability to co-create self-binding procedures but also the willingness to take over the responsibility for those procedures. Citizens who aim at sustainable action goals bear the self-responsibility for the implementation of the creating measures, which enable the pursuit of these goals. *Self-binding* depends on *self-responsibility*.[25] Jon Elster has shown that there are two types of self-responsible self-binding (Elster 1990: 104). Actors can influence their environment causally and change it. Or they can determine their self within the existent environment anew and change themselves (Taylor 1989). The first type of self-binding consists of the external design of structures and processes by which – as in the case of Ulysses' captivation by his companions – the freedom of action is restricted in order to achieve one's aims more easily. The second type of self-binding consists of the inner recreation of the self, that – by public promises and consistent saving plans, for example – tries to influence his desires and prefer-ences so that these aims are more likely to be achieved (see also Schelling 2001). The first case is an *exogenous* form of self-binding that aims at the manipulation of the realizable range of actions, the second case is a *endogenous* form of self-binding that aims at the manipulation of one's own character. Exogenous self-binding is mainly based on the limitation of freedom of action, endogenous self-binding on the limitation of free will.[26]

In both cases the process of self-binding consists of realizing the aims of action, that otherwise would not have been realized, by a *limitation of external and internal options*.[27] On their own responsibility, actors give up part of their freedom in order to achieve goals they consider to be especially important. This usually happens by the *delegation* of the self-binding procedures to *institutions* that are on one hand authorized to perform these procedures and on the other hand able to implement the necessary self-obligation. The purpose of these institutions is not only to support "incidental constraints" which – like the environmental laws or ecological incentives – exist already and have current advantages for the major-ity of actors, but particularly to promote "essential constraints," which – like the shift towards regenerative energy and electro-mobility – do not have a direct advantage for current actors, but will generate their sustainable benefit only in the future.[28]

The central achievement of self-binding institutions consists of implementing *essential constraints* with the help of which the current members of society volun-tarily limit their freedom in order to realize a sustainable expected benefit in the future that does not, or only partially, benefit themselves. The *voluntariness* of sustainable self-binding is given, if the accompanied limitations of the citizens' freedom is not just privately wanted but can also be publicly justified. Long ago, Claus Offe pointed out that democratic institutions in modern risk and scarcity societies have to be designed in a way that they promote the "self-binding of citizens" (Offe 1989: 744) by providing rules of "intelligent self-restriction" (Habermas 1985: 160) that make members of liberal communities pursue sustainable aims of public welfare against their tendency towards self-interest and short-term planning.

To this purpose *sustainable democracies* have to institutionalize sustainable "principles of responsible self-constraint" (Offe 1989: 747) and build up effective barriers that protect social actors from the consequences of their incomplete rationality in form of "passion, preference change and ... time-inconsistency" (Elster 2000: 1). In order to "overcome the liberal weakness of potentially deficient welfare orientation of citizens ... deliberative forms of rational self-binding" (Schaal and Ritzi 2009: 56) have to be developed that contribute to social actors taking on "a strategic attitude against their own preferences in the future as well as against the development over time" (58). On the one hand, this requires public decision-making processes by which collectively binding welfare aims are determined by discursive procedures (cf. Aaken 2006: 16). But, on the other hand, as it is not guaranteed that social actors stick to the sustainable welfare aims in the long run, there has to be democratic participation in the installing of *deliberative self-binding procedures* (Heidbrink and Reidel 2011: 155; Heidbrink 2013: 33). It is not enough that citizens and social actors agree to the change of preferences in the argumentative way and agree on the implementation of sustainable welfare aims in the course of a discursive decision-making process. In order to work against the risk of shortsightedness and motivational overload, society members have to be included in the design of the choice architecture that shall ease the implementation of sustainability goals.

8. Bounded freedom

Self-binding procedures consist of the limitation of one's own freedom in order to realize self-chosen goals. Actors give up part of their freedom to achieve aims they consider to be particularly important. Procedures of self-binding are suitable measures for the promotion of sustainable action if they are legitimized not only argumentatively and discursively but are also co-designed and implemented by those actors. The realization of sustainable public welfare aims by self-binding requires not only democratic deliberation but also collective participation. For actors to voluntarily limit their freedom for the benefit of long-term aims, institutional forms of participation are necessary.

In her research on common-pool resources, Elinor Ostrom has shown that the sustainable cultivation of common goods is not achieved by external coercion but by "credible commitments" (Ostrom 2006: 43) that actors stick to because there is a common interest in the use of common goods and social mechanisms of mutual observation. Actors are particularly prepared to show quasi-voluntary compliance if they are given a chance to take part in the design of the rules and if the majority of the other actors are willing to follow these rules.[29] Regulative self-organization and conditional cooperativeness are two main requirements for the sustainable handling of scarce common goods and for the solution of collective problems of action.

Thereby, has a way been found to support the willingness of actors to act sustainably without interfering with their autonomy? Can the risks of libertarian paternalism of intruding manipulatively into the freedom of social actors be reduced by the discursive and participatory extension of self-binding processes? Is the communal self-organization of the sustainable use of resources a more effective means than governmental control with eco-political nudges?

Concerning the last question there are indeed similarities between the self-organized cultivation of common goods and the promotion of sustainable behavior by the political design of publicly relevant decision architectures. The rules of the commons administration can be understood as nudges that help actors to match their own interests with common welfare aims without having to invest more costs than the resulting benefits.[30]

The question on the protection of individual and collective autonomy is more difficult to answer. It is a principle question, the answer depends on normative – and in a broadest sense – ethical pre-decisions. Just like libertarian paternalism is based on the assumption that people are characterized by deficient rationality and behavior anomalies that have to be compensated for by nudges in their own interest, every form of political welfare promotion is characterized by normative premises that are the basis for the chosen measures and means. Questions of the long-term welfare economy and sustainable support of public welfare can only be decided ultimately on the basis of the personal and political self-conception of a society.[31]

If this self-conception features a strong understanding of autonomy there have to be explicit criteria when procedures of self-binding are allowed to limit personal and political freedom. Libertarian paternalism, as has become clear, has difficulties in determining precise criteria for the limitation of freedom. The proposal of this chapter, therefore, is to understand nudges as instruments of institutional self-binding through which actors implement mechanisms of self-control in the present that will be behavior-effective in the future. This preferably happens in a way of *assisted self-binding* in which informal and formal institutions self-responsibly authorized by actors control self-imposed obligations (North 1990). The paradox of self-binding, therefore, is not solved by Hobbesian governmental control but by the delegation of control to social institutions that are legitimized by involving actors to regulate the relation of external binding and self-binding in a way that secures the long-term self-determination of the actors.[32]

In this sense, nudges can be understood as *mandates* that are given to institutional control mechanisms in order to enable voluntary self-control over time.[33] It is possible that liberal societies disassociate themselves from their former autonomy conception and restrict the freedom of their members more fiercely to master the challenges of sustainability in the long run. Conceivably, the limitation of growth propagated today, the rejection of an energy-intensive lifestyle, aims of sufficiency and of a post-material consumption culture can only be achieved by a strong limitation of spheres of freedom. Apart from the question of whether such degressive processes of transformation are actually followed in the future and lead to the desired success, even a strong limitation of freedom is not a problem as long as it is guaranteed that it is based on democratic majorities and originates in autonomous decision-making processes of the participants.

The guiding principle of autonomy is based on normative premises that have a cultural and ethical basis. This can change over time. The limitation of individual and collective freedom does not contradict the norm of autonomy if the measure for the support of sustainable transformation processes originates in deliberative and participative procedures of self-binding and is based on self-determined decisions. Self-determined decisions do not necessarily require freedom, but are – as Harry Frankfurt showed – characterized by actors identifying themselves by "second order volitions",[34] with the attitudes underlying their action decisions. This results in the fact that the responsibility of actions is not necessarily based on alternative possibilities,[35] but is compatible with constraints of freedom if these are considered sufficiently important from an internal perspective and are meaningful for the lifestyle of actors.[36]

Actors therefore can be considered autonomous persons as far as they decide and live under circumstances of *bounded freedom*. For the protection of their autonomy it is not relevant that they can decide freely and have fully rational reasons for their decisions but that they are able to accept existent limitations in reflexive learning processes and the development of meta-preferences for the reason that they find their motivational *agreement* and are in *accordance* with their self-conception (Heidbrink 2007: 277).

The criteria for the legitimacy of nudges as a means of self-binding are therefore not to be found, as libertarian paternalism believes, in the simplification of decision processes, minimization of costs, reversibility of measures and the opportunity of opting-out (Sunstein 2013: 190). The criteria lie in fact in the question of whether nudges provide enough transparent information, enough space for self-responsible decisions and respect the choice and are in conformity with the self-conception of actors (White 2013: 127, 149; Hausman and Welch 2010: 134; Reiss 2013: 294).

This results in the following conclusion: The design of choice architectures for the promotion of sustainable action is based on the considerations of autonomy and of public welfare purposes. Nudges are legitimate and effective means of control if they are designed openly and transparently, support the self-responsibility of actors and allow for learning processes. The constraints of individual and collective freedom by governmental interventions and political influence on behavior can be justified if the actors' ability to bind themselves to sustainability aims of their own will is supported.

On the practical side, this results in the requirement that actors should be more consistently supported by political regulations, socio-cultural practices, and subsidiary settings in implementing their own interest in an environmentally friendly and socially acceptable consumption behavior. The promotion of sustainable behavior belongs to the sector of consumer and environment policy that helps consumers follow their sustainability goals with monetary incentives such as emission trading, car toll and climate taxes, but also with informational instruments such as traffic light food labeling systems, eco-labels, the carbon footprint, or the use of smart meters in households.[37] On the other hand, sustainable consumer behavior can be promoted by a societal environment in which ecological lifestyles exist and peer groups set an example of sustainable consumption practices so that consumers meet offers and goods that accommodate their own interests and motivate them at the same time to choose sustainable alternatives (Devinney *et al.* 2012). By embedding consumption processes in sustainable milieus, the promotion of self-responsible decision processes and the involvement in the administration of scarce public resources citizens and consumers can be supported in aiming at social and environment-friendly goals that they want to achieve by their own account.

Notes

1 The term "sustainable action" is used in this article for actions that are in line with a long-term, fair distribution of limited but essential goods and resources: cf. Heidbrink and Schmidt 2011: 31; Voget-Kleschin, Baatz and Ott 2015.

2 The term originates with LaPiere 1932. See also Newholm/Shaw 2007, Carrington et al. 2010.

3 On this development see Heidbrink and Hirsch 2007.

4 Nudges are defined as "regulatory tool" with "high benefits and low costs" (cf. Sunstein 2013: 9).

5 For comments on the inevitability of rules by the example of the chess game see Thaler and Sunstein 2008: 10. For the American employee pension as an example for default rules see Thaler and Sunstein 2003: 176.

6 On the following see Sunstein and Thaler 2003: 1184.

7 Cf. Sunstein and Thaler 2003: 1174. On the cafeteria example see Thaler and Sunstein 2008: 1; Sunstein 2013: 58.

8 "A regulation is asymmetrically paternalistic if it creates large benefits for those who make errors, while imposing little or no harm on those who are fully rational" (Camerer *et al.* 2003: 1212) On the political arguments see ibid.: 1221.

9 Title by Camerer *et al.* 2003.

10 Very similar to that, Norbert Elias spoke of "societal coercion to self-constraint" which helps people in highly developed civilizations to stick to social rules: "This, particularly, is characteristic for the change of the psychic apparatus in the course of civilization, that the differentiated and stable regulation of the individual's behavior is more and more cultivated as an automatism from an early age, as a self-constraint which he cannot fend off, even if he consciously wants to" (Elias 1991: 317).

11 On the discussion on the expected utility approach in form of a classic "experiences utility" and a modern "decision utility" see Kahneman and Thaler 2006. On the criticism of clinging to the neo-classic rationality ideal see especially Rebonato 2012: 36.

12 See also Sunstein 2005.

13 Cf. Carlin *et al.* 2009; also Veetil 2011.

14 Cf. Whitman who developed a self-control approach on the basis of the externalization model of Coase (2006: 5).

15 See Hayek (1960: 61): "It would hardly be exaggerating to say that in the eyes of those British philosophers [i.e. Locke, Hume, Smith *et al.*] man is lazy and remiss, reckless and lavish and that he was only persuaded by the power of circumstances to act economically and learned how to adjust his means to his purposes carefully." Cf. on that also Klein 2004: 263.

16 Cf. Aaken 2006:2; Beck 2010: 145; Rebonato 2012: 118, who is talking of the "exploitation of cognitive biases."
17 On the following see Sunstein and Thaler 2003: 1199; Thaler and Sunstein 2008: 235.
18 *Constraints* stand for legitimate forms of limitation of the freedom of action, *interventions* and *influences*, too. Illegitimate forms of limitation of freedom of action can be characterized as *coercions*.
19 Cf. Whitman 2006: 9; with reference to Ainslie 2001.
20 On adaptive preference development see Elster 1985: 109. On strategies of aspiration adaption see also Selten 2002.
21 "Alternate possibilities and moral responsibility" (Frankfurt 1995: 10).
22 See also Hobbes: "Nor is it possible for any person to be bound to himself; because he that can bind, can release; and therefore he that is bound to himselfe onely, is not bound" (2003: 211).
23 Cf. on the phenomenon of *mental accounting* Thaler 1999.
24 Cf. Schnellenbach (2012: 27), who points at the favoritism of short-term preferences in self-binding.
25 Thereby not the self-responsibility for the keeping of advantageous rules of the game are meant as it is represented in economical ethics: Homann and Blome-Drees 1992: 35.
26 See Elster (1990: 103) who distinguishes three groups altogether.
27 The respective basic definition of Elster (1990: 39) is "To bind oneself is to carry out a certain decision at time t_1 in order to increase the probability that one will carry out another decision at time t_2."
28 On the distinction of *incidental constraints* and *essential constraints* see Elster (2000: 4).
29 Cf. Ostrom, who names further"design principles illustrated by long-enduring CPR institutions" (2006: 90).
30 See, as an example, the rotation system of the collective control of watering and fishing (Ostrom 1999: 124).
31 Norton et al. 1998; Rebonato 2012: 242. On the term of self-conception see Langbehn 2012: 27.
32 On the relation of *binding oneself*, *being bound* and *binding others* see Elster (2000: 276).
33 On the relationship between nudges and mandates see Frank (2008: 206).
34 "Freedom of the will and the concept of a person" (Frankfurt 1995: 16).
35 "Alternate possibilities and moral responsibility" (Frankfurt 1995: 9).
36 "Three concepts of free action" (Frankfurt 1995: 55); "Identification and wholeheartedness" (172). On the differentiation of different types of constraint see also Frankfurt (1995: 26), ("Coercion and moral Responsibility").
37 See Ratner et al. 2008; Fischer and Sommer 2011; Reisch and Hagen 2011; Sunstein 2014. On the juridical side see Smeddinck 2011.

References

Aaken, A. 2006. *Begrenzte Rationalität und Paternalismusgefahr: das Prinzip des schonendsten Paternalismus*. Reprint of the Max Planck Institute for Research of Collective Goods, No. 2006/3, Bonn.
Ainslie, G. 2001. *Breakdown of Will*. New York.
Ariely, D. 2008. *Predictably Irrational*. New York.
Beck, H. 2009. "Wirtschaftspolitik und Psychologie: Zum Forschungsprogramm der Behavioral Economics." In: *ORDO. Jahrbuch für die Ordnung von Wirtschaft und Gesellschaft*, Bd. 60. Stuttgart, 119–151.

Beckmann, M. and Pies, I. 2009. "Freiheit durch Bindung – Zur ökonomischen Logik von Verhaltenskodizes." In: Pies, I. *Moral als Produktionsfaktor. Ordonomische Schriften zur Unternehmensethik.* Berlin, 157–191.

Borgstedt, S., Christ, T. and Reusswig, F. 2010. *Umweltbewusstsein in Deutschland 2010. Ergebnisse einer repräsentativen Bevölkerungsumfrage.* Heidelberg,Potsdam.

Camerer, C., Issacharoff, S., Loewenstein, G., O'Donoghue, T. and Rabin, M. 2003. "Regulation for Conservatives: Behavioral Economics and the Case for Asymmetric Paternalism." *University of Pennsylvania Law Review*, 151, 1211–1254.

Carlin, B. I., Gervais, S. and Manso, G. 2009. "When Does Libertarian Paternalism Work," NBER Working Paper Series. *Working Paper 15139.* Cambridge.

Carrington, M. J., Neville, B. A. and Whitwell, G. J. 2010. "Why Ethical Consumers Don't Walk their Talk: Towards a Framework for Understanding the Gap between the Ethical Purchase Intentions and Actual Buying Behaviour of Ethically Minded Consumers." *Journal of Business Ethics*, 97 (1), 139–158.

Devinney, T. M., Auger, P. and Eckhardt, G. 2012. "Can the Socially Responsible Consumer Be Mainstream?" *Zeitschrift für Wirtschafts- und Unternehmensethik (ZfWU)*, 13/3, 227–235.

Di Fabio, U. 1999. "Unternehmerische Selbstbindung und rechtsstaatliche Fremdbindung." In: Peter Ulrich (ed.), *Unternehmerische Freiheit, Selbstbindung und politische Mitverantwortung. Perspektiven republikanischer Unternehmensethik.* Munich, 85–96.

Dworkin, G. 2010. "Paternalism." In: *Stanford Encyclopedia of Philosophy.* Available at: http://plato.stanford.edu/entries/paternalism.

Elias, N. 2000. *The Civilizing Process: Sociogenetic and Psychogenetic Investigations.* Oxford.

Elster, J. 1985. *Sour Grapes: Studies in the Subversion of Rationality.* Cambridge.

Elster, J. 1990. *Ulysses and the Sirens: Studies in Rationality and Irrationality.* Cambridge.

Elster, J. 2000. *Ulysses Unbound: Studies in Rationality, Precommitment, and Constraints.* Cambridge.

Feinberg, J. 1986. *The Moral Limits of the Criminal Law, Vol. 3: Harm to Self.* New York.

Fischer, M. and Sommer, B. 2011. "Mentale und soziale Infrastrukturen – Voraussetzungen verantwortungsvollen Konsums im Kontext der Nachhaltigkeit." In: Ludger Heidbrink, Imke Schmidt and Björn Ahaus (eds), *Die Verantwortung des Konsumenten. Über das Verhältnis von Markt, Moral und Konsum.* Frankfurt, 183–202.

Flügel-Martinsen, O. 2010. "Libertärer Paternalismus? Bemerkungen zu Richard H. Thalers und Cass R. Sunsteins Nudge." In: *Der moderne Staat – Zeitschrift für Public Policy, Recht und Management*, H. 1/2010, 235–244.

Frank, R. H. 2008. "Richard H. Thaler and Cass R. Sunstein, Nudge: Improving Decisions about Health, Wealth, and Happiness." *Ethics* 119(1), 202–208.

Frankfurt, H. 1995. *The Importance of What We Care About.* Cambridge.

Habermas, J. 1985. *Die Neue Unübersichtlichkeit.* Frankfurt.

Hausman, D. M. and Welch, B. 2010. "To Nudge or Not to Nudge." *The Journal of Political Philosophy* 18(1), 123–136.

Hayek, F. A. 1960. *The Constitution of Liberty.* Chicago.

Heidbrink, L. 2007. "Autonomie und Lebenskunst. Zu den Grenzen der Selbstbestimmung." In: W. Kersting and C. Langbehn (eds), *Kritik der Lebenskunst.* Frankfurt, 261–286.

Heidbrink, L. 2013. "Leben nach dem Fortschritt. Zur nachhaltigen Gestaltung der Zukunft." In: Ulf Kilian (ed.), *Leben // Gestalten in Zeiten endloser Krisen.* Berlin, 24–35.

Heidbrink, L. and Hirsch, A. (eds) 2007 *Staat ohne Verantwortung? Zum Wandel der Aufgaben von Staat und Politik*. Frankfurt.

Heidbrink, L. and Reidel, J. 2011. "Nachhaltiger Konsum durch politische Selbstbindung. Warum Verbraucher stärker an der Gestaltung von Entscheidungsumwelten mitwirken sollten." *Gaia* 3, 152–156.

Heidbrink, L. and Schmidt, I. 2011. "Das Prinzip der Konsumentenverantwortung. Grundlagen, Bedingungen und Umsetzung verantwortlichen Konsums." In: Ludger Heidbrink, Imke Schmidt and Björn Ahaus (eds), *Die Verantwortung des Konsumenten. Über das Verhältnis von Markt, Moral und Konsum*. Frankfurt, 25–56.

Heidbrink, L. and Seele, P. 2008. "Greenwash, Bluewash und die Frage nach der weißen Weste. Begriffsklärung zum Verhältnis von CSR, PR und Unternehmenswerten." *Forum Wirtschaftsethik* 2, 54–56.

Hobbes, T. 2003. *Leviathan: A Critical Edition*, G. A. J. Rogers and K. Schuhmann (eds). Bristol.

Homann, K. and Blome-Drees, F. 1992. *Wirtschafts- und Unternehmensethik*. Göttingen.

Jones, R., Pykett, J. and Whitehead, M. 2010. "Governing Temptation: Changing Behaviour in an Age of Libertarian Paternalism." *Progress in Human Geography* 35(4), 483–501.

Kahneman, D. 2011. *Thinking, Fast and Slow*. New York.

Kahneman, D. and Thaler, R. H. 2006. "Anomalies: Utility Maximization and Experienced Utility." *The Journal of Economic Perspectives*, 20(1), 221–234.

Kahneman, D. and Tversky, A. (eds) 2000. *Choices, Values, and Frames*. Cambridge.

Kersting, W. 2009. *Thomas Hobbes zur Einführung*. Hamburg.

Klein, D. B. 2004. "Statist Quo Bias." *Econ Journal Watch* 1(2), 260–271.

La Piere, R. T. 1932. "Attitudes vs. Actions." *Social Forces* 13(2), 130–137.

Lades, L. K. 2012. *Impulsive Consumption and Reflexive Thought: Nudging Ethical Consumer Behavior*. Papers on Economics and Evolution, No. 1203, Max Planck-Institute of Economics, Jena.

Langbehn, C. 2012. *Vom Selbstbewusstsein zum Selbstverständnis. Kant und die Philosophie der Wahrnehmung*. Paderborn.

Newholm, T. and Shaw, D. 2007. "Studying the Ethical Consumer: A Review of Research". *Journal of Consumer Behaviour* 6, 253–270.

North, D. C. 1990. *Institutions, Institutional Change and Economic Performance*. Cambridge.

Norton, B., Costanza, R. and Norton R. C. B. 1998. "The Evolution of Preferences. Why 'Sovereign' Preferences May Not Lead to Sustainable Policies and What to do About It." *Ecological Economics* 24, 193–211.

O'Donoghue, T. and Rabin, M. 2003. "Studying Optimal Paternalism: Illustrated by a Model of Sin Taxes." *American Economic Association Papers and Proceedings* 93, 186–191.

Offe, C. 1989. "Fessel und Bremse. Moralische und institutionelle Aspekte, intelligenter Selbstbeschränkung." In: Axel Honneth et al. (eds), *Zwischenbetrachtungen. Im Prozeß der Aufklärung. Jürgen Habermas zum 60. Geburtstag*. Frankfurt, 739–774.

Ostrom, E. 2006. *Governing the Commons. The Evolution of Institutions for Collective Action*. Cambridge.

Ratner, R. K. et al. 2008. "How Behavioral Decision Research can Enhance Consumer Welfare: From Freedom of Choice to Paternalistic Intervention." *Marketing Letters* 19, 383–397.

Rebonato, R. 2012. *Taking Liberties. A Critical Examination of Libertarian Paternalism*. London.

Reisch, L. A. and Hagen, K. 2011. "Kann der Konsumwandel gelingen? Chancen und Grenzen einer verhaltensökonomisch basierten sozialen Regulierung." In: Ludger Heidbrink, Imke Schmidt and Björn Ahaus (eds), *Die Verantwortung des Konsumenten. Über das Verhältnis von Markt, Moral und Konsum.* Frankfurt, 221–244.

Reiss, J. 2013. *Philosophy of Economics. A Contemporary Introduction.* New York.

Rizzo, M. 2005. "The Problem Of Moral Dirigisme: A New Argument Against Moralistic Legislation." *NYU Journal of Law and Liberty* 1(2), 781–835.

Rizzo, M. J. and Whitman, D. G. 2009. "The Knowledge Problem of the New Paternalism." *Brigham Young University Law Review* 2009(4), 905–968.

Saint-Paul, G. 2011. *The Tyranny of Utility: Behavioral Social Science and the Rise of Paternalism.* Princeton.

Schaal, G. S. and Ritzi, C. 2009. "Rationale Selbstbindung und die Qualität politischer Entscheidungen – liberale und deliberative Perspektiven." In: G. S. Schaal (ed.), *Techniken rationaler Selbstbindung.* Berlin, 55–95.

Schelling, T. 2001. "Self-Command in Practice, in Policy, and in a Theory of Rational Choice." *American Economic Review* 74(2), 1–11.

Schelling, T. 2006. *Strategies of Commitment and Other Essays.* Cambridge.

Schnellenbach, J. 2012. "Nudges and Norms: On the Political Economy of Soft Paternalism." *European Journal of Political Economy* 28, 266–277.

Selten, R. 2002. "What is Bounded Rationality?" In: Gerd Gigerenzer and Reinhard Selten (eds), *Bounded Rationality:. The Adaptive Toolbox.* Cambridge, 13–36.

Smeddinck, U. 2011. "Regulieren durch 'Anstoßen'. Nachhaltiger Konsum durch gemeinwohlverträgliche Gestaltung von Entscheidungssituationen." *Die Verwaltung* 44(3), 375–395.

Sugden, R. 2008. "Why Incoherent Preferences do not Justify Paternalism." *Constitutional Political Economy* 19, 226–248.

Sugden, R. 2009. "On Nudging: A Review of *Nudge: Improving Decisions About Health, Wealth and Happiness* by R. H. Thaler and C. R. Sunstein." *International Journal of the Economics of Business* 16(3), 365–373.

Sunstein, C. R. 2005. *Law of Fear: Beyond the Precautionary Principle.* Cambridge.

Sunstein, C. R. 2006. "Boundedly Rational Borrowing." *The University of Chicago Law Review* 73 (1). *Symposium: Homo Economicus, Homo Myopicus, and the Law and Economics of Consumer Choice,* 249–270.

Sunstein, C. R. 2013. *Simpler: The Future of Government.* New York.

Sunstein, C. R. 2015. "Behavioral Economics, Consumption, and Environmental Protection." In: Lucia Reisch and John Thøgersen (eds), *Handbook of Research on Sustainable Consumption.* Cheltenham.

Sunstein, C. R. and Thaler, R. H. 2003. "Libertarian Paternalism Is Not an Oxymoron." *The University of Chicago Law Review* 70(4), 1159–1202.

Taylor, C. 1989. *Sources of Self. The Making of the Modern Identity.* Cambridge MA.

Thaler, R. H. 1999. "Mental Accounting Matters." *Journal of Behavioral Decision Making* 12(3), 183–206.

Thaler, R. H. and Sunstein, C. R. 2003. "Libertarian Paternalism." *American Economic Review* 93(2), 175–179.

Thaler, R. H. and Sunstein, C. R. 2008. *Nudge: Improving Decisions About Health, Wealth and Happiness.* London.

Umweltbundesamt. 2009. *Umweltbewusstsein und Umweltverhalten der sozialen Milieus in Deutschland.* Available at: www.umweltbundesamt.de/publikationen/umweltbewusstsein-umweltverhalten-sozialen-milieus

Veetil, V. P. 2011. "Libertarian Paternalism is an Oxymoron: An Essay in Defence of Liberty." *European Journal of Law and Economics* 31, 321–334.

Voget-Kleschin, L., Baatz, C. and Ott, K. 2015. "Ethics and Sustainable Consumption." In: L. Reisch and J. Thøgersen (eds), *Handbook of Research on Sustainable Consumption*. Cheltenham.

White, M. D. 2013. *The Manipulation of Choice. Ethics and Libertarian Paternalism*. New York.

Whitman, G. 2006. "Against the New Paternalism Internalities and the Economics of Self-Control." *Policy Analysis* 563, 1–16.

Wohlgemuth, M. 2001. "Klassisch-liberaler Paternalismus? Das Beispiel von F.A. von Hayek." In: Volker Gadenne and Reinhard Neck (eds), *Philosophie und Wirtschaftswissenschaft*. Tübingen, 155–177.

11 The "missing link"

Polarization and the need for "trial by jury" procedures

Adrian-Paul Iliescu

Since true representation of the preferences/priorities of future generations is impossible, what we primarily miss is not representative institutions (ombudsman, guardian, committee etc.), but rather methods of reconciling present and future generational priorities; and, given the antagonistic character of the dilemma "protect future generations or satisfy present needs," what we most urgently need are adversarial instruments of comparing, balancing and opting among alternatives. What is thus needed is a trial by jury-mechanism of solving controversies between protectors (of future generations) and promoters (of risky technologies, of economic development and of the priorities of present generations).

1. Introduction

The aim of this chapter is to argue for "trial by jury" type decision procedures on matters that are supposed to affect future generations. Such procedures, I submit, can be seen as a "missing link" in contemporary institutional decision-making systems. The argumentation will rely upon two main points: First, that, contrary to a widespread conviction, what we sorely and primarily miss is not representation of future generations, but rather methods of reconciling present and future justified generational priorities; second, that, given the antagonistic character of the dilemma to "protect future generations or satisfy present needs," what we most urgently need are adversarial instruments of comparing, balancing and opting between various alternatives.

2. Background

The background of my discussion is quite familiar. Enormous attention has been paid to the representation of interests/rights of future generations. Generally speaking, this has been beneficial since it has stimulated a better exploration/understanding of these interests/rights and an increased awareness of the dangers created by ignoring them.

But preoccupation with "giving a voice to future generations" has also created a dominant feeling that *representation* (more precisely, that failure to represent adequately future generations inside our decision making) is the main obstacle to

an ethical attitude towards the future. It is thus often claimed that "what is missing is a voice with legal authority; a voice with the force of the law to protect our
environment and our future."[1]

That might seem obvious and uncontroversial for all those concerned by our
lack of responsibility towards the future; but many commentators go further than
that. The need for representation is often taken as the most important and the
most pressing: "The principal problem is that future generations have no person
to represent their interests," claims Howell-Moroney (2013).

In my opinion, that evaluation is wrong. Representation, I would like to say
most emphatically, is *not* the main problem.

3. Vulnerabilities of the idea of "representing future generations"

No matter how important and deeply justified the concern for the well-being of
our descendants is, the idea of *representation* appears to be very problematic when
applied to future generations, especially as regards the distant ones. In order to
see that, the starting point might be the following observation: *representation* is
inseparable from *mapping* – representing implies a capacity to map correctly what
is to be represented. Thus, talking about "representing future generations" in
contemporary public debates naturally implies that one could somehow "map"
the specific interests/priorities of these generations and defend them in present
political debates.

But such a "mapping" is something one obviously cannot do for distant future
generations. Since we know so little about the particulars of their
epoch/context/situation, we are far from able to draw, even vaguely, a map of
their specific interests/priorities. The difficulties confronting present attempts to
grasp and reconstruct rationally these interests and priorities have been often
invoked by enemies of intergenerational justice and critics of the received views
in the field, especially by those coming from libertarian or neo-conservative
camps. Typically, these authors aim to prove, in the words of Jan Narveson, that
"the remote future ... is much better left to take care of itself" (Narveson 2011:
12). I do not intend to foster such a nihilistic, or at least narrow-minded, position. But I think the arguments put forward by these critics should be
distinguished from their general aims. While the aims (of putting an end to
investigations of future generations' interests/rights/priorities) might or should be
rejected, the huge obstacles confronting such investigations cannot be dismissed:
they should be carefully taken into account and analyzed.

The difficulties faced by any attempt to reconstruct the interests and priorities
of future generations are of several kinds. The most obvious are the *epistemologi-
cal* difficulties generated by our incapacity to predict many of the relevant
particulars of the situations in which future generations are going to find themselves. Less visible, but not less important, are the *logical* difficulties. Any
tentative effort to synthesize future interests and priorities would imply a capacity to compare and aggregate preferences characterizing different members or
groups of the same generation (who will inevitably disagree on several matters)

but also the members in the same group (who always have a great variety of preferences, not necessarily harmonious). As several well-known logical results since Arrow's famous theorem have shown, there might be no objective method of aggregating these preferences into a unique and coherent final set. Moreover, according to the same results, even if a method of aggregation could be found, it will surely rely upon some *subjective* (hard to guess, for us) options to be made in the future (for instance, on some particular meta-preferences among preferences, justified by particular circumstances known only to the generation involved). But as far as we can fail to synthesize the various, possibly non-harmonious, preferences of some future generation into a coherent final map, how can we hope to be able to establish their major interests/priorities in order to represent them in present political debates?

It is not my aim here to develop these arguments. What I shall do instead is to insist a little bit on a *conceptual* argument. The idea of a *representation* of future generations is obviously inspired by our usual experience with representing present generations. We are somehow committed to some sort of reasoning by analogy: "If present generations can be represented, why shouldn't we try to also represent, at least in part, future generations?" The question certainly makes sense. But the analogy on which it is based is exposed to some risks – as Wittgenstein famously insisted, we always run the risk of extending an analogy too far. The familiar situations in which we apply the idea of *representation* are characterized by the following traits:

- One can genuinely examine the actual interests/preferences of certain people (either by talking to them, or by interacting with them in practice or, at least, by studying their actual behavior); one can also gather statistical data on their choices, which presumably reflect their interests/preferences/priorities; shortly, *one is not bound to rely upon abstract deduction* or upon *hypothesizing*, because one can *learn* about the true interests/priorities which should be represented.
- One can establish a contractual relationship of representation, and rely on the accord of the people to be represented.
- One can get some feedback from these people. They are able to approve or disapprove the way in which they have been represented; a dialogue is in principle possible (even if many representatives do not care to engage in it), misunderstandings can be eliminated, errors can be rectified (in due time, not just retrospectively).
- The feedback of those involved can, in special circumstances, amount to a proof that their interests/priorities have, or have not, been correctly mapped and defended. It is thus possible to draw a distinction (in due time) between *representing genuinely* the interests/priorities of some people and *attributing some interests/priorities to some people and defending them, even though they are not their genuine interests/priorities*. It is precisely this possibility that enables representatives to correct their misinterpretations and errors as soon as they have been committed.

It cannot be denied that these traits are not to be found in the representation of future generations as it is usually understood. One can, of course, claim that any understanding of the interests of other people always includes some sort of *attribution*, and that consequently any act of representation is based upon attribution – which might be taken by some as an objection against the distinction in the last trait mentioned above. But the objection is weak. Precisely because in usual cases representation includes a possibility to get feedback from those represented, the distinction makes perfect sense: Representatives can correct their mistakes in case they have misinterpreted the interests/priorities to be represented. This is not the case for representatives of future generations. They are prone to remain entrapped in their own interpretations of what future generations will need, want or prefer. The distinction between *representing interests* and merely *attributing interests* is not one that applies to the representation of future generations.

It is not my intention here to dismiss the idea of *representing future generations* altogether. I am content to conclude that its use, however familiar that has become, is problematic and that we should ask ourselves whether this use might not be another example of the typical philosophical error described by Wittgenstein as 'extending an analogy too far.'

4. An alternative proposal

In order to get a better picture of our endeavor to care about the interests of future generations we should (I submit) make use of another analogy than the ones usually implied.

The situation we are in with respect to future generations can be better compared to the situation of a deeply ignorant "representative to be." Suppose a Western diplomat is suddenly, out of the blue, asked to represent (with no further delay) the small faraway island state X, about which he knows nothing, in an UN General Assembly meeting. The diplomat's first concern should of course be to gather information on X and its population. But before any precise information has been obtained, what could he do (if required to act effectively and immediately as a representative of that state)? He can only rely upon one's general idea of what rational human beings are expected to desire. The diplomat can safely suppose that the population of that state, regardless of its peculiarities, is probably interested in: freedom (to decide for themselves), not in being compelled to obey orders from abroad; more access to natural resources than in less access; more protection from risks created by natural disasters or by human activity than in less protection etc. Consequently, at the very beginning of his job he can simply state these interests/priorities as constituting the minimal set of requests of X. Does he actually represent the population in X? Not really; he rather promotes some *general interests/priorities of all rational human beings* (at least according to the common idea of rationality), which supposedly are also characteristic for that particular population. In the following days, as he gathers more and more information on X and gets acquainted with the particularities of the situation of the people in that country, the diplomat can actually start to *represent* the population in X, by really promoting the particular interests and priorities that follow from the mapping (he has managed to acquire) of the specific situation of X. But before that, although technically a "representative of X," he was only a representative of the general human interests he had attributed (probably rightly) to the population of X, as he would have attributed to any other population.

What is the point of invoking this admittedly wild and oversimplified imaginary case? The suggestion is that, when preoccupied by the concerns of distant future generations, we are pretty much in the same situation as the diplomat when first engaging in his unexpected task. We know much too little about the particulars of their situation to be able to represent distant future people properly; we cannot actually map their particular interests and priorities, since we do not know their particular situation/context. But we can nevertheless remember what rational beings cannot but desire and request.

What we can do is to focus on some important preferences (preferences that cannot be neglected, since they create duties for others) that we can hardly avoid attributing to rational human beings. We can hardly imagine that future human beings would not prefer more rather than fewer opportunities to make their own choices, more rather than less access to natural resources, more rather than less biodiversity, more rather than less protection from natural disasters, climate change, or anthropogenic risks generated by nuclear or chemical waste.

The interests/priorities we attribute to distant future generations are not deduced from genuine knowledge of the particularities of their situation, from a good grasp of their real priorities or of their true concerns at some specific moment in the future, but from what we know now about the preferences of rational human beings in general.[2] When we claim that "the voice of future generations should also be heard," we cannot reasonably mean that we could somehow guess or predict their precise particular concerns and requests in a certain context; what we mean is simply that some general preferences of all generations should be respected also when distant future generations are at stake. Representing future generations boils down to claiming that these fundamental general preferences should be respected by present generations, in such a way that no unnecessary risks would be imposed upon descendants.

It seems thus reasonable to conclude that we should not claim we could really represent future generations. What we should actually aspire to is not "effective representation" of future generations (which is in fact impossible), but rather "effective prevention" of unnecessary risks to future generations.

This might seem uncontroversial and harmless enough, but the key word here is "unnecessary." Various social or interest groups, political parties and governments will almost inevitably make different, and even opposing, judgments upon "what is actually a risk worth taking," and thereby we reach the main point. It is not difficult to imagine that future generations will have the preferences above mentioned, but it is very difficult to commensurate their preferences (and the strength of their preferences) with the relevant preferences of present generations. For example, it is quite easy to imagine that future generations will prefer to avoid having to spend money in order to neutralize chemical or nuclear waste left by us, but it is very difficult (if possible at all) to commensurate the opportunity costs of their activities to neutralize waste with our opportunity costs of eliminating or neutralizing waste from the very beginning.

It seems thus obvious that the trickiest problem is not representing future generations, but rather conciliating their justified preferences with other justified preferences manifested by present generations.

5. A working hypothesis

My working hypothesis is that:

> the main obstacle to protecting future generations and to promoting environmental values is not insufficient representation, but rather the difficulties to balance interests/rights/priorities of present generations and interests/rights/priorities of future generations.

There is an obvious polarization between experts, politicians and public opinion on these matters, and this is what creates the biggest difficulties. The justification of adopting this hypothesis might include the following arguments:

1. It has been noticed that the institutions meant to "represent" future generations cannot actually achieve that (there cannot be a binding mandate of present generations to decide for future generations), so that "rather than seen as truly representing future generations, they should be understood as alarm mechanisms, or watchdogs" (Gosseries 2007: 110). This suggests the need for a change of priorities, from "speaking in the name of future generations" to "finding just solutions for intergenerational justice problems": "the very idea of a mandate could be dropped altogether and simply replaced by the need to act in an intergenerationally fair way" (111). "Just solutions" imply balancing the priorities of future generations and the ones of present generations.

2. In some ways, representing future generations is either a hopeless or a superfluous task: for, on the one hand, many of the exact immediate priorities of future generations can hardly be pinned down (since they depend on particulars that can hardly be foreseen), and, consequently actually cannot be represented; and, on the other hand, some of their preferences are obvious to us, reflecting what we actually think that is in general preferable (more natural resources rather than less; more biodiversity rather than less; more safety from dangers created by anthropogenic changes in the environment, rather than less safety; a less degraded environment rather than a more degraded one, etc.) and need no special voice or dedicated "representation." What they actually need is just respect and consideration.

Representation of future generations is thus caught in a sort of "between Scylla and Charybdis" situation, i.e. between two opposing risks: a task which cannot be fulfilled by us (we cannot predict exactly and map correctly future priorities) and one that is superfluous – since general interests/preferences of all generations, being perfectly familiar to everybody, need no special institution dedicated to representing them; they belong to common knowledge and should automatically be taken into consideration in any sound reasoning about the future. On the other hand, those who reject treating such general priorities/preferences of future generations as priorities for us don't do so because these preferences are unknown to them or inadequately represented, but because they think we do have other, higher, priorities; so that the main problem is, once again, comparing and balancing priorities.

Opinions on the priority or urgency of public policies dedicated to future generations are extremely divided, which indicates that the main difficulty is lack of consensus on what should be done; and consensus cannot be reached simply by better representing future generations. Therefore, the main focus of both theoretical and practical attention should be directed from representation to conciliation between priorities/interests/rights of present generations and future generations; the real "missing link" in our institutional decision-making systems is not the "representative" ingredient, but the "balance/conciliation" ingredient.

This does not imply that exploration of the interests/rights/priorities of future generations, promoted by specialized representative institutions, were useless and should be abandoned. It only implies that seeking conciliation is more urgent and more important, and should be prioritized over mere "representation."

It follows, however, that, given the adversarial characteristic of the controversies between defenders of interests/rights of future generations and defenders of interests/rights of present generations – given the existing deep polarization on that matter – an institutional ingredient is needed capable of: (a) applying efficiently an adversarial logic; and (b) finding solutions, or reaching enforceable decisions.

6. A guiding example and a proposal

Lennart Sjöberg describes two different typical roles played by experts who deal with risks, the *protector* role and the *promoter* role:

> A Protector considers his or her role to be that of warning people about a risk that they do not know about or neglect to protect themselves from with sufficient vigor. Protectors wonder why people are so uninterested in their own safety and regrets that so little money is spent on saving lives. Protectors are found among experts on the following: many medical problems, fires, tornadoes, earthquakes, radon, ultra-violet radiation, and some economic problems. Promoters, on the other hand, regret that people are too much concerned about risks and ask how they can be convinced that those risks are not so large and that they certainly are worth taking. Promoters are found in the fields of the following: nuclear power, pesticides, genetic engineering, and crime policy (at least in Sweden).
>
> Sjöberg 1999: 4

The proposal would be to acknowledge the existence of a similar protector–promoter distinction, and a widespread polarization accordingly, in the area
of discussions concerning future generations. Many of these discussions revolve
around the priority problem: should promotion of some environmentally
unfriendly technologies, or of economic development and/or of urgent present
needs to be prioritized, or should prevention of risks for future generations and
protection of interests/rights of these generations, be prioritized?

Indeed, the most intense controversies concerning future generations seem to
take place between participants who play the role of protectors of (interests,
rights, or priorities of) future generations and participants who promote certain
technologies (despite their possible bad consequences for the future), or
economic development (despite its bad effects on the environment, or resources)
and/or priorities of present generations (despite their negative consequences on
the priorities of future generations).

I thus take the promoter-protector distinction as a *very general* one (not just
one between expert roles, but rather one between roles played in general in
controversies about future generations). But I am not supposing that all people
fall sharply or permanently into one of the two categories. Obviously, there are
also people who are undecided, or eclectics who combine some elements of both
roles. I suppose, however, that the difficulties encountered by our attempts to
deal fairly with future generations spring to a great extent from opposition of
promoters who think that priority should be given to efficient use of some technologies or to development or to urgent needs of present generations instead to
interests/rights/priorities of future generations.

There is no doubt that in many cases the objections raised by promoters are
inspired by generational selfishness, or by special hidden interests etc. But it can
hardly be said that that is always the case. The possibility might be left open that
some objections raised by promoters are, at least prima facie justified, possibly
sound and morally acceptable, so they should not be dismissed automatically as
expressions of mere generational selfishness or self-centeredness.

7. "Trial by jury" procedures

The present institutional systems are indeed deficient as regards responsible
examination of, and consideration for, the interests/rights of future generations.
But if the opposition between protectors and promoters is at the very core of our
controversies over future generations, then what is primarily needed is a mechanism to deal with this opposition. Such a mechanism should not only assess the
weight of the objections and arguments of both parties, but also provide a decision on the matter. And since the matter is an adversarial one (protectors and
promoters oppose each other, see each other as "enemies" or at least as activists
militating for "dangerous" aims, and try to "win" the case against each other), the
mechanism should be one capable of dealing with adversarial issues.

The best, or the most successful, mechanism to deal with adversarial matters
that has been invented is the "trial by jury" procedure, developed for many

centuries inside various justice systems. This might suggest that in order to solve the controversies over future generations, what is needed is not just a representative institution (ombudsman, guardian, committee, or the like), but rather a trial by jury mechanism of solving controversies between protectors (of future generations) and promoters (of risky technologies, of economic development and of the priorities of present generations).

This mechanism could take the form of a Grand Jury for Intergenerational Justice, in front of which controversial decisions and policies (presumably affecting future generations) would be brought. Such a jury could work as an institutional machine:

- focusing on future generations' interests/priorities/rights, on possible risks for future generations;
- specializing in problems concerning conflicts of interests/rights among present and future generations, concerning possible tradeoffs between aims of various generations;
- examining at length evidence provided by experts and arguments/counterarguments advanced by protectors and promoters;
- debating extensively and processing the pros and cons invoked in the relevant controversies;
- assessing the necessary tradeoffs (between preferences and priorities of various generations), balancing possible risks;
- reaching collectively conclusions on "acceptable/unacceptable" risks to future generations, on "morally admissible/inadmissible" present options, activities and policies (from the point of view of the well-being of future generations).

The advantages of such a jury could, in principle, be: representativeness (for the various sections of the present population and of public opinion), official status, focus, specialization, access to the best evidence available, support from specialists/experts, a capacity of systematic examination of the relevant problems and arguments, a capacity to use extensively adversarial logic methods – and consequently less subjectivism and fewer biases. These advantages are, in fact, nothing else than the characteristic advantages of all "trial by jury" procedures.

During the debates taking place in front of such a jury, the protectors (playing the role of "accusers," since they accuse some decisions and policies of being harmful to future generations) and the promoters (playing the role of "defenders," since they defend some contemporary decisions or policies as legitimate) would make their respective cases, while an adequately selected jury would make decisions: "too risky" or "not too risky" (for future generations), "too dangerous" or "not particularly dangerous," "acceptable" or "unacceptable" (from the point of view of our duties to future generations).

Designing a successful mechanism of this type is, of course, a very tricky affair and I do not think this can be achieved through individual efforts and imagination, or from scratch. I am thus not aiming at providing here a general sketch for such a mechanism. Instead, I shall just try to clarify the idea and to argue for the usefulness of "trial by jury" procedures.

The idea that a court or some sort of judicial institution would be necessary for the protection of future generations' rights/interests is, of course, not new. Especially since the publishing of the classic *In Fairness to Future Generations* by Edith Brown Weiss (Weiss, 1989), this idea has been defended and developed in many ways. But in general its advocates insist both on the aim of *representation* and on the importance of *rights*. My fear (as I have already suggested above and as I shall briefly argue below, when tackling some possible objections) is that emphasis on both elements is bound to generate difficulties.

A Jury for Future Generations need not be, in fact, a proper tribunal or a formal component of the existing legal system. Its task need not be to produce sentences on "crimes against future generations" and to decide upon legal retribution – obvious facts such as "lack of sufficient relevant norms" and "lack of sufficient evidence" make such sentences impossible anyway; neither need it be to decide upon the constitutionality of some piece of legislation or on some policy. The jury should be seen, I think, more as an adversarial processing machine meant to compare, weigh and balance priorities, than as a judicial instrument.

But this relaxation does not, of course, eliminate the relevance of the legal aspects altogether. Members of the jury can themselves be influenced by what they take to be "sound rules", or the "law". But they won't be asked to use laws and rules as standards or yardsticks, but just to decide whether something is (morally and socially) *acceptable* from the point of view in which the sort of future generations is at stake.

The main tasks of such an institutional arrangement could be the following:

- creating an official specialized forum for examining the relevant evidence, for processing (testing, comparing, balancing) the pros and cons, for debates and decisions on risks that our activities, policies and lifestyles generate for future generations;
- separating concerns for justified interests/justified priorities/rights (of both future and present generations) from concerns that are strongly dependent on issues loaded with particular ideological assumptions and shaped by immediate political aims and worries, by the fight for political power etc., and thereby allowing present generations to concentrate on concerns regarding future generations;
- compelling the jury and indirectly public opinion to confront/compare/ weigh priorities of future generations with priorities of present generations, and hopefully to compare (if possible) the respective opportunity costs of relevant activities (e.g. "how great our sacrifices would be in case we took some substantive measures *to prevent* future floods generated by anthropogenic climate change, and how great the sacrifices required from future generations in order *to cope* with floods, in case we failed to take the necessary preventive measures");

- compelling directly the members of the jury, and indirectly public opinion, to confront the arguments/reasons/evidence provided by protectors with the arguments/reasons/evidence provided by promoters;
- compelling the jury to apply the adversarial logic (based on confrontation between pro and cons, between the arguments of the "accusation" and those of the "defense") to the controversial issues that are relevant for future generations;
- compelling the jury to reach a decision ("too risky for the well-being of future generations, and thus unacceptable"– "not too risky, and thus acceptable") that might have a strong (even if not a decisive) influence on political life and social attitudes.

In fact, the debates taking place in front of such a jury (political parties, social movements, specialists, associations, NGOs, might make their respective cases in front of the jury) would try to encapsulate the debates in our society, to represent the clash of opinions in our society – but with a difference. While the debates in society might continue infinitely and fail to reach a conclusion, the "encapsulated" debates would be limited in time and asked to reach a verdict that public policies should respect. In this respect, the debates in front of the jury might "represent" our general public debates, the clash of opinions in front of the jury would represent the clash of opinions in society. The Grand Jury would be representative, not for future generations, but for our worries concerning future generations and for the possibility to conciliate these worries with other important worries that we have. That seems to be the right kind of "representativeness" that we can rationally aspire to.

The jury should not be composed of specialists, but (like other juries) of ordinary citizens, selected in such a way that the whole body be characterized by representativeness for the population. It will not be asked to produce a whole map of the interests/needs/preferences of future generations, but only to make piecemeal decisions on particular measures, acts or policies. I am not claiming that such a jury would have a particularly good competence at balancing interests, but only that, if representative for the population, it would be a good forum in which public debate on that matter could take place in such a manner that a verdict can be reached. It would also be some sort of laboratory where interests of future generations clash with other present interests, the clash is examined and analyzed, so that one can see to what extent compromise and balance can be found.

8. Objections

But don't we have enough institutions and mechanisms? Shouldn't we apply the wisdom of Occam's razor, rather than indulge in imagining *ad libitum* various new institutions? Institutional innovation does constitute a very delicate subject matter. Engaging in institutional invention is risky, because here unbound imagination can easily take the upper hand over realism and pragmatism. And it might be claimed that no new institution or mechanism was needed in order to deal with the risks for future generations, because we already have a lot of useful instruments that can be successfully used for the same task (parliaments, constitutional courts, ombudspersons, commissioners, various boards, committees and commissions, agencies, public debates etc.). Above all, there seem to be plenty of political institutions that could play such a role. It might be claimed, for instance, that the priorities of present people are sufficiently well represented by parliaments etc., so that there is no real need to have another mechanism for balancing both kinds of interests. The institutions specialized in representing future generations would defend the interests of these generations, while parliaments etc. would defend the interests of present generations – and the interaction between these two kinds of institutions might guarantee the good functioning of the adversarial logic needed in the debate on present/future generations' interests.

According to this point of view, what we really need is not a new mechanism or institution, but rather effective and fertile dialogue between representative (existing) institutions. Indeed, such a dialogue might work quite well, were parliaments and other existing political representative institutions dedicated exclusively to defending the interests/rights of present generations. But, in fact, they are not exclusively dedicated to directly representing present interests, for they are structurally designed to promote political ideologies and to win some particular political battles. While the positions taken by some institutions specialized in protection of future generations (ombudsmen, commissioners, dedicated bodies) can, at least in principle, be considered genuinely inspired exclusively by concerns for the future generations' welfare, the positions taken by parliaments, political parties etc. can never be considered genuinely inspired exclusively by concerns for the present generation's welfare. What parliaments and other similar bodies choose to do/decide is always reflecting not just present interests and rights, but also, on one hand, complex political ideologies, particular (religious, philosophical, moral) commitments and, on the other, pragmatic (narrower) aims such as getting to/staying in power, defeating political enemies/rivals, winning particular political battles, imposing some policies etc.

Political decisions too often reflect purely political tensions, power relationships, narrow tactical interests, parochial or contextual peculiarities, fear (to lose a certain battle) or hope (to take advantage of some circumstances) etc., rather than a correct representation of the interests/priorities/needs of the present generation. Political bodies are indeed meant to provide optimal decisions on such interests/priorities, but being shaped by various partisan commitments and loyalties as well as by narrow pragmatic considerations ("what we need to do in order to win the next elections"), can hardly be taken as reliable sources of relevant information and sound judgment on such a particular topic as intergenerational justice. Moreover, political parties and parliamentary groups dedicate themselves to promoting "packages" of options, so that their acts and attitudes, shaped by various interlocking concerns and reasons, can never be taken as a faithful mirror of the interests/rights of present generations.

Consequently, the profile of the existing bodies and mechanisms is both much too general (since they don't focus enough on representing the present generations' interests, as diverging/converging with interests of future generations, since they dissipate in too many other activities) and simultaneously much too parochial (since they focus too much on immediate, particular, political tasks, and not on strategic aims such as conciliating present and future interests/rights) to be able to generate a fertile and conclusive dialogue with the protectors of future generations.

But what about "specific *institutions* aimed at defending the interests and rights of future generations," such as enumerated by Gosseries?

> A set of *reserved seats* in one of the parliamentary chambers, setting up a specialized second chamber, appointing a commissioner directly attached to one of the chambers (*Knesset* model), or instituting specialized administrative bodies such as a guardian/ombudsman or a specific agency.
>
> Gosseries 2008: 446

Why wouldn't these institutions be enough? What reasons do we have to ask for more?

One reason follows from the very aim of all these institutions or mechanisms: they are all meant to protect, and they have, so to say, an inbuilt bias (a "role-biased judgment"), so that they cannot function as impartial courts meant to decide by considering all the reasons and the arguments brought forward by both the protectors and the promoters. These well-known (although rarely kept alive) institutions all can, of course, defend future generations, but they are not prepared to explore impartially the tensions, and to bridge the gap between, the interests of these generations and the priorities of present people.

It is the same with institutions such as The World Future Council, which are presented as "closing the gap" between the present or the status quo (the interests of which are well represented) and the interests of future generations (von Uexkull 2009). They can close no gap, since they are role biased. Inside such institutions specializing in representing future generations, the interests/rights/priorities of present generations are not equally well represented and an impartial debate is hardly possible.

There is thus no true symmetry between the representative nature of an ombudsman/commissioner/board for future generations, and the representative nature of political parties or parliaments. While an ombudsman for future generations can, at least in principle, focus exclusively on interests of future generations and adopt political positions/decisions accordingly, a parliament is always promoting packages of interests, and the electorate is always compelled to vote for packages of interests – the so called "bundle options" – never for the mere genuine representation of interests of present generations – and consequently, its positions/decisions never just reflect general interests of present generations, but always also other more specific, parochial, aims. One can, for instance, expect that a certain parliamentary majority adopts a certain stance not because that stance reflected the genuine interests of the majority of voters, but because it was useful in a certain political context, in a certain political battle, in order that a second mandate be gained, or in order that a certain political minority be kept in opposition etc.

Another objection of the type "there already are a lot of democratic institutions; no extra ones are needed" can invoke, not the official agencies, but the popular, informal, ones. It might be said that there are, though, several kinds of democratic institutions and mechanisms – such as "citizens juries", or "les conférences de citoyens" or specialized NGOs promoting public debates – which could play the role of forums in which contrasting interests are compared and balanced. But such institutions and mechanisms are purely deliberative and consultative, so that their decisions are not authoritative and powerful enough. What we need is a link in the official institutional system, not "additional" associations like NGOs, popular committees, etc.

9. Legal instruments

But do we really need a special Jury for Future Generations? Couldn't some existing judicial institutions, for instance constitutional courts, play the role of defending the interests of future generations? Shouldn't we simply "go to (some existing) Court"? Unfortunately not. Although a court is indeed prepared to process some specific adversarial issues, and moreover (which is very important) to make enforceable decisions, it is though not the best place for solving problems of public policy.

Sometimes a court can even decide on priorities among equally justified interests, as many examples show.[3] But it is obvious that courts are not expected to specialize in such decisions and to focus on interests and conflicts of interests, or on conciliating opposing priorities, but only on respect for well-defined rights and positive laws. The court focuses on the legal aspects, not on the policy/social/ethical ones; it is meant to judge upon legality, not on social desirability/rationality/moral acceptability of social options.

The court is used to relying upon legal documents, not on general utilitarian considerations concerning what is socially preferable, or what is moral from a social point of view, or what kind of public choice is rational.

It is, indeed, sometimes acknowledged that regular courts cannot solve such problems:

> despite courts' best efforts, the need to balance the rights of present and future generations and the reality of finite resources they sometimes make future generations' interests more aspirational concepts than self executing and judicially enforceable obligations.
>
> *The International Human Rights Clinic* 2008: 14

Courts work with presumptions such as "the innocence presumption" (no one should be deemed guilty before adequate proof is provided and due process achieved) and the presumption that "anything that is not forbidden is permitted," which are not relevant/adequate here.

Constitutional courts are not good enough either, for the same reasons that other legal institutions are not good enough. Assessing decisions and public policies from the point of view of future generations is not a matter of detecting accord or disaccord with the positive law, or with the "Founding Fathers" original intentions' etc., but rather of assessing the existing risks, comparing the relative weights of opposing considerations, and judging the moral aspects of some possible harms. It's not just a matter of legal rights or obligations, but also a matter of moral decision, of risks worth taking etc.

Another objection to a Jury for Future Generations might be that a jury of this type would not be competent enough to judge upon the delicate matters involving conflicts of interests/priorities between present and future generations, tradeoffs between justified divergent aims of various generations etc. After all, even if assisted by experts, what resources can such a jury appeal to in order to reach wise decisions, other than *common sense*? And should mere common sense be relied upon?

The force of such an objection comes from the vague feeling that we could have a full representation of the interests/priorities of future generations and that precisely upon such a representation (not on mere common sense) our assessments and decisions to protect future generations should rely. Once we acknowledge that no full map of the interests of future generations can be at our disposal and that we don't have access to some "scientific" representation of the priorities of future people, the idea that we have to rely on common sense does not appear as scandalous any more. In fact, all juries rely on common sense, and a Jury for Future Generations would not constitute an exception. Juries relied upon in court are in exactly the same situation: as there is no certain representation of "what really happened" and no certain knowledge of "who is actually the culprit," juries are required to assess the evidence, to compare the pros and cons, to balance opposing reasons and to reach a conclusion based using common sense, not some special kind of technical wisdom. The point of all attempts to resort to juries is precisely that juries can provide decisions based on common sense in complicated cases where there is no other specialized competence capable of delivering ultimate certainties. In the same way, where no reliable map of "what exactly will actually happen in the distant future" and of "what certain distant future generation will specifically reclaim" is available, we are compelled to appeal to common sense.

10. Referendum

It might be objected that the true democratic mechanism through which *all* our concerns can truly manifest and express themselves is a "direct representation," one like a referendum. Why wouldn't we put all our policies and measures (which can be suspected to affect future generations) to the genuine test of referendum?

Leaving aside the obvious technical difficulties, the main problem is that a referendum helps people to express themselves, but does not compel them to compare/weigh/conciliate their concerns for the future and their concerns for the present. In a referendum, people who are inclined to act as protectors (of future generations) will vote for protective steps, while those who are inclined to be promoters (of possibly dangerous technologies, or of economic development) will of course vote for promotion strategies. Systematic examination of relevant evidence, confrontation of arguments and counterarguments, the full application of adversarial logic are not guaranteed by the very existence of a referendum. A referendum certainly provides a democratic decision, but does not necessarily create the framework for processing the pro and cons that are relevant to the wellbeing of both present and future generations; it might intensify public debates, but the suggestion here is that what we need is not just an intense public debate: it is some sort of processing of the pros and cons, based on adversarial logic, which pertain to the conflict of duties we might have to face when both our commitments to the present and to the future generations must materialize.

11. Conclusion

It seems, thus, that no existing institutional mechanism is likely to be able to play successfully the role that a Jury for Intergenerational Justice should play. While political bodies are prepared to make social and political decisions, taking into consideration a variety of reasons (including, in principle, also moral ones), but have very limited prospects for objective, balanced judgment, legal institutions, on the contrary, specialize in objective, balanced judgment, but are not all meant to provide optimal social and political assessments (but only evaluations on rights, broken rights, etc.). On the other hand, political bodies can make decisions, but they are deeply biased, while "citizens juries" or some NGO-type organizations, which might be neutral or at least less biased, cannot make enforceable decisions.

What we should try to reach is thus not just a synthetic representation of the interests of future generations, but a representation of our relevant certainties about the future generations, of our doubts on future generations, of our dilemmas concerning them. We need all these to be represented in front of a jury, so that the jury can reach a verdict; to encapsulate all the relevant elements and to process them adversarially, so that a relevant decision might be reached.

What is needed, then, is a sort of institution that combines the propensity of legal institutions towards objectivity and balanced judgment with the propensity of political bodies towards strategic social and political decisions; as well as the capacity to process clashes between pros and cons, between arguments and counterarguments in a (more) objective manner, which might be found in public debates and perhaps in activities of some "citizens juries", with the capacity to make decisions characterizing political bodies. A Jury for Intergenerational Justice, supported by the state and exposed to critical examination of public opinion, can hopefully materialize such a combination of aspirations.

Notes

The work on this chapter has been done in the framework of the research program: "Rights to a Green Future: Uncertainty, Intergenerational Human Rights and Pathways to Realization (ENRI Future)," supported by The European Science Foundation. I am pleased to express my gratitude, both to The European Science Foundation and to my colleagues participating in the project, for their kind support. I am particularly indebted to Dr. Axel Gosseries, from the Chaire Hoover for Economic and Social Ethics (at the Catholic University of Louvain-la-Neuve, Belgium), who has kindly read and commented on an earlier draft of this chapter, making a series of very useful suggestions that, due to time limits, I was only partially able to follow. All the remaining errors or lacunae are, of course, mine and only mine.

1   www.futurejustice.org/our-work/ombudspersons-for-future-generations/. Retrieved on 1 July 2013.
2   Jan Narveson (2011) has suggested that the rights we tend to attribute to future generations are inspired by "the common humanity" shared by both present and future generations. Here I am not concerned with rights, but in interests and preferences.
3   J. L. Mackie has analyzed an interesting example of such a decision on priority of public interests in Mackie 1995.

References

Gosseries, A. 2008. "Should They Honour the Promises of Their Parents's Leaders?". In C. Barry, B. Herman and L. Tomitova (eds), *Dealing Fairly with Developing Country Debt*, 99–125. Hoboken, NJ: Wiley-Blackwell.

Gosseries, A. 2008. "On Future Generations' Future Rights." *Journal of Political Philosophy* 16(4), 446–474.

Howell-Moroney, M. 2013. "Future Generations." In Dustin Mulvaney (ed.), *Green Politics: An A to Z Guide*, 184–186. Thousand Oaks, CA: Sage.

International Human Rights Clinic at Harvard Law School 2008. *Models for Protecting the Environment for Future Generations*. Science and Environmental Health Network. Available at: www.sehn.org, www.law.harvard.edu/programs/hrp (acccessed: 1 July 2013).

Mackie, J. L. 1995. "The Third Theory of Law." In J. Feinberg J. and H. Gross (eds), *Philosophy of Law*, 5th edn. 162–168. Belmont CA: Wadsworth.

Narveson, J. 2011. "Duties to, and Rights of, Future Generations: An Impossibility Theorem." Available at: www.cpsa-acsp.ca/papers-2011/Narveson.pdf (accessed: 1 July 2013).

Sjöberg, L. 1999. "Risk Perception by the Public and by Experts: A Dilemma in Risk Management." *Human Ecology Review* 6(2), 1–9.

von Uexkull, J. 2009. "Representing Future Generations." In: L. Zsolnai, Z. Boda and L. Fekete (eds), *Ethical Prospects*. Springer, 233–234.

Weiss, E. B. 1989. *In Fairness to Future Generations: International Law, Common Patrimony, and Intergenerational Equity*. Tokyo: United Nations University.

12 Parliaments and future generations

The four-power-model

Jörg Tremmel

Democracy, as it has been conceived of and practiced until now, has to a large extent ignored the problem of 'presentism'. The main objective of this article is to suggest an extension of the age-old separation of powers between the legislative, executive and judicial branch. It is argued that in order to make the political system more future-oriented, there is a need for a new (fourth) institution that ensures that the interests of future generations be taken into account within today's decision-making process. The chapter argues in favour of an institution with rights of initiative in the legislative process, integrating the competences of this new institution with those of parliament.

1. Introduction: endemic presentism

Since the 1990s, political scientists have been engaged in a lively debate about the 'presentism' of the democratic form of government, and its most important institution, parliamentarianism (Dobson 1996; Lafferty 1998; Kielmansegg 2003; Eckersley 2004; Schmidt 2006; Thompson 2010; Stein 1998). 'Presentism', the preference towards present-day interests, is a more precise word for what is generally understood as a lack of sustainability. To be sure, the concepts of 'presentism', 'short-sightedness' and 'short-term nature' do not mean the same. The first two, 'presentism' and 'short-sightedness', are in sharp contrast to the noble idea of 'sustainability/intergenerational justice',[1] but the same is not true for the phrase 'short-term.' A generation's long-term commitments, for example with regard to a certain energy system (such as nuclear power, energy from fossil fuels, or renewable energy), necessarily restrict the possibilities of future generations to revise them; in other words, short-term rerouting might not be feasible due to previously made (or not made) investments. The political right of generations to self-determination has been discussed regularly, and at great length, in political philosophy, for example by Jefferson, Madison and Paine during the foundation of the United States.[2] Jefferson argued that every constitution ought to become invalid after 19 years, so that each new generation, just like its predecessors, would be free to organize the terms of its coexistence however it saw fit. Madison objected by pointing to the insecurity that would thus arise. Thomas Paine took Jefferson's side and famously remarked that 'Every age and generation must be as free to act for itself in all cases as the age and generations which preceded it' (Paine 1996: 261) This right was even embedded in the French constitution of 1793.[3] Article 28 thereof stated that no generation was to force future generations to comply with its laws. (Godechot 1979).

Even though Jefferson's concept did not prevail, his idea that 'short-term' commitments need not necessarily have a negative impact on future generations deserves to be taken seriously. Therefore, this chapter will limit itself to criticize the concept of 'presentism'. What exactly does it mean for present-day democracy to be accused of 'presentism'?

(1)

Voters, as well as the elected, tend to seek advantages that can be realized in the present or the near future, or at the very least within their own lifetimes. From this diagnosis, some studies arrive at conclusions that can be taken as a critique of elected politicians or the political class. This chapter, in contrast, will turn its attention first to the 'presentism' of the electorate (the voters). Faced with the choice between receiving a certain state benefit (or tax concession) either now or at a slightly later point in time – e.g. in a year – most people opt for the present day for what appear to be anthropological reasons. With respect to larger time differences, Kielmansegg finds:

> A voter is thus doubly discounted in his political decision, first because the future is the future and not the present, and second because and in so far as it involves the future ... The bottom line is that with regard to their responsibility towards the future, there is no evidence that direct-democratic decision-making procedures are inherently superior to representative democracy.
>
> Kielmansegg 2003: 586

In fact, it would be inappropriate to equate more direct democracy with less 'presentism'. It comes as no surprise that in direct democracies such as Switzerland, a 'presentism' of the electorate can easily be ascertained (Bonoli and Häusermann 2010). The empirical reality thus confirms the assumption that 'presentism' affects representative and direct democracies in pretty much the same way.

(2)

In democracy, opposition politicians take an interest in being elected, as do governing politicians in their being re-elected. This is not to say that as a group, politicians are exclusively motivated by power, positions and privileges. Even those who seek to shape sensible policy have to exert power to do so; and the only way to obtain that kind of power is by holding an office (or mandate). Therefore, during campaigns, political parties have to focus on the current preferences of the current electorate. Future people cannot vote today, and they cannot be included in the calculus to maximize votes. Political competitions between two politicians, one of whom promises some benefits to occur in the near future, while the other one pledges the same but in the further future, will not end in favour of the latter – at least not as long as the electorate is presentist.[4] The fact that some political decisions lean towards 'presentism' is not primarily due to a lack of future-awareness amongst politicians; rather, it is a structural consequence of majority rule. For this reason, appeals to the conscience of politicians, asking them to consider the interests of future people more deeply, are likely to go unheard. It is only natural for democracy that its rhythm conforms with the timing of election periods (i.e. periods of four to five years). Therefore, it exhibits structural incentives for a politics of 'glorifying the present and disregarding the future' (Richard von Weizsäcker, cf. Friedrich *et al.* 1998: 53). Mutatis mutandis, John Stuart Mill's insight from 1861 still holds true today:

> Rulers and ruling classes are under a necessity of considering the interests and wishes of those who have the suffrage; but of those who are excluded, it is in their option whether they will do so or not; and, however honestly disposed, they are, in general, too fully occupied with things which they must attend to have much room in their thoughts for any thing which they can with impunity disregard.
>
> Mill 1958: 131

In order to 'outwit' the presentist part of the electorate, as it were, the future-orientated part of the political class should take a genuine interest in amending the rules of the game so as to include a self-commitment of the entire political class.

(3)

The scarce representation of future generations means that conflicts of interest are decided upon by the majority of eligible voters and not by the affected party. The normative justification of democracy actually includes the promise that all those ruled by a government and affected by its decisions have a say on the laws that rule their lives.[5] Due to their divergence in time, effects brought about by the current generation will affect only future generations. Thus, a special form of 'representation gap' comes into being. This gap is entirely different from the lack of electoral representation for societal minorities or other groups whose lack of representation is often lamented, such as women, the elderly, foreigners, and minors. These groups are present in the here and now; they can take part in political discourse, write letters, appear on talk shows, and in many cases vote in elections. None of this applies to future generations. If future generations were able to claim their interests in the political decision-making process, the majority stakes in important political decisions would be different. Consider the example of energy policy: the current form of energy production, with its empha-sis on fossil energy sources, enables a high standard of living in the present. However, with such an investment comes grave disadvantages in the mid-term (50–100 years) future. Post-1990 – the year in which the IPCC's *First Assessment Report* assessed a connection between anthropogenic carbon dioxide emissions and climate change with a 90 per cent probability – presently living generations can no longer legitimately claim ignorance of the consequences of their actions. Scientific analyses indicate that current energy policy intensifies the natural greenhouse effect and causes the global average temperature to rise. Even to date, anthropogenic climate change has cost hundreds of thousands of human lives. And this number of casualties among future people is expected to be a multiple. Assuming that only those born within the next 200 years from now were to have a say on energy policy in the next general election, all political parties would have to rewrite their programs in order to facilitate a much faster reduction in greenhouse gas emissions. State debt would also be reduced much faster than is currently foreseen.[6]

It is only since the twentieth century that the pace of humankind and the environment have started to fall apart. In environmental issues, more than else-where, the effects of current actions reach far into the future and can have a deeply negative impact on the quality of life of numerous future generations (for examples, see Tremmel 2009: 2). Prompted by humanity's unprecedented ability to influence its geophysical surroundings, scientists have recently begun to speak of the beginning of a new geological period, the anthropocene.[7] Naturally, this transition into a new phase of geology also necessitates a further advancement of our form of government.

2. Lack of liability for inadequate performance in office

There is yet another issue that amplifies the orientation towards the present: in democracies, the governmental responsibility borne by politicians is limited in time. Indeed, this is one of the advantages of the democratic type of government. However, it also means that an elected official does not have to assume that her own short-sighted decisions will catch up with her twenty or thirty years later. As soon as a new government comes into power, she is no longer liable.

It is quite a novelty that, and for what reason, a lawsuit was brought against the former prime minister of Iceland Geir Haarde in June 2011. Haarde was the prime minister in office when the country's financial system broke down. The *Althing*, Iceland's parliament, voted in favour of a lawsuit against Haarde because he had failed to take action during the financial crisis of 2008 that led to the collapse of the country's economy.[8] He was actually convicted in 2012 on one of four counts, namely for not holding cabinet meetings at the height of the crisis. However, he was acquitted from the heavier charges of neglecting his duties.[9] Regardless of one's take on the question of guilt concerning the financial crisis, such a case is a unique approach that has not been considered even remotely by other countries affected by the financial crisis (Greece, Portugal or Ireland). The introduction of a criminal offence statute that would make political decision-makers liable for knowingly creating policies that put future generations at a disadvantage has no chance of being implemented on a broader scale.[10] Such thinking would pose too much of a risk by inviting partisan-motivated reckoning with the policies of deselected incumbents.

3. Democracy as a political legacy for future generations

After the failed UN climate conference in Copenhagen in 2009 and the divisive follow-up conferences in Cancun 2010, Durban 2011 and Warsaw 2013, there was an increase in contributions to the debate, giving rise to the question of whether democracy is in general the best form of government to cope with ecological challenges (see, for example, Shearman and Smith 2007; Pötter 2010; Leggewie and Welzer 2009 a, b). This provocative question is misleading, however, whether it is answered in the affirmative or not. At any rate, the international climate conferences are a bad case in point, given that not only democratic, but also non-democratic states contributed to the failure of the negotiations (Saretzki 2011: 42). Comparative studies have shown that the environmental performance of authoritative regimes is far worse than that of democracies.[11] Reforming democracy, to be sure, does not mean putting it into question. Churchill's famous line 'Democracy is the worst form of Government except all those other forms that have been tried from time to time', points to the heart of the matter. Democracy as a form of government is one of the most valuable legacies that future generations can inherit from present generations.

4. Insufficient posterity protection clauses in constitutions

The growing acceptance of future responsibility has led to the trend of including posterity protection clauses in constitutions. Insofar as constitutions were newly adopted, for example in Eastern Europe and Central Asia after 1989 or in South Africa after the end of apartheid, a regard for generations was inscribed in almost all of these cases. Even well-established constitutions were changed, thus reflecting an increasing prominence of future ethics.[12] Around 30 constitutions exhibit such a generational regard, including those of France, Germany, Argentina, Brazil and South Africa. Only five constitutions speak explicitly of 'rights of future generations': Norway (Article 110b), Japan, Iran (Article 50), Bolivia (Article 7) and Malawi (Article 13) (Article 11). In other cases, the interests of future generations (e.g. Georgia) or, alternatively, their needs (e.g. Uganda) are addressed.

The number of constitutions with posterity protection clauses is already considerable, and it continues to grow. But has it made any difference? A sobering conclusion seems in order. The introduction of such clauses resulted neither in the phasing out of nuclear power nor in serious climate action in the respective countries. Constitutional courts are obviously not optimal to serve as the guardians of future generations' interests. They cannot represent such interests with full commitment for the simple reason that they have no mandate to do so.

It makes a substantial difference whether a new institution is created with its own budget, whether people come to hold new positions and whether new office spaces and logos are required – or whether, by contrast, existing courts are entrusted with new tasks by legal extensions. The approach advocated below is based on the need to create a new organization or institution for the representation of interests of future generations.[13]

5. Paradigm shift from a three- to a four-power-model

What is required in the anthropocene is nothing less than a paradigm shift. The new paradigm would entail a 'future branch', representing the interests of future generations in the legislative process, and regard it as a legitimate and necessary part of a democratically constituted community.[14] The linchpin of this paradigm would be that the age-old separation of powers into legislative, executive and judicial branches is no longer appropriate today. The present-day demos of the twenty-first century can affect the living conditions of a future demos far more than it used to do in former times. Just like in the eighteenth century, when in the course of first establishing a democracy in a large territorial state, the *Federalist Papers* considered a system of 'checks and balances' to protect minorities against the 'tyranny of majority' (Tocqueville), so today, we are in need of 'checks and balances' against the tyranny of the present over the future.

According to Jellinek's three-element doctrine, a state is constituted by state territory, state population and state power. The basic idea of the separation of powers is that they should be distributed between several institutions so as to prevent each one of them from becoming too powerful. Article 20 II of the German Basic Law protects the separation of powers in Germany. The new paradigm would require that Article 20 be amended as follows (new words in italics):

> All state authority emanates from the people. It is exercised by the people through elections … and through specific legislative means, executive power, jurisdiction *and the representation of future generations.*

These are just a few more words on paper – but they would be associated with many prerequisites and consequences. There would be many prerequisites because the purpose of such a constitutional amendment would have to be justified by extensive considerations before work on it could get started. Such a constitutional amendment would also be almost revolutionary and entail far-reaching consequences. The separation of powers into legislative, executive and judiciary – the 'trias politica'– was conceived by thinkers in the seventeenth and eighteenth century and is now universally established in Western democracies.[15] Scholars speak of a common 'commitment of *all* democratic constitutional states to three-power structured constitutional order' (Möllers 2008: 13). If a fourth institutional level were to be added now, this would not only be a major qualitative development of democracy. Due to the necessary coordination of the competences of all powers, this would also necessitate a revision of numerous articles of the constitution, at least in some versions of the four-power-model.

The idea of extending the separation of powers model provides an answer to the so-called problem of motivation in the context of intergenerationally just policies. This problem is understood by philosophers, psychologists and political scientists as the hitherto unresolved question of how to motivate individuals and our society as a whole to act in intergenerationally just and sustainable ways. The extension of the separation of powers model solves this problem. In adopting such an extension, a constitutive people coerces itself into acting sustainably. The German term 'Vierte Gewalt' (literally 'fourth force', identical with the less martial English concept 'Fourth Branch') speaks for itself.

6. The historical roots of the separation of powers and the extension of the concept in the present

The historical roots of the separation of powers are usually associated with the political theorists John Locke and Charles de Montesquieu. However, even a thinker as early as Aristotle already recommended a mixed constitution, or, more specifically, a mixture of democracy and oligarchy designed to prevent an excessive concentration of power, which he called 'polity'. According to Aristotle, a constitution is more durable the more it is mixed because the mixture keeps the different forces in balance (Strohmeier 2004: 32). In his *Two Treatises of Government*, published in 1690, John Locke distinguishes between legislative and executive, but leaves no room for an independent third judicial power. Locke introduces a clear hierarchy of powers when he writes that 'this *legislative* is not only the *supreme power* of the common-wealth, but sacred and unalterable in the hands where the community has once placed it' (Locke 1924, 183–184). Charles de Montesquieu, the actual 'father' of the separation of powers doctrine, applies the classical tripartite division of legislative, executive and judiciary power in his *De l'esprit des lois* of 1748. In the sixth chapter of the 11th book, which mainly deals with the English constitution, he is concerned with the sharing and balancing of powers. Montesquieu writes: 'In every government there are three sorts of power: *the legislative; the executive, in respect to things dependent on the law of nations; and the executive, in regard to things that depend on the civil law*' (Montesquieu 2001: 173. Emphasis in original) Following this statement, Montesquieu explains that this latter power is to be referred to as the judiciary. This brings us to the classic tripartite division of legislative, executive and judicial power (Mastronardi 2007: 268).

While the idea of a 'horizontal' separation of powers with its three-pillar principle has a long history, more attention has been directed recently towards the 'vertically' directed separation of powers. In Germany, for example, the federalization of political systems means the division of labour between federal states and from a local level upwards, complemented by the European Union. The term 'separation of powers' is therefore in need of interpretation. In order to obtain at least a core in terms of a working definition, the term shall be used here primarily for the horizontal separation of powers. This seems to offer the most options for an extension that institutionalizes the interests of future generations. Lest it be misunderstood: this horizontal separation of powers can be found on quite different federal levels – in Germany, the *Länder* have state governments, parliaments and constitutional courts. But overloading the term 'separation of powers' is of little use. Neither the separation of powers according to Harrington into an advisory and a decision-making body, nor the separation of power according to John Locke into legislative, executive and federative forces, has prevailed historically. The media is also often referred to colloquially as 'the fourth power'. To some extent, interest groups such as trade unions or employers' associations act as a 'fifth power' because they try to influence politicians through lobbying. The terminology I use counts only the 'branches of government' (not society) and adds a fourth such branch to the existing three. What some modern scholars (e.g. Steffani 1997: 98) call 'additional levels of power separation' may be readily referred to as subsystems of society. Needless to say, the power of the political system does not penetrate all other areas such as business, science, media, religion or private relationships. Since these systems are autonomous, political power is limited. However, the term 'separation of powers' should continue to refer to the organization of state power to prevent confusion.

7. Who constitutes the demos?

Are there any counter-arguments against the establishment of a powerful institution for the representation of future generations? The backdrop of this is one of the great questions in political theory: 'Who constitutes the demos?'[16] The idea of who is part of the electorate is subject to historical change. Two hundred years ago, in most democracies, the demos was formed of those men who paid the 'right' tax revenue, had the 'right' skin colour, and were of the 'right' religion and the 'right' age. Today women, for example, vote, but future generations are still left out. It is crucial that for reasons of logic, the issue of the original composition of the demos cannot be decided democratically. Goodin (2007: 47) writes: 'It is logically incoherent to let the composition of the initial demos be decided by a vote of the demos, because that demos cannot be constituted until after the demos votes.' To illustrate this point, one might imagine the 1959 vote on women's suffrage in Switzerland: two thirds of the men refused the extension and thus defined themselves as, alone, the voting demos, at that time and also in the future. Today, hardly anyone would consider this decision to be legitimate.[17] Rather, the consideration of upstream normative principles must form the basis of deciding how the demos should be constituted. The *all-affected principle* leads to the conclusion that both current and future citizens can be considered as bearers of popular sovereignty. But it might make sense to replace today's principle of *one person, one vote* with a principle of proportionality for future, still unborn citizens. The more the life of a future person will be affected by a particular decision, the more their voice would be taken into account, for example, by 50 per cent per decade. Even if the practical problems of such proportional suffrage seem insurmountable, this could be an interesting theoretical principle to guide the design of a future branch. For, if the *all-affected principle* is taken seriously, every political decision is thought to affect another circle of people. Given that, for example, the consequences of nuclear waste accumulation extend much further into the future than the issue of sprawling public debt. The future electorate's 'No' against the current electorate's majority in favour of both these presentist policies would be much louder in the case of nuclear waste, if the votes of future people would be anticipated in both cases, respectively.

But, it might be asked, is it not the case that the principle of representation is generally incompatible with the idea of democracy? In a world in which most democracies happen to be *representative* democracies, the struggle for the principle of representation itself (as it prominently features in Kant's distinction between the republic and democracy) has long been settled. According to a dictum ascribed to Abraham Lincoln, democracy is characterized by 'government of the people, by the people, for the people'. However, most democracies today are based on the principle of representation: government of *all (with few exceptions)* members of the people, by *some* elected representatives from the people, for *all* members of the people. Thus, in accordance with common knowledge, representation and democracy do not seem to conflict. Extending the principle of representation to future citizens merely amounts to a consistent extension of the principle of representation. 'Representation, in the broadest sense, means making the invisible visible and the absent present', writes Göhler (1992: 109). Taking the same stance, Thaa adds that representation should be understood as the 'visualization of the absent' (2011: 151). Even though these statements might be taken out of their original context here, they resonate nicely with the problem of future generations' lack of representation.

To be sure, unlike the disenfranchisement of living people (such as those living abroad or those of a certain race, gender, nationality, class, or age),[18] the case of unborn citizens raises a number of questions which hitherto have been addressed by philosophers rather than by political scientists:

1. the *uncertainty* or *ignorance* with respect to future developments, the preferences of future people, or the impact of present-day decisions on future generations' quality of life;
2. the *non-identity problem*;
3. the rich-future thesis.[19]

Even though (2) and (3) make for complex problems, it is reasonable to assume, in view of the pertinent literature, that both of them are solvable.[20] The uncertainty argument, however, is nowhere as easy to refute, as we shall see later in light of some practical examples.

8. Core questions

As justified above, the conception of a four-power-model that includes a future branch is a central task of our time. It should not be forgotten, however, that the idea of the *trias politica* currently varies from country to country as a result of different traditions of political thought. Take the example of France: to this day, popular sovereignty is equated much stronger with parliamentary sovereignty in France than it is in Germany. The powers exercised by Germany's constitutional court continue to astonish many in France.[21] Given that the three-power-model varies from democracy to democracy, we might need many different configurations of the fourth branch; that is, for numerous kinds of future branches. There cannot be a *one-model-fits-all* solution for the representation of future generations; rather, it seems apt to conceive differently of such a representative body for each country. Keeping this in mind, the remainder of this chapter will design a representative body for future generations' interests for a specific country, Germany. The core questions about such an endeavour are the following:[22]

- Should the representative body for future generations be entitled to propose legislation, to put a suspensive veto on it, or even to quash it for good?
- Should the domain of the new institution be limited to certain areas of policy, and if so, which ones?
- How should the new institution be constituted, who should have the right to convene it, and how often?
- For how long should the new institution's members be in office, how many members should it have and to what kind of resources should they be entitled? Who should determine its members' allowances? Should they enjoy indemnity/immunity, or should it be easy to have them dismissed from office in cases of misconduct? By whom?
- How exactly would the constitution of a particular country have to be amended in order to establish an assertive fourth branch?

Throughout the globe, there is by now a considerable number of organizations with a mandate for sustainability and intergenerational justice. However, most of these enjoy merely consultative status and thus exercise little actual power in a Weberian sense.[23] A decisive touchstone is whether or not such institutions have the right to intervene in legislative procedures. Among the eight institutions mentioned in a UN report,[24] only four exhibit these competences. One of the main issues here is whether or not the new institution should be entitled to prevent or propose new legislation: should it rather act as the legislative or the judicative branch? In the first case, for instance, a number of seats in parliament could be reserved for representatives of future generations, or certain organizations outside parliament could be endowed with a right of initiative. In the second case, one might think of introducing either a third senate to the Federal Constitutional Court or, alternatively, a new ombudsperson. This chapter argues in favour of a future branch for Germany that holds a right of initiative. Thus, the question of democratic reform becomes one of reforming parliamentarianism. This is the route that is pursued in the remainder of this chapter. Further characteristics of this proposal include an appeal to consider path dependencies, to prevent another 'veto player', and to render moot the charge of an 'eco-dictatorship'.

Nowadays, the separation of powers is an important structuring principle in every democratic state under the rule of law. The legislative passes the law, the executive implements it, and the judiciary controls its abidance. The separation of powers is meant to create an internal control mechanism among the government bodies so as to prevent the abuse of power.[25] At the same time, the separation of powers better not diffuse the state authority to the effect that the state itself becomes powerless, for a powerless state will find itself unable to guarantee the liberty, security and equality of its citizens.[26] In the best case, the separation of powers amounts to a sort of division of labour. In the worst case, the different branches neutralize each other as 'veto players',[27] thereby making it impossible for any governing to take place at all. Germany's multi-level parliamentarianism, in particular, features a number of veto players such as the *Bundesrat* (the 'upper house' representing the country's 16 *Länder*), the Federal Constitutional Court, the Federal President, and the people itself, insofar as it makes itself heard through referenda. There is certainly a risk that creating the new institution will also mean creating an additional veto player. What is more, any future branch with veto power would be subject to charges of fostering a democratically illegitimate 'eco-' or 'future-dictatorship.'

In designing the German 'future branch', it is helpful to consult experiences from other countries. There is a large consensus in the literature that Hungary and Israel deserve credit for taking the most serious efforts to realize a representational body for the interests of future generations. In Israel, the institutional makeup of the country has been supplemented in 2001 by a Commission for Future Generations, which lasted until 2006. Hungary installed an Ombudsman for Future Generations in early 2008, but largely deprived him of his powers only three years later. Even though both institutions exerted considerable degrees of influence, controversies arose over their authority to suspend legislation and other governmental activities.

In Hungary, the position of the Parliamentary Commissioner for Future Generations was created after 20 years of discussing the idea, by means of a constitutional amendment. Formally, the Hungarian institution was embodied by a special ombudsperson, the Future Generations Ombudsman (FGO).[28] The Hungarian system of ombudspersons originally consisted of the 'general ombudsperson' primarily in charge of civil rights, and two 'special ombudspersons' in charge of ethnical minorities' rights, data privacy, and freedom of information. Hence, the FGO was third in the line of 'special ombudspersons'. The first incumbent was Sándor Fülöp, a lawyer, who (after securing his appointment by the parliament when several other candidates had failed to do so in three rounds of voting) held the office from May 2008 to 2011. In the general election of 2010, the coalition of the national-conservative Hungarian Civil Alliance (Fidesz) and the Christian Democratic People's Party (KDNP) earned a two-thirds majority of seats in the Hungarian parliament. The right-wing populist government under Viktor Orbán passed a constitution that was to become effective on January 1, 2012, and in which the ombudsperson's authority and resources were severely curtailed, causing Fülöp to step down. The position was not entirely abolished, however, but restructured to the effect of there being only one ombudsperson to remain, and several deputies. One of these deputies is the future generations ombudsman. The new incumbent, Marcell Szabó, a professor of law, was appointed by parliament in September 2012.

The remarks that follow refer to the wide-ranging mandate that the FGO had from 2008–2011. The FGO's office was staffed with 35 employees, among them 19 lawyers, two economists, one engineer, two biologists, an expert on climate change and a physician.[29] There were four departments: for legal matters, strategy and science, international affairs and coordination. The office's financial endowment amounted to 260 m Forint, or 858,000 euro (Ambrusné 2010: 19).

The task of the FGO was mainly environmental: to protect the health and living conditions of present and future generations, and to preserve the common heritage of humanity as well as the quality of life and the unhindered access to natural resources. The FGO's tenure of six years exceeded that of the parliamentarians by two years. To be elected, or prematurely discharged from his mandate for exceptional circumstances, a two-thirds majority in the *Országgyűlés*, Hungary's parliament, was required. The bulk of the FGO's activities consisted of mediation and intervention – similarly to his fellow ombudspersons in Germany, who, alongside petition committees, support citizens in asserting their rights against public administration.[30] It was not because of these, however, that the FGO got disempowered. In addition to the former, Fülöp was endowed with a number of powerful and very specific authorities reminiscent of those of an Attorney General, comparable to the position of the Federal Prosecutor in the Brazilian *Ministério Publico*.[31] The regulations added to the Ombudsman Act in 2007 authorized the FGO 'to repeal the enforcement of governmental decisional, if otherwise the environment were to suffer from severe damages" (Fülöp 2014: 73). Apart from this powerful weapon, which the FGO used but once, he also had the right to participate in certain civil and administrative trials. This could happen either by his initiating a lawsuit himself, or by joining a lawsuit initiated by a third party as an 'amicus curiae'. During his tenure, Fülöp made use of both options about seven times a year. The courts, however, had the last word, so it remains open to debate whether the institution 'FGO' qualified as an extension of the classical three-power model. But still, the FGO was to be consulted on every draft bill and government initiative that could have an impact on the environment and sustainable development. He could argue his case in parliamentary committees and had the right to speak in plenary sessions. He did both. In this, the FGO came to the conclusion that the 2010 budget represented an economical model of growth that would diminish the prospects of future generations. (Ambrusné 2010: 24).

How did the FGO deal with the problem of uncertainty? How could he know which alternative political action would prove (most) advantageous to future generations? In what was seen as particularly controversial at the time, the FGO deployed all legal instruments at his command in order to prevent a huge biomass facility made up for 50 MW in the buffer zone of Tokay, a wine region and a World Cultural Heritage site. Biomass or rural conservation, which one serves posterity more? In cases like these, it is almost impossible to determine objectively how the needs and interests of future generations would be served best.[32]

Evidence suggests that the 'uncertainty argument', as it has been advanced in the literature on intergenerational justice, deserves to be taken seriously. This, however, does not belittle the credit of those states who first installed representatives of future generations, and in doing so, altered the institutional setting of their respective political landscapes in a both spirited and innovative way.

9. A practice-oriented proposal for a future branch in Germany

Göpel lists five criteria for a future branch which are 'universally important for an effective mandate' (Göpel 2014: 98): independence, right of access, transparency, legitimacy, and effectiveness. Even though these are inspiring test criteria, this chapter takes a different approach. The key criterion suggested here is 'constructive input' in the sense of a right to *propose* legislation, as opposed to the possibility of destructive input, that is, all rights intended to suspend laws and activities temporarily or permanently. This approach proceeds from the existing infrastructure of advisory boards and councils of experts as a reservoir for possible new arrangements. Given that conflicts between the interests of present-day and future generations can be most virulent in environmental and financial policy, these two areas are primarily taken into account here. With the Council for Sustainable Development (RNE), the German Advisory Council on the Environment (SRU) and the German Advisory Council on Global Change (WBGU), three councils appointed by the federal government exist simultaneously to offer their advice on environmental and sustainable matters. Added to this is the Parliamentary Advisory Council on Sustainable Development (PBNE), which recruits its members from the *Bundestag* and whose task is to accompany the federal government's national sustainability strategy. Since the remits of said councils partly overlap – given that, for instance, they are all are engaged with the national sustainability strategy – it seems sensible to merge them into one central 'Ecological Council'.[33] Likewise, there are several independent councils on financial policy. Best known is the German Council of Economic Experts (SVR), whose members are colloquially referred to as the 'Five Sages of Economy'. Finally, the advisory boards of the federal ministries of finance and economics deserve notice. These councils should be merged into a new body, the 'Financial Council'. The key innovation for the political system would be to endow both the new 'Ecological Council' and the new 'Financial Council' with a right of initiative, allowing them to introduce legislation into the *Bundestag*. In order to this, the *Bundestag*'s Rules of Procedure would have to be revised accordingly. Currently, it states that bills have to be signed either by a fraction or by five per cent of all members of the *Bundestag*, unless the Rules of Procedure prescribe or allow something else (cf. § 75, § 76). The new institutions, albeit separated both personnel-wise and organizationally, would jointly form the 'future branch', that is, the new fourth power for Germany. By limiting itself to a purely constructive role, the legitimacy of the new institution is ensured. The charge of an 'eco-dictatorship' only makes sense when talking about organizations with veto rights, for only these can override decisions made democratically by parliament.

To repeat, according to this approach, the PBNE, RNE, SRU and WBGU are all supposed to merge. While the latter three mentioned organizations are purely consultative, the PBNE, at least in theory, already enjoys legislative powers, since its members are simultaneously members of the *Bundestag*. However, it is in fact precisely this doubling which prevents the PBNE from growing into the role of a future branch.[34]

Insofar as the model suggested here relates to environmental issues (the most important policy area of the anthropocene), it is both compatible to and distinguishable from proposals made earlier in the literature. Tine Stein and Johannes Rux, for example, have both independently called for the establishment of an 'Ecological Council'. Stein proposes to conceptualize the council as a kind of third chamber with a suspensive veto right, 'so as to throw an ecological wrench in the works of norm setting' (2014: 59). Thus equipped, the Ecological Council should be able to block legislation that fails the test of intergenerational justice. Stein dismisses further powers such as granting the Ecological Council an absolute veto or rights equal to those of the legislative bodies: the democratic legitimacy of the council, whose members are to be elected by the legislative bodies (such as the *Bundestag* and the *Bundesrat*), would simply not be strong enough (cf. Stein 2014: 60). According to the proposal made by Rux, the Ecological Council likewise would not only be entitled to put down draft laws and other resolutions in the *Bundestag*, but, agreeing with Stein, would also be empowered to block the decisions of other government bodies with the help of a suspensive veto right (Rux 2003: 473). One last proposal for future branches with a right of veto is put forward by Andreas Troge, a former president of the Federal Environment Agency, who suggests turning the federal president into an 'advocate of sustainability' with the new role to refuse appending his signature to draft proposals which seemingly violate the ideals of intergenerational justice (Troge 2011). While this solution would not create an additional veto player, its disadvantage lies in that an individual would hold an extremely salient position.[35] When collective bodies such as the Ecological and Financial Council formulate draft proposals, pitfalls like these are avoided in favour of collective intelligence. Of course, the internal decision process of the 'fourth branch' would have to reflect the majority principle.

Going forward, the question arises as to how the composition of the future branch should be determined, or whether a change in the appointment procedure is called for. While a general election by the entire population would maximize the formal independence of the council's members vis-à-vis the legislative, executive and judicial branches, there also would be several drawbacks. Thus, an appointment procedure similar to what is currently practiced looks more sensible.

It would be naïve to believe that the legislative power will take up and implement every proposal made by the fourth branch. What is rather to be expected is that parliament will refer most of both councils' draft proposals to committees in order to have them die a silent death by non-treatment.[36] But there is a valid hope that the new institution for the representation of future generations will gain the support of both the press and public opinion. The more its voice is heard in public, the less parliamentarians are going to be able to simply ignore its constructive draft proposals. Therefore, when compared with its alternatives, this suggestion is in some ways more modest even if more ambitious in others.

The concept of a separation of powers is not only appropriate for models in which all branches are equally powerful, but also for those in which one branch is significantly less powerful than the others. Maybe the suggestion made above, then, is best characterized by labelling it a 'three-and-a-half-powers-model'.

Notes

1   For an overview of these partly overlapping terms, see Tremmel 2014a; 2012; 2009.
2   Kley 2003 retraces this debate nicely.
3   This very progressive constitution never came into being. It was boycotted by the Jacobins, who kept a terrorist rule over France from autumn 1793 until summer 1794.
4   Alleged tools of political education such as the German *Wahl-o-Mat* play their part in this. For their seeming objectification of the vote decision lead to a concentration on one's own interests ("What would your purse choose?"), and not to an increased consideration of the common good.
5   For different versions of the so-called 'all-affected principle', see Beckman 2013: 778; Dryzek 1999: 44; Dobson 1996: 124; Shapiro 1996: 232 and above all Goodin's ground-breaking article (Goodin *et al.* 2007). Goodin's question of whether people in other states, which are also affected by a decision in State A, should be considered in an election in State A can be omitted here. This chapter is about the lack of participation of unborn citizens who will come into the world according to the demographic forecasts of State A.
6   The problem of 'presentism' in democracies is not limited to environmental issues. Long before the advent of the modern environmental movement, excessive public debt was a prime example of the careless use of the future. In a letter to John Taylor, Thomas Jefferson wrote on May 28, 1816: 'Funding I consider as limited, rightfully, to a redemption of the debt within the lives of a majority of the generation contracting it; every generation coming equally, by the laws of the Creator of the world, to the free possession of the earth he made for their subsistence, unencumbered by their predecessors, who, like them, were but tenants for life … And I sincerely believe … that the principle of spending money to be paid by posterity, under the name of funding, is but swindling futurity on a large scale' (Jefferson 1816). Underinvestment in education or lack of adjustments to social security systems are other examples of a lack of future orientation in political systems.
7   The term 'anthropocene' was coined by the ecologist Eugene F. Stoermer and effectively elaborated on by the climate researcher and Nobel Prize winner Paul Crutzen (see Crutzen 2011).
8   Haarde was the first person having to answer to the *Landsdomur*, an Icelandic special court created in 1905 for lawsuits against Icelandic ministers of state.
9   Haarde pleaded 'not guilty' and had called his case the first politically motivated lawsuit in the history of Iceland (BBC 2012).
10 A corresponding, but immature, proposal can be found in Jodoin 2011.
11 Weidner and Jänicke 2002. Jänicke 1992,1996 is right to consider democracy a premise for solving the global environmental problems.

12 For overviews of posterity protection clauses, see Earthjustice 2008; Tremmel 2006: 192–196; Weiss 1989. On the question of whether the German Basic Law also takes into account the interests and needs of future citizens, in addition to the interests of living people, see Häberle 1998; Lux-Wesener 2003; Boelling 2003; Tremmel 2005, 2004. Regarding the European level, see Göpel and Arhelger 2011.

13 In much of the literature, the bodies described below (e.g. the 'Commission for Future Generation" in Israel, or the 'Parliamentary Commissioner for Future Generations' in Hungary) are referred to as 'institutions'. In the social sciences, there are a variety of conflicting definitions of the term 'institution'. Some theories define the term so as to not cover organizations. In the following, however, a concept of institutions is employed which also includes organizations or permanently organized associations of individuals.

14 Neither citizens nor politicians are aware of the idea of a new branch in the separation of powers model, nor is it much discussed within political science. At least, the 2011 main survey of the WBGU also argued for a fundamental paradigm shift. It coined the heuristic concept of 'Great Transformation' which describes a paradigm shift that would be substantial in size and comparable to only two previous transformations in the history of mankind, the Neolithic Revolution in 12,000 BC and the Industrial Revolution (WBGU 2011: 87). Even though the WBGU has not called for a four-power-model, both approaches agree that the transformation of our society today must go beyond marginalia.

15 The view of our present three-power-model changes when we learn about the evolution from a two- to a three-power-model in the approaches of Locke and Montesquieu. The most important lesson from the history of ideas seems to be that even the supposedly definitive present is only a stage between past and future.

16 Goodin (2007: 40) prefers this framing of the question to a formulation such as 'inclusion problem', since the latter might lead us to think of an existing authorized decision group and thereby block out the more decisive question of how the original composition of an authorized group can be justified. The question of the constitution of the demos was already central to political thinkers in ancient and medieval times. In modern times, it has still occupied generations of political scientists. It is reminiscent of Robert Dahl's still relevant quote: '[The problem of inclusion] is an embarrassment to all normative theories of democracy, or would be were it not ignored' (1982: 98).

17 In Germany, a contradictory provision is still in force: section 2 (2) of the Scrutiny Act (*Wahlprüfungsgesetz*) specifies that only eligible voters are able to challenge the validity of an election. Thus, the part of the German people to whom the right to vote is denied on grounds of age is unable to challenge its situation by taking legal action.

18 On the last question, see Tremmel 2014b.

19 A counter-argument put forth by the opposing side holds that nation-state institutions are rather useless for getting a grip on global problems. This objection, however, is refuted convincingly by Tine Stein (2014: 48). The most important decisions about day-to-day life continue to be made on a national level. This also holds true for global problems such as climate change.

20 See Tremmel (2012: 72–92, 119–212) or Tremmel (2015) for an in-depth discussion with more sources.

21 In the midst of the euro crisis, many French rubbed their eyes in disbelief when the European Stability Mechanism (ESM) threatened to fail at the hands of the Federal Constitutional Court.

22 An attempt to give a more detailed answer is made in Tremmel 2015a. This chapter merely seeks to ask the right questions, and to give some preliminary answers at best.

23 'Power means every chance in a social relation to have one's own will even again the resistance of others' (Weber 1972, § 16).

24 On the UN level, the report brings the creation of a 'High Commissioner for Future Generations' into discussion. On a national level, the most influential future institutions worldwide are said to be the following: Finland, Committee of the Future; Germany, Parliamentary Advisory Council on Sustainable Development; Israel, Commissioner for Future Generations; Hungary, Ombudsman for Future Generations; Canada, Principal for Sustainable Development Strategies; Wales, Commissioner for Sustainable Futures; Norway, Ombudsman for Children; New Zealand, Parliamentary Commissioner for the Environment. See UN 2013.

25 A purely horizontal separation of powers without subsequent re-entanglement exists only in theory and has proven unsuitable in practice. Germany's parliamentary democracy relinquishes a strong separation of powers in many regards – first by having the chancellor (executive branch) elected by the *Bundestag*. Moreover, the *Bundestag*, by virtue of being a legislative body, can remove the chancellor from office by means of a 'constructive vote of no confidence.' The *Bundestag* also takes part in electing the Federal President and the judges of the Federal Constitutional Court. In addition, many members of government are simultaneously members of parliament, which makes for a personnel entanglement of powers and thus for a softening of the 'classical' separation of powers. Another striking disruption of the principle of separation of powers follows from the constitutional court's authority to enact decisions with the force of law, thereby interfering with the realm of the legislative branch. In general, the classical branches are separated more strongly in presidential systems than in parliamentary democracies. In the United States, for example, the president and Congress are elected separately. Both the president (by virtue of his veto power) and Congress (by way of an impeachment trial) exert only limited influence over the respective other. See Mastronardi 2007: 268.

26 The models of Locke and Montesquieu were primarily engaged with limiting the abundance of power held by an absolutistic ruler. The constitutional authors of the late eighteenth and nineteenth century struggled with more complex constraints on basic liberties. They were also concerned with the tyranny of legitimate institutions, namely the parliamentary majority (in the US) or the courts (in France). This shows that the basic idea behind the separation of powers cannot only be held against the executive branch, but against all three powers.

27 Cf. Tsebelis 2002. Tsebelis's approach is an interesting theory of the inability to reform political systems. Traditionally, institutionalists examine dichotomous classifications (unitary vs. federalist, parliamentarian vs. presidential etc.). By contrast, Tsebelis regards all political competitions as equal and asks how many actors must consent to a decision or are able to veto it and thus count as 'veto players'. This enables Tsebelis to predict the further development (or gridlock) of a political system in the terms of game theory.

28 Owing to the better literature available, and for reasons of space, the following is limited to a presentation of the FGO. For more information on the CfG, see Shoham and Lamay 2006, Shoham 2010 and Urler 2010. The CfG's sharpest weapon was a right to delay, not unlike the Filibuster.

29 For a very good account on the scope and limits of the competencies, see Ambrusné 2011. Even though the competencies of the FGO were laid out in full detail in the Ombudsman Act of 1993 and, respectively, in its specific amendment of 2007, they had to be concretized time and again by the courts, and remained disputed until his disempowerment in 2011. For example, the FGO declared itself competent in the case of a reordering of the public water supply, while his opponent, a state holding, denied this very competence (Ambrusné 2011: 23).

30 Apart from the FGO's very far-reaching right of access to information, such as his being entitled to access all premises and records during his inquiries without adjudication.

31 In an interview with the German magazine *DER SPIEGEL*, Fülöp himself characterized his task as follows: 'I am, so to speak, a state prosecutor for the citizens, called into action whenever the government fails' (Utler 2010: 2). With regard to the environment department, Fülöp was quoted as follows: 'Environment ministers don't always meet the requirements of professional independence; it is common for them to represent the politics and economic interests prevalent in their ministries rather than the eco-political stances of the government. Hence, independent state institutions, such as parliamentarian commissioners, could be a useful supplement to the governmental system' (Fülöp 2014: 70).

32 Likewise, the Israeli commissioner once exhausted his far-reaching competencies in a case in which the perspective of intergenerational justice could be claimed by both sides. Simply put, he advocated a law for the inclusion of handicapped young people, which the finance minister had rejected for cost reasons. See Shoha and Lamay 2006: 248.

33 Likewise, the final report of the finding commission *Growth, Wealth, Quality of Life – Paths Towards Sustainable Economics and Societal Progress in the Social Market Economy* (Enquete-Kommission 'Wachstum, Wohlstand, Lebensqualität – Wege zu nachhaltigem Wirtschaften und gesellschaftlichem Fortschritt in der Sozialen Marktwirtschaft') takes a critical stance towards the current myriad of councils and advisory boards, each of which exhibits only a limited efficacy (Deutscher Bundestag 2013: 285).

34 The PBNE was first constituted in 2004. In the current 18th parliamentary term, the PBNE consists of 17 full and 17 deputy members, of which, respectively, eight belong to the CDU/CSU, five to the SPD and two to each the Left and the Greens. It is presided over by Andreas Jung (CDU/CSU), whose deputy is Lars Castellucci (SPD). Its tasks are laid down in its appointment resolution, dating from 19 February 2014 and backed by all factions of the *Bundestag*. Among these tasks are the parliamentary support of the national sustainability strategy and the support of sustainability measures on the UN level. The PBNE is entitled to give advisory opinions, for example to other parliamentary committees. In addition, the PBNE assesses the sustainability evaluation of the Federal Government. In doing so, it submits the result of its assessment to the committee in charge. Currently, the PBNE does not enjoy rights equal to the other parliamentary committees, mainly because it is not entitled to draft bills.

35 Another suggestion, made by the World Future Council (www.worldfuturecouncil.org), envisages the creation of an ombudsperson. This suggestion might be sensible for many countries, but not so for Germany. This statement should not be misunderstood as opposing existing or conceived institutions for the representation of future generation in countries other than Germany, and which are (or used to be) endowed with a suspensive or absolute right of veto.

36 It was in this manner that an attempt to adopt a stronger reference to future generations in the Basic Law also failed – an attempt that had been undertaken in the years 2003–2009 by young members of parliament and which had been initiated by the Foundation for the Rights of Future Generations. For further readings on the initiative for an Intergenerational Justice Act, which had considered several formulations, but never a direct intrusion into the separation of powers model, see Tremmel 2009 (57–59), 2005 and Wanderwitz *et al.* 2008.

References

Ambrusné, É. T. 2010. 'The Parliamentary Commissioner for Future Generations in Hungary and its Impact'. *Intergenerational Justice Review* 1/2010, 18–24.

BBC 2012. 'Iceland ex-PM Haarde "partly" guilty over 2008 crisis'. Available at: www.bbc.co.uk/news/world-europe-17817174.

Beckman, L. 2013. 'Democracy and Future Generations: Should the Unborn Have a Voice?' In: Merle, J.-C. (ed.), *Spheres of Global Justice, Bd. 2: Fair Distribution – Global Economic, Social and Intergenerational Justice*. Dordrecht: Springer, 775–788.

Boelling, A. C. 2003. 'Ist die ökologische Generationengerechtigkeit in guter Verfassung?' In: SRzG (ed.), *Handbuch Generationengerechtigkeit*. Munich: oekom, 441–470.

Bonoli, G. and Häusermann, S. 2009. 'Who Wants What from the Welfare State? Socio-Structural Cleavages in Distributional Politics: Evidence from Swiss Referendum Votes'. In: Tremmel, J. (ed.), *A Young Generation under Pressure? The Financial Situation and the 'rush hour' of the Cohorts 1970–1985 in a Generational Comparison*. Berlin/Heidelberg: Springer, 187–205.

Crutzen, P. F. 2011. 'Die Geologie der Menschheit'. In: Crutzen, P. F. (ed.), *Das Raumschiff Erde hat keinen Notausgang*. Frankfurt am Main: Suhrkamp, 7–10.

Dahl, R. A. 1982. *Dilemmas of Pluralist Democracy*. New Haven, CT: Yale University Press.

Deutscher Bundestag 1980/2014. *Geschäftsordnung des Deutschen Bundestags in der Fassung der Bekanntmachung vom 2.7.1980*, zuletzt geändert am 23.4.2014. Berlin, § 76.

Deutscher Bundestag 2013. *Schlussbericht der Enquete-Kommission "Wachstum, Wohlstand,Lebensqualität – Wege zu nachhaltigem Wirtschaften und gesellschaftlichem Fortschritt in der Sozialen Marktwirtschaft"*. Drucksache 17/13300.

Dobson, A. 1996. 'Representative Democracy and the Environment.' In: Lafferty, W. M. and J. Meadowcroft (eds), *Democracy and the Environment*. Cheltenham: Edward Elgar, 124–139.

Dryzek, J. 1999. 'Transnational Democracy'. *The Journal of Political Philosophy*, 7, 30–51.

Earthjustice 2008. *Environmental Rights Report 2008*, Available at: www.earthjustice.org/library/references/2007-environmental-rights-report.pdf.

Eckersley, R. 2004. *The Green State: Rethinking Democracy and Sovereignty*. Cambridge, MA: MIT.

Foley, M. 1989. *The Silence of Constitutions: Gaps, 'Abeyances' and Political Temperament in the Maintenance of Government*. London: Routledge.

Friedrich, H. M., Mändler, M. and Kimakowitz, E. von 1998. *Die Herausforderung Zukunft: Deutschland im Dialog. Ein Appell der jungen Generation*. Berlin: Ullstein.

Fülöp, S. 2014. 'Die Rechte, Pflichten und Tätigkeiten des ungarischen Parlamentsbeauftragten für zukünftige Generationen'. In: Gesang, B. (ed.), *Kann Demokratie Nachhaltigkeit?* Wiesbaden: Springer, 67–84.

Global Humanitarian Forum 2009. *Human Impact Report. Climate Change: The Anatomy of a Silent Crisis*. Geneva: Global Humanitarian Forum.

Godechot, J. (ed.) 1979. *Les Constitutions de la France depuis 1798*. Paris: Garnier-Flammarion.

Göhler, G. 1992. 'Politische Repräsentation in der Demokratie'. In: Leif, T. (ed.), *Die politische Klasse in Deutschland. Eliten auf dem Prüfstand*. Bonn/Berlin: Bouvier, 108–125.

Goodin, R. E. (ed.) 2007. 'Enfranchising All Affected Interests, and its Alternatives'. *Philosophy and Public Affairs* 35, 40–68.

Göpel, M. 2014. 'Ombudspersonen für zukünftige Generationen: Diktatoren oder Bürgervertreter?' In: Gesang, B. (ed.), *Kann Demokratie Nachhaltigkeit?* Wiesbaden: Springer, 89–108.

Göpel, M. and Arhelger, M. 2011. 'How to Protect Future Generations' Rights in European Governance'. *Intergenerational Justice Review* 1/2010, 3–10.

Häberle, P. 1998. 'Ein Verfassungsrecht für künftige Generationen'. In: Ruland, F. (ed.), *Verfassung, Theorie und Praxis des Sozialstaats. Festschrift für Hans Zacher zum 70. Geburtstag*. Heidelberg: Müller, 215–233.

IPCC (ed.) 1990. *Climate Change: The IPCC Scientific Assessment*. Cambridge: Cambridge University Press.

Jänicke, M. 1992. 'Conditions for Environmental Policy Success: An International Comparison'. *The Environmentalist* 12, 47–58.

Jänicke, M. 1996. 'Democracy as a Condition for Environmental Policy Success'. In:Lafferty, W. M. and Meadowcroft, J. (eds), *Democracy and the Environment*. Cheltenham: Edward Elgar, 71–85.

Jefferson, T. 1816. *Letter to John Taylor* (28.5.1816). Available at: http://teachingamericanhistory.org/library/index.asp?document=letter-to-john-taylor/.

Jodoin, S. 2011. 'Crimes against Future Generations: Implementing Intergenerational Justice through International Criminal Law'. *Intergenerational Justice Review* 1/2010, 10–17.

Kielmannsegg, P. G. 2003. 'Können Demokratien zukunftsverantwortlich handeln?' *Merkur*, 57, 583–594.

Kley, A. 2003. 'Die Verantwortu gegenüber künftigen Generationen – ein staatsphilosophisches Postulat von Thomas Jefferson'. In: Hänni, P. (ed.), *Mensch und Staat. Festgabe der rechtswissenschaftlichen Fakultät der Universität Freiburg für Thomas Fleiner zum 65. Geburtstag*. Fribourg: Univ.-Verl., 505–523. Available at: www.rwi.uzh.ch/lehreforschung/alphabetisch/kley/container/jefferson_pages_50 5_523.p

Lafferty, W. M. 1998. 'Democracy and Ecological Rationality: New Trials for an Old Ceremony'. *Aufsatz für CPSA/IPSA Roundtable*. Quebec City. Available at: www.prosus.uio.no/publikasjoner/Andre_pub/1.html.

Leggewie, C. and Welzer, H. 2009a. *Das Ende der Welt, wie wir sie kannten. Klima, Zukunft und die Chancen der Demokratie*. Frankfurt am Main: Fischer.

Leggewie, C. and Welzer, H. 2009b. 'Können Demokratien den Klimawandel bewältigen?' *Transit* 36 (online edition). Available at:www.iwm.at/index.php?option=com_content&task=view&id=108&Itemid=178

Locke, J. 1924. *Two Treatises on Government*. London/New York: Everyman.

Lux-Wesener, C. 2003. 'Generationengerechtigkeit im Grundgesetz?' SRzG (ed.), *HandbuchGenerationengerechtigkeit*. Munich: oekom, 405–440.

Machiavelli, N. 1990. *Politische Schriften*. Frankfurt am Main: Fischer.

Mastronardi, P. 2007. *Verfassungslehre: Allgemeines Staatsrecht als Lehre vom guten undgerechten Staat*. Stuttgart: UTB.

Manin, B. 1994. 'Checks, Balances and Boundaries: The Separation of Powers in the Constitutional Debate of 1787'. In: Fontana, B. (ed.), *The Invention of the Modern Republic*. Cambridge: Cambridge University Press, 27–62.

Mill, J. S. 2004. *Considerations on Representative Government*. Edited with an Introduction by Currin V. Shields. New York: Liberal Arts Press.

Möllers, C. 2008. *Die drei Gewalten*. Weilerswist: Velbrück Wissenschaft.

Montesquieu, Charles de 2001. *The Spirit of Laws*. Translated by Thomas Nugent. Batoche Books.

Paine, T. 1973. *Die Rechte des Menschen*. Frankfurt am Main: Suhrkamp.

Paine, T. 1996. 'Dissertation on First Principles of Government'. *The Writings of Thomas Paine. Bd. III 1791–1804. Gesammelt und hrsg. von Moncure Daniel Conway*. London: Routledge/Thoemmes, 256–277.

Pötter, B. 2010. *Ausweg Öko-Diktatur? Wie unsere Demokratie an der Umweltkrise scheitert*. Munich: ökom.

Rux, J. 2003. 'Der ökologische Rat – Ein Vorschlag zur Änderung des Grundgesetzes'. *Stiftung für die Rechte zukünftiger Generationen. Handbuch Generationengerechtigkeit. 2., überarb. Aufl.* Munich: ökom, 471–490.

Saretzki, T. 2011. 'Der Klimawandel und die Problemlösungsfähigkeit der Demokratie'. In: Schüttemeyer, S. S. (ed.), *Politik im Klimawandel. Keine Macht für gerechte Lösungen?* Baden-Baden: Nomos, 41–63.

Schmidt, M. G. 2006. 'Die Zukunft der Demokratie'. *Zeitschrift für Parlamentsfragen* 37, 812–822.

Schmidt, M. G. 2008. *Demokratietheorien. Eine Einführung.* 4. überarbeitete und erw. Auflage. Wiesbaden: VS Verlag.

Shapiro, I. 1996. *Democracy's Place.* Ithaca, NY: Cornell University Press.

Shearman, D. and Smith, J. W. 2007. *The Climate Change Challenge and the Failure of Democracy.* Westport, CT: Praeger Publishers.

Shoham, S. 2010. *Future Intelligence.* Gütersloh: Verlag Bertelsmann Stiftung.

Shoham, S. and Lamay, N. 2006. 'Commission for Future Generations in the Knesset: Lessons Learnt'. In: Tremmel, J. C. (ed.), *Handbook of Intergenerational Justice.* Cheltenham: Edward Elgar, 244–262.

Steffani, W. 1997. *Gewaltenteilung und Parteien im Wandel.* Opladen/Wiesbaden: Westdeutscher Verlag.

Stein, T. 1998. 'Does the Constitutional and Democratic System Work? The Ecological Crisis as a Challenge to the Political Order of constitutional Democracy'. *Constellations* 4, 420–449.

Stein, T. 2014. 'Zum Problem der Zukunftsfähigkeit der Demokratie'. In: Gesang, B. (ed.), *Kann Demokratie Nachhaltigkeit?* Wiesbaden: Springer, 47–63.

Strohmeier, G. 2004. 'Ideengeschichtlicher Überblick über die Entwicklung der Gewaltenteilung'. In: Gellner, W.and Galtzmeier, A. (eds), *Macht und Gegenmacht – Einführung in die Regierungslehre.* Baden-Baden: Nomos, 41–61.

Thaa, W. 2011. *Politisches Handeln. Demokratietheoretische Überlegungen im Anschluss an Hannah Arendt.* Baden-Baden: Nomos.

Thompson, D. F. 2010. 'Representing Future Generations: Political 'Presentism' and Democratic Trusteeship'. *Critical Review of International Social and Political Philosophy* 13, 17–37.

Tremmel, J. 2004. 'Institutionelle Verankerung der Rechte nachrückender Generationen'. *Zeitschrift für Rechtspolitik* 37, 44–46. Troge, A. 2011. 'Ein Anwalt für die Zukunft. Nachhaltigkeit ist ein gern genutzter Begriff. Ein Vorschlag, wie daraus endlich Politik werden könnte'. *Zeitonline.* Available at: www.zeit.de/2011/03/Nachhaltigkeit-Staatsziel.

Tremmel, J. 2005. 'Verankerung von Generationengerechtigkeit in der Verfassung'. *Aus Politik und Zeitgeschichte,* 8/2005, 18–28.

Tremmel, J. 2006. 'Establishment of Intergenerational Justice in National Constitutions'. In: Tremmel, J. (ed.), *Handbook of Intergenerational Justice.* Cheltenham: Edward Elgar, 187 214.

Tremmel, J. 2009. *A Theory of Intergenerational Justice.* London: Earthscan.

Tremmel, J. 2014a. 'Nachhaltigkeit'. In: Sturma, D. (ed.) *Handbuch Bioethik.* Stuttgart: J. B. Metzler. Im Erscheinen.

Tremmel, J. 2014b. 'Demokratie oder Epistokratie? Das Alter als Kriterium für das Wahlrecht'. In: Hurrelmann, K. and Schultz, T. (eds.), *Wahlrecht für Kinder?* Weinheim: Beltz Juventa, 45–80.

Tremmel, J. 2015. *Zukunftsverantwortung in der Politik.* Wiesbaden: Springer.

Tsebelis, G. 2002. *Veto Players: How Political Institutions Work.* Princeton: Princeton University Press.

UN 2013. *Intergenerational Solidarity and the Needs of Future Generations.* A/68/322.b

Availale at: http://sustainabledevelopment.un.org (accessed on 12 January 2014).

Utler, S. 2010. 'Wir blicken zu ängstlich in die Zukunft'. Available at: http://ml.spiegel.de/article.do?id=728070.

WBGU (Wissenschaftlicher Beirat der Bundesregierung Globale Umweltveränderungen) 2011. *World in Transition – A Social Contract for Sustainability*. Available at: www.wbgu.de/en/flagship-reports/.

Wanderwitz, M., Friedrich, P., Lührmann, A. and Kauch, M. 2008. 'Changing the German Constitution in Favor of Future Generations – Four Perspectives from the Young Generation'. In: Tremmel, J. (ed.) *Demographic Change and Intergenerational Implementation of Long-term Thinking in Political Decision-Making*. Berlin/Heidelberg: Springer, 163–173.

Weber, M. 1972. *Wirtschaft und Gesellschaft: Grundriss der verstehenden Soziologie*, 5. rev. Aufl.; besorgt von Johannes Winckelmann. Tübingen: Mohr-Verlag.

Weidner, H. and Jänicke, M. (eds) 2002. *Capacity Building in National Environmental Policy: A Comparative Study of 17 Countries*. Berlin: Springer.

Weiss, E. B. 1989. *In Fairness to Future Generations*. New York: United Nations University/Transnational Publishers.

World Bank 2013. *Turn Down the Heat: Climate Extremes, Regional Impacts, and the Case for Resilience*. Washington, DC: World Bank.

World Health Organization 2009. *Global Health Risks. Mortality and Burden of Disease Attributable to Selected Major Risks*. Geneva: World Health Organization.

Index

Printed in the United States
by Baker & Taylor Publisher Services